CITY OF REMEMBERING

Oldest Cemetery, St. Louis No. 1, New Orleans, La.

CITY OF REMEMBERING

A HISTORY OF GENEALOGY IN NEW ORLEANS

SUSAN TUCKER

UNIVERSITY PRESS OF MISSISSIPPI JACKSON

www.upress.state.ms.us

The University Press of Mississippi is a member of the Association of American University Presses.

Title page: Book cover, Joseph Bryan commonplace book and genealogical notes, Bryan Family Papers, Mss 1 8408a. Courtesy of the Virginia Historical Society, Richmond.

Portions of chapter 8 appeared in an earlier publication, "Tacitly the Work of Women: Personal Archives and the Public Memory of Families," in *Women's Archives Reader*, edited by Tanya Zanish-Belcher (Chicago: Society of American Archivists, 2013).

Manufactured in Malaysia

First printing 2016
∞

Library of Congress Cataloging-in-Publication Data

Names: Tucker, Susan, 1950– author.
Title: City of remembering : a history of genealogy in New Orleans / Susan Tucker.
Description: Jackson : University Press of Mississippi, 2016. | Includes bibliographical references and index.
Identifiers: LCCN 2015034527| ISBN 9781496806215 (cloth : alk. paper) | ISBN 9781496806222 (ebook)
Subjects: LCSH: New Orleans (La.)—Genealogy.
Classification: LCC F379.N557 T83 2016 | DDC 976.3/35—dc23
LC record available at http://lccn.loc.gov/2015034527

British Library Cataloging-in-Publication Data available

To Winston De Ville

CONTENTS

ACKNOWLEDGMENTS

This book is a beginning step. Not much work has been done on the history of genealogy, especially its varying local histories. For this reason, I feel particular gratitude that I was able to begin to study the work on the practices of New Orleans genealogists. I could never have done so without the help of genealogists themselves. My most profound gratitude goes to those family historians who have spoken to me over the past ten years. I thank you all. Many of you are cited by name in the work that follows; many others did not wish to be listed by name. I will always appreciate your generosity, passion, and sincerity. I will always be grateful for the time you spent with me.

I thank also the dedicated and congenial New Orleans community of archivists, librarians, and museum staff who have helped me learn more about the records used by family historians: Chris Harter at the Amistad Research Center; Lee Leumas and Dorenda Dupont at the Archives of the Archdiocese of New Orleans; Alfred Lemmon at the Historic New Orleans Collection; Greg Lambousy, Sarah-Elizabeth Gundlach, Anna Gospodinovich, Erin Roussel, and Michael Leathem at the Louisiana State Museum; Jessica Strawn and Sally Reeves at the Notarial Archives; Sean Benjamin and Samantha Bruner at the Louisiana Research Center, Tulane; Florence Jumonville at the University of New Orleans; Irene Wainwright and Yvonne Loiselle at the Louisiana Division of the New Orleans Public Library; and Chloe Raub from the Newcomb Archives. You all make me cognizant of the good fortune we have to work together with the history of the place in which we live. Thank you especially to Yvonne Loiselle and Dorenda Dupont, who went beyond what I expected to help me learn more about records. In the archival community, I also thank Beth Yakel for her eloquent scholarship.

Farther afield, I thank Tim Salls of the New England Historic Genealogical Society; Jaclyn Penny of the American Antiquarian Society; Matthew Rutherford of the Newberry Library; Jamison Davis and John McClure from the Virginia Historical Society; James Sweany and Anne Toohey of the Library of Congress; Judy Bolton and Tara Zachary Laver of Hill Memorial at LSU; Sharalyn Howcroft of the LDS Church History Library; and Eric Grundset and Anne Ruta of the National Society Daughters of the American Revolution.

My first inkling for this type of study began in 2002 in Lund, Sweden, where I was part of the Committee on Outreach and User Services of the International Council on Archives. For participation in my early thinking, I thank Christer Bogefeldt, Antonio Lechasseur, Daniela Ferrari, Olga Muzychuk, and Coleman Chua. Antonio, especially, has been a consistent presence in my professional life, even from afar, building as he was then the National Library and Archives of Canada's Genealogy

Centre. A research fellowship grant in 2003 and 2004 from the National Historical Publications and Records Commission (NHPRC) allowed me to develop other beginning work on perceptions of archivists on the work of genealogy, and I am grateful for that opportunity. In 2005, the flood that followed Hurricane Katrina brought a three-week stay at the Newberry Library in Chicago, for which I am appreciative, especially since I had then spent months moving materials out of a damaged building and thinking a great deal about family history in a less welcoming way. After hurricane recovery, Tulane University offered me a research enhancement grant in the winter of 2007. I am grateful to the university for this grant, which made it possible for me to conduct related work on this project, especially on the private archives of Mary Anne de Boisblanc and Carolyn Ivy Shimek. I am also grateful to Sally Kenney and my other colleagues at the Newcomb College Institute for allowing me a sabbatical year in 2010–2011 to work on this and other projects. I also thank the Interlibrary Loan Department at Howard-Tilton Memorial Library, especially Patricia Windham and Hayden Battle for their amazing efforts in amassing so many different sources on family history.

Looking to France, I thank François Weil for his question about the characteristics of New Orleans genealogy that were different from those elsewhere. Looking to the Netherlands, I thank Selma Leydesdorff for her questions about women and memory, José van Dijck for her questions about religion and family history, Rob Kroes for his questions about gender and the place of men in family photographs, and most of all, Eric Ketelaar. Without Eric's scholarship and his collegiality, none of this work would have been accomplished.

A visit to Salt Lake City in 2011 made for a special inquiry into the history of family history. For that time of learning, I thank Russ Lynch, Wayne Morris, Larry Telford, and Kahlile Mehr.

I thank others who also asked very good questions about my work. Francesca Morgan is a reader beyond parallel whose own work on the history of genealogy I have long admired. Sally Reeves knows more than almost anyone about the records of New Orleans. Thank you again, Sally, for the generosity of time in reading drafts of this work. Your example too has been important to the whole of my professional life. Greg Lambousy is another colleague to thank doubly since his knowledge of the city and its collections contributed to this book, and to my happiness, as well.

I thank as well yet other helpers: Elizabeth Shown Mills for questions answered; Winston De Ville for an overview of the whole of the project; Mary Allen Johnson and Susan Johnson for their skills with footnotes and proofreading; Harriet Swift and Alisa Plant for early comments on writing; Bea Calvert for conversations on DNA; Yuka Petz for photographs and help with images and digital problems; Jan Gilbert and Kevin McCaffrey for insights into art; Anne Atkinson and Mary Ann and John

Travis for last-minute reading of chapters; Beth Willinger for being always generous and supportive; and Wendy Wolf and Hugh Van Dusen for such a long and good friendship that started around books.

Thanks also go to friends who offered me time in their welcoming homes, or kindnesses left on my doorstep: Myrte and Rein Breeman; Tina Dove; Marie-Christine Format; Michel Goisque; Myriam Huet; Becky and Jonny Jordan; Peggy Kohlepp; Linda Lehmil and Eric Hanemann; Marston Luce; and Françoise, Patrick, and Antoine Perié.

Among my own family, I thank my sisters and their husbands, children, and grandchildren. I thank my daughter Franny, her husband Drew, and their beautiful daughter, Tilly. My cousins, Shannon Miller Lord and Sophia Hunter Ethier, were both alive when I began this work and are now deceased. Yet they also deserve thanks; they taught me about our family and our resilient happiness.

There are not many professions in which one's duties always involve gratitude for those who have saved materials that now tell about the past. The professional work of archivists always does, and also involves the writing of thanks for collections new to one's oversight. So it is with special pleasure that I end my acknowledgments with gratitude in general to my own ancestors, especially my step-grandmother, father, and mother, who always told me that the most important part of life was to be useful and to acknowledge those who helped us to be so. That I did so in archives makes me all the more grateful to them and to the world in general. I thank you all who read here, for that, as well.

CITY OF REMEMBERING

CHAPTER ONE

Introduction

This is a book about practices and histories of genealogy and its more informal version, family history. It is not a traditional history but rather a personal and professional journey. Genealogy is defined most simply as the study of lineages, or more accurately in regard to today's endeavors, as "the study of an entire family unit, including collateral as well as direct line descendants."[1] I think of family history as encompassing more than biological descent, as involving the neighborhoods in which people lived, or some sense of a few key elements that made up daily lives. Overall, family history becomes a gift of remarkable generosity, not just to one's immediate kin but also to a wider world, to cousins across time and space.

I learned to think like this from genealogists I've interviewed and worked among during the past ten years.[2] What they reminded me about often was that very little is left to us from past lives, from our kin or anyone really. So, this is also a book about what does remain behind: records, stories, and artifacts. Of course, there are other "remainders." We have the great histories of nations, cities, and organizations. But usually they are not what we use as touchstones of our living. Asked to choose what items they would take when leaving a home in an emergency, most people tell of items from family life: photographs, needlework, a child's artwork, a letter, a book with an inscription. These material objects remind us that life is a continuing process, that something can be passed on that is unique and is at once private and universal in love. The practice of family history does that in daily doses.

I begin in New Orleans since it is the place where I have learned about such means and matters, humble and grandiose. I often think about what it means to live among records, to live too in a particular climate, since I am an archivist. The city's hot, humid weather is notoriously unkind to paper. Yet the foundation of much of the majesty and the less visible but unassuming, ordinary local life is formed from sepia photographs of the city's immigrant families, the sturdy pages of birth registrations from Saint Louis Cathedral, the small scraps of the earliest French Superior Council records, the elegant and weighty leaves of papers used by notaries, and ledgers from the judicial deliberations of the Illustrious Spanish Cabildo. This book is about these local distinctions as seen within the context of a larger national history of genealogy.

Begin with the self. That is one of the first dictates of genealogy.[3] I have never traced my own family's history, but it figures in my interest in the

FIGURE 1.1
Emily Croom Norris, John Houston Mifflin, ca. 1835. Oil on canvas. Photograph by Yuka Petz.

FIGURE 1.2
Calvin Norris, John Houston Mifflin, ca. 1835. Oil on canvas. Photograph by Yuka Petz.

paths that others have taken to know their ancestors. I started to think of my own life as going by (unrecorded, more or less) when I inherited two nineteenth-century portraits that now hang in my New Orleans home. Their story begins when John Houston Mifflin, a Philadelphia portrait painter, journeyed to the South in the 1830s.[4] One of the places where he stopped was at the Marengo County, Alabama, home of my fifth great-grandmother and grandfather. Mifflin painted their likenesses in oil on large canvases, twenty-four by thirty inches. They were named Emily Hare Croom Norris (1817–1866?) and Calvin Norris (1806–1853).[5]

I know something about the portraits since I have always been the guardian of documentation on our family. My mother passed me a folder on Mifflin, at some point, with her notes that he had been a student of Thomas Sully (1783–1872). As genealogists say, "Every family has someone appointed as recordkeeper."

My possession of the portraits suggests another story too that is common to many families. I was the one to get the portraits after our mother's death because of another legacy, this time of circumstance and behavior. I had the smallest house; I could not accommodate the larger legacies of furniture that my sisters could.

Genealogists often talk about gifts of generosity within families and within the reading rooms of libraries where they work. Like the acts of sharing they told me about, my sisters' gift of thoughtfulness itself derives from a sort of birthright: our mother's mother and her extensive family had been Quakers, a group that countless histories have described as quiet and meditative people. This family also carried, and still carries, a gene for a disease that restricts breath. Even those not affected by the disease are socialized by people whose voices can often be faint. As one of my cousins once said to me, the adjective "soft-spoken" is written in many descriptions of family members.

This family, my mother's maternal grandmother and grandfather, came to the United States in the 1870s. My great-grandfather and his brother were known in their Scottish village as enterprising people, and so they were hired by an English lord who gave them money to buy up timberland and start a lumber business in the American South. In the classrooms of my childhood, such people were called carpetbaggers, who, after the Yankees had done their damage, further destroyed the plantation way of life. This education was another kind of inheritance.

One of these great-grandparents brought the genetic disease to this side of the Atlantic. People with this disease are often lethargic, although in our family we say "complacent," and people with this disease sleep more than others do. These symptoms fated us for parenting and family life that, for at least two generations and likely more, had been understated; had been marked by gratitude for good health; and, as far as I could ever tell from my grandmother and her sisters, had been accepting of ill health, the placement of it under the category of "everyone is different." This meant that we, the lucky ones who thrived, were also given a lot of freedom and—I have come to believe—the chance to be reflective enough to be considerate. All this boiled down to my current custody of the portraits.

FIGURE 1.3
Helen and Billy Hunter, with their mother, May Prince Hunter, ca. 1910. Studio print. Collection of the author. Helen was one family member who had a more pronounced form of myotonic dystrophy. That said, she did not display symptoms until her late teens, and here one sees something of the normalcy, and hence likely the thought of the future involved with having a studio print made of her, her mother, and brother.

My step-grandmother called the genetic illness "the horrible disease." Although we always knew that it was a form of muscular dystrophy, only when I was in my forties did I learn its name: myotonic dystrophy.

As genealogists often told me, one's mother's family often holds the most crucial place in one's knowledge of the past. This was true for my sisters and me, and also for our mother: we thought of ourselves as primarily descended from her maternal side of the family rather than from the side of my father or even from my maternal grandfather, whose great-grandmother and grandfather were Emily and Calvin Norris of the portraits.

My mother's mother, our granny, had divorced our grandfather in the mid-1920s. They had had their first child in 1916, and they knew from the very beginning that she was a sickly child. Today we would know that she had the juvenile onset of myotonic dystrophy, but then there was not enough medical information to tell them so. They chose to think or

FIGURE 1.4
Helen Hunter (right) and friend, ca. 1930. Family snapshot. Collection of the author. Helen needed a wheelchair by the time she reached her late twenties. In their albums, families often leave out images that show evidence of disabilities.

were told to think that she had some other, unnamed condition. Even when others in the family were diagnosed with muscular dystrophy, they thought of this disease as passed on the male line only and did not know about the other manifestations, such as heart problems that this child had, as associated with a genetically linked problem. Not knowing then what we know now, my grandparents decided to stay together long enough to have another child, a healthy one. Both my mother and my grandfather's second wife—again, our step-grandmother—would even boast about this gamble they took. Their passion for life, their confidence, their entrepreneurial daring seemed to be epitomized by this decision to have a second child, who would, as they never doubted, be healthy, even though, or perhaps especially since, they also planned to divorce once this child was born.

We know today that myotonic dystrophy is transmitted with a predictable and pitiless statistical frequency to both male and female descendants: if you have the disease, you have a fifty-fifty chance of passing it to any child you might have. You can also possess varying degrees of the disease. Some people might have only mild symptoms: the sleepiness and softness of voice I have described, or early cataracts, or, in men, early balding. Still, a mildly affected parent *may* have a severely affected child.[6]

My grandmother and my grandfather did not know these chances. They dared to have another child. In 1920, they had my mother.

She did not have the disease. My grandmother and her friends did not say the word "healthy." They said, about our mother, that she was fun and lively; an early talker; a popular child who smiled easily, was good at art and math, and was easy to take on a trip around town. Much later, in 1998, a genetic test would show she did not have even a mild form of the disease. They knew they were lucky but not as lucky as *we* know that they were.

In addition to this healthy child who became my mother, my grandparents had a friendly divorce. My sisters and I moved easily between them. The grandmothers (my real grandmother and my step-grandmother) talked to each other almost every day. This civility was another legacy passed on to us.

I was named Susan for the child who had the disease—Sue Norris, who would live into her twenties but who was never healthy, never normal. There is evidence that she lived a fairly good life. She went to school, she made trips, she read books and kept scrapbooks. My mother became an artist, she said, because her sister would not or could not play with other children, could not run and jump, and would not or could not easily communicate; painting pictures on their front porch, my mother could console her sister.

Sue Norris signed her name in books, wrote about the movies she saw as she pasted magazine clippings in scrapbooks, and collected dolls. These ephemeral items attest to the story she could weave on daily life, reasons to get up in the morning, and delight in living itself. Genealogists made me see all these little items differently, made me place them as products of both family and worldly habits as well as family and worldly diseases.

My grandmother clearly always valued the belongings from her daughter's life. We know that because our own house burned to the ground in 1955, and anything that survived is rimmed with black edges and the smell of smoke. So when my grandmother died in 1959, my mother could not part with the things her mother had saved, and she took them to our new house. One box that I am sure had not been opened in decades contained a list Sue Norris made of ten collected dolls. I found this list in 2009 and read over its description of chosen names, outfits worn and outfits that could be created, and visions about the world (here a Scandinavian doll, here an American Indian), but also information on who gave her each doll, and, in microcosm, a picture again of family and neighborhood.

That sort of dating of memories too is something many genealogists told about. In describing the artifacts of their families, they took on the responsibility of knowing who saved what and when.

When I look up at Emily and Calvin, I sweep through these memories told to me. They hold other accounts of individual acts that made my mother who she was, and thus made me, my sisters, and our children. The portraits say to me, *we are part of your grandfather, who dared to have your mother.*

I know at the same time that these thoughts always indicate some sort of adjustment, some sort of calibration with the present. The disease was difficult, and other difficulties too were present, always and for everyone. Then I jump to a bigger context: The portraits of Emily and Calvin hold more for me than these family stories. They set in motion a form of "mnemonic synchronization," part of the politics of genealogy that involves what one scholar calls "cutting and pasting" among other categories where one "chooses" ancestors. One focuses on a certain line, a particular lineage, and ignores others.[7] But there are always parts that are difficult to ignore. Even if I try some sort of rearrangement in my mind of what I have inherited, the portraits still say to me "slavery."

Emily and Calvin are beautiful and calm as people there in the gilded wooden frames. Their clothes are crisp, here, satiny, there—and these luxuries and more are evidence of their place in the hierarchy of master, mistress, and slaves. They make me wonder about other lives that circled about the room where they sat for the paintings, where they undertook this passive role that also told of their entitlement in the very act of being able to afford portraits. What were the compensations, strengths, and weaknesses in these other lives in the room? How was time shaped for these slaves and how did they eke out some time of their own? Where was joy for them, or perhaps only, what did they think about the leisure to sit for a portrait?

Emily and Calvin's daughter Susan traveled to Mobile and married into a family of physicians. Her husband would be a surgeon in the Confederate Army, defending this way of life that imprisoned people of African descent. In turn, that Susan and her doctor husband had another Susan, who married into a family who had come to Mobile in the 1820s from Pennsylvania. They, like my mother's mother's family, had been Quakers, although I know not if they continued to practice Quakerism in the South. In Mobile, they had a brickyard. Court records can tell me where it was located, and from a clipping, I know that these ancestors donated bricks for the construction of one of the city's first African American churches. This gift is a more favorable memory, synchronized and socialized, than the memory of the other side of the family, their ownership of slaves and fighting for the Confederacy.

These inheritances—some preferred, some not—have made me all the more intrigued by family histories. My profession makes me frame these histories, my own and others, in other terms as well. For archivists, stories and artifacts are part of the context of records, which we define as "data or information that has been fixed on some medium." To be permanent evidence, records must show the circumstances of their creation, be created in a structure that lasts, and possess content that a given society considers worthy of retention (of archiving). These properties of context, structure, and content must be combined in such a way that they can be used as an extension of human memory "to demonstrate accountability."[8] Most importantly, records must continue to exist as sources, must move in an array of knowledge across time, and must be accessible and known across time. I have organized this book around this archival vocabulary, slightly reordered to deal with the contexts, structures, contents, and continuum of genealogical practices.

In chapters 2 through 4, I discuss national and local New Orleanian histories of genealogy. Chapters 5 and 6 introduce formats of materials used and loved by family historians, again nationally and locally. Chapters 2 through 6 also offer generalities told to me by family historians, while chapters 7 and 8 deal with specific families, their genealogical stories, and the influence of gender and technologies on the ways they remember the past. Chapter 9 concerns the continuum of records, the work of genealogists in the transmission of the past though documentary sources.

I have alternated the local with the national in imitation of the work of genealogists who gather records across many boundaries. All their activities represent a particularly American pursuit. Genealogy in the United States concerns the beauty of hope as well as the sadness within migration. We have gained, the genealogists have taught me, in our movements. We have gained the wisdom of leaving clues behind us, practices of creation as well as practices of historical research, empathy for those in the present as well as the past, and even imagination of the future.

CHAPTER TWO

Foundations of One City in a Nation of Genealogy

In 1822, the trustees of Saint Louis Cathedral in New Orleans commissioned a portrait of a priest who had served their church almost continuously since 1781. Born in Sedella in southern Spain, Antonio Moreno y Arze (1748–1829) was called most often by his French name, Père Antoine. The trustees, also referred to often enough by their French designation, the *marguilliers,* wanted to show their respect and loyalty for someone who had been a valiant, if sometimes contentious, figure.[1]

Names tell family stories, genealogists told me, and these choices of French names were no exceptions.[2] In the city that could adjust its languages to fit philosophies of culture and families, late eighteenth- and early nineteenth-century residents could have called the Saint Louis Cathedral priest Père Antoine, Padre Antonio, or even Father Anthony; for the trustees, they could have chosen *fabriciens* or *administrateurs.*[3] People seemed to have chosen the names most associated with older French rule: watch that, genealogists said, societies and individuals have reasons to change the way they call themselves.

Contemporaries of Père Antoine and later scholars also called him less benign names. He was the "scourge" of the Church in Louisiana, a rebel in the face of both ecclesiastical and secular authorities, a titular representative of the Spanish Inquisition, "a law unto himself," father to a child by his mulatto housekeeper, and finally beloved caregiver of the poor and the enslaved.[4] These varying opinions reflected something else that genealogists wanted me to see: New Orleans can be not only multicultural, as all family history is, but also accommodating to many sentiments.

Père Antoine's name has lasted until today as part of the overall aura of the city, without the necessity of a portrait. But artist Edmund Brewster still left an important clue not often noted about the priest, yet certainly attached to the story of American genealogy: he painted Père Antoine with his right hand resting on a book.

As genealogists told me, the history of genealogy in New Orleans revolved first and foremost around such a book that we can interpret as a sacramental register. Family historians in the city focused their first attention and their considerable pride on these religious records of births, marriages, and burials.

FIGURE 2.1
Père Antoine, Edmund Brewster, 1822. Oil on canvas. Courtesy of the Archdiocese of New Orleans, on loan at the Louisiana State Museum. This larger-than-life portrait, almost eight feet high, captures the commanding presence of the Capuchin priest, today almost always called Père Antoine. He was a recordkeeper's recordkeeper in that he began a preservation program and also, from time to time, annotated his entries in sacramental registers.

FIGURE 2.2

Baptismal index draft, Saint Louis Cathedral, 1796–1802, Personal Documents Series, Collection 525 (13), Louisiana Research Center, Tulane University.

Père Antoine and his assistant, archivist Rufino Thomas Fernandez, likely created this draft index to sacramental records. Genealogists know well the importance of indexes and throughout the twentieth century undertook many painstaking and protracted projects to provide access to family history materials.

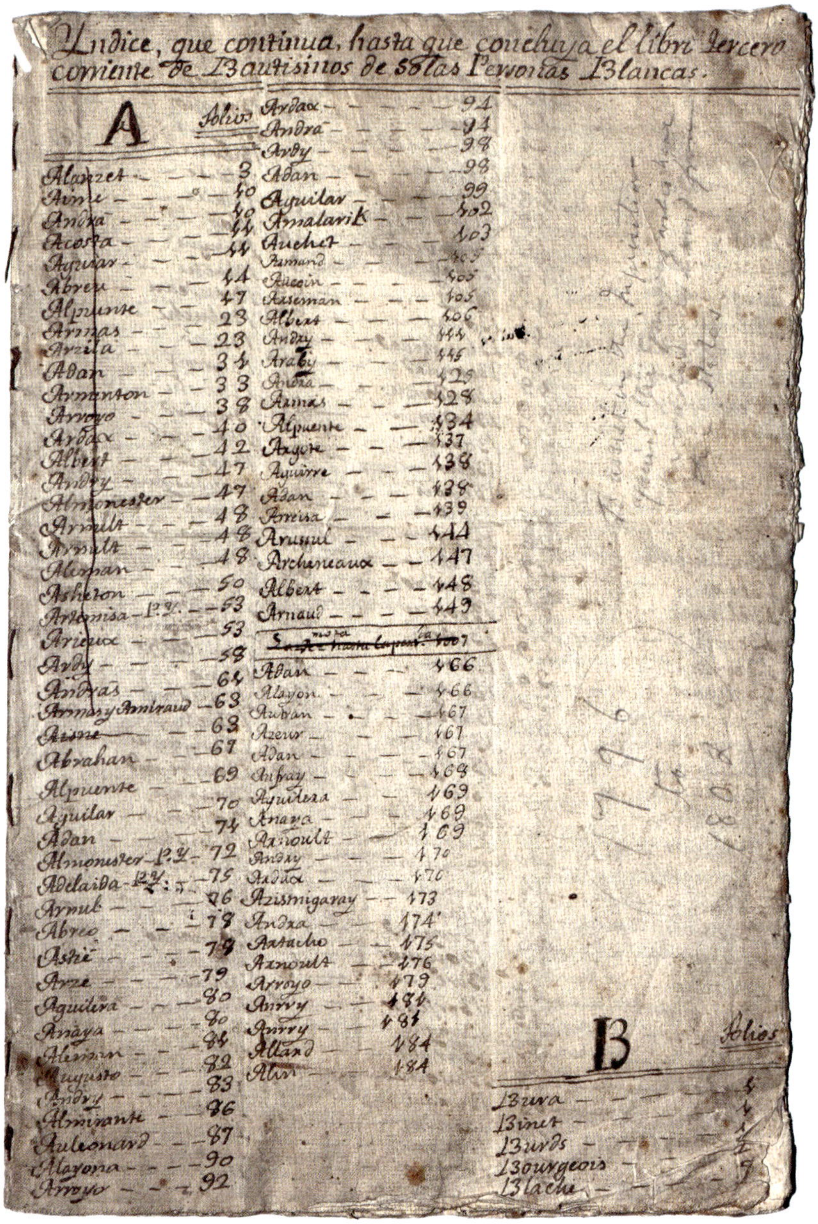

Yndice, que continua, hasta que concluya el libro tercero corriente de Bautismos de solas Personas Blancas.

A	Folios		
Alanzet	3	Ardax	94
Aime	10	Andra	94
Andra	10	Ardy	98
Acosta	11	Adan	98
Aguilar	11	Aguilar	99
Abreu	11	Amalarik	102
Alpuente	17	Auchet	103
Armas	23	Aumand	104
Arzila	23	Aucoin	105
Adan	31	Auseman	105
Armenton	33	Albert	106
Arroyo	38	Andry	111
Ardax	40	Araby	115
Albert	42	Andra	125
Ardry	47	Armas	128
Almonester	47	Alpuente	134
Arnult	48	Azgote	137
Arnult	48	Aguirre	138
Aleman	48	Adan	138
Asheton	50	Arreisa	139
Artemisa-P.Y.	53	Arnaut	144
Arieux	53	Archenaux	147
Ardy	58	Albert	148
Andras	64	Arnaud	149
Armas y Amiraud	63	Adan	166
Aime	63	Alayon	166
Abrahan	67	Audan	167
Alpuente	69	Azeur	167
Aguilar	70	Adan	167
Adan	74	Aufray	169
Almonester-P.Y.	72	Aguilera	169
Adelaida-P.Y.	75	Anaya	169
Arnul	76	Arnoult	169
Abreo	78	Andry	170
Ashé	78	Andrac	170
Arze	79	Azismigaray	173
Aguilera	80	Andra	174
Anaya	80	Antacho	175
Aleman	84	Arnoult	176
Augusto	82	Arroyo	179
Andry	83	Anry	184
Almirante	86	Anry	184
Auleonard	87	Alland	184
Alayona	90	Alain	184
Arroyo	92		

B	Folios
Bura	4
Binet	4
Burds	4
Bourgeois	[illegible]
Blache	[illegible]

1796 a 1802

Père Antoine did not write the first religious record of the city (a sacramental entry for a marriage in 1720), but he saved it, or rather he saved the information in it. Sometime in his beginning years in the city, in the 1780s, he established the state's first known preservation program. He ordered the copying of the sacramental registers that had been completed by priests who had come before him. He explained his process in the newly copied registers. Not only that, but weeks or months, maybe even years before the fire of 1788 that burned most of the city, he had had time to consider that it might be wise to place the originals and the copies in

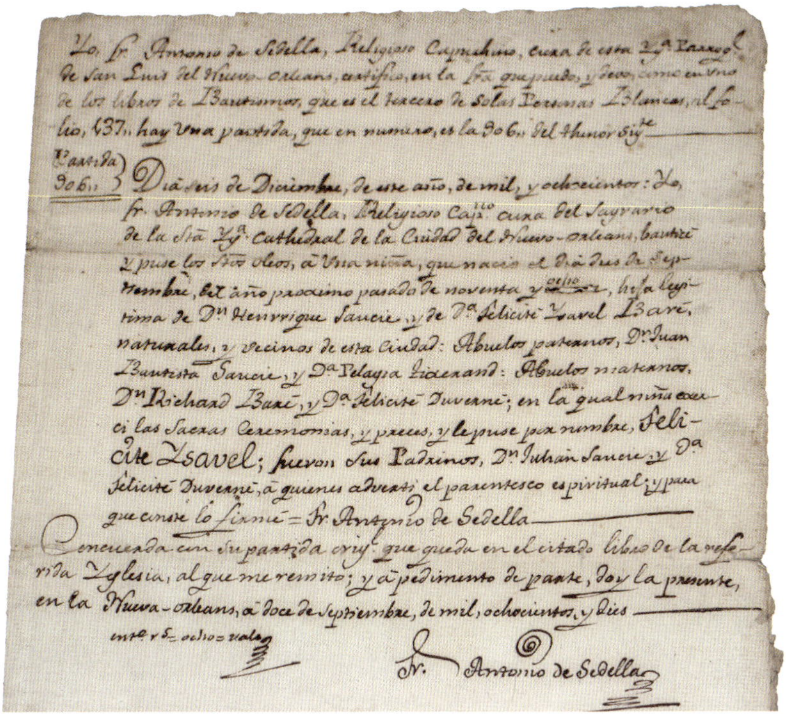

Yo, fr. Antonio de Sedella, Religioso Capuchino, cura de esta Sta. Parroq.l de San Luis del Nuevo-orleans, certifico, en la forma que puedo, y devo, como en uno de los libros de Bautismos, que es el tercero de solas Personas Blancas, al folio, 137,, hay una partida, que en numero, es la 906,, del thenor sig.te —

Partida 906,, Dia seis de Diciembre, de este año, de mil, y ochocientos: Yo, fr. Antonio de Sedella, Religioso Cap.no cura del Sagrario de la Sta. Yg.a Cathedral de la Ciudad del Nuevo-orleans, bautizé y puse los Stos. oleos, a una niña, que nació el dia doze de Septiembre, del año proximo pasado de noventa y ocho, hija legitima de Dn. Henrrique Saucie, y de Da. Felicité Ysavel Baré, naturales, y vecinos de esta Ciudad: Abuelos paternos, Dn. Juan Bautista Saucie, y Da. Pelagia Lizenard: Abuelos maternos, Dn. Richard Baré, y Da. Felicité Duverne; en la qual niña exerci las Sacras Ceremonias, y preces, y le puse por nombre, Felicite Ysavel; fueron sus Padrinos, Dn. Julian Saucie, y Da. Felicité Duverne, a quienes adverti el parentesco espiritual; y para que conste lo firmé = fr. Antonio de Sedella —

Concuerda con su partida orig.l que queda en el citado libro de la referida Yglesia, al que me remito; y a pedimento de parte, doy la presente, en la Nueva-orleans, a doce de Septiembre, de mil, ochocientos, y dies —

entre r s = ocho = vale

fr. Antonio de Sedella

FIGURE 2.3
Certificate of baptism of Felicité Isavel Saucier, dated September 12, 1819, Spanish, by Fray Antonio de Sedella, which he extracted from the original entry in Saint Louis Cathedral Baptism Book 3, part 2, folio 138, No. 906. From the family papers of Jack Belsom, New Orleans.

separate locations. He took the 1720 original to the home of the director of tobacco. He kept the copy in the church. Then, on the day of the fire, when he was called to help the Ursulines save their convent from destruction, he threw the copy and other papers into a pile in the Plaza de Armas (later Jackson Square, another name choice). The copies survived; the originals did not.[5]

Layers of Records

In noting this fire, I am sent on a trail of others who saved records so that genealogists can do their work today. Again, this is the most important of all points about how we know the past: records must be saved so that access to them will be granted, so that familiarity with them will be spread, generation to generation. Père Antoine acted as only one tiny element in this archival universe when he registered births, marriages, and deaths. He followed the rules of the Catholic Church, begun in increments from the late 1400s and institutionalized by the Council of Trent in 1563.[6] Contemporaries (in other outposts of the European colonizers and in towns, cities, and tiny hamlets in Europe) also created and saved their registers, their ledgers, their pieces of paper. They wrote names on censuses, ship manifests, marriage contracts, land grants, troop rolls, poll tax listings, and more obscure lists, everything from attestations of purity to payments of chimney taxes. Users of these records, in turn, created indexes to these materials, produced yet other lists, or recopied and in due course filmed materials. It is easy to forget that these recordkeepers and family historians did most of this work within only the past 500 years, with the bulk of the work done in the past 150 years, from the late nineteenth century until today. Now, with a keystroke, many of their efforts, their points of entry into names, have been scanned, and so have many of the original records from which their compilations first came.

These recordkeepers and family historians made materials that today can likely be found in the largest genealogical library in the world, the Family History Library in Salt Lake City. Here, there are "over 2.4 million rolls of microfilmed genealogical records; 727,000 microfiches; 356,000 books, serials, and other formats; over 4,500 periodicals; and 3,725 electronic resources."[7] There are also other records to add to these numbers, from other repositories, family materials, and oral accounts. The Family History Library does not hold them all. Local sources remain central to genealogy, records like those created by Père Antoine, which are not in the huge databases.

Such vast numbers and varying types of sources to uncover could easily intimidate. Ignore scale, one family historian wisely told me. Start with one or at the most four people.[8] Follow them. I have tried to use this limitation of four, but ended up with more in the genealogy of genealogy in New Orleans. Still my list is pared down. It is five, by some counts, at least.

Foundational Figures and Institutions

First, there is the Catholic Church and especially Père Antoine. He, alongside his assistant, the cantor and archivist Rufino Thomas Fernandez, remain evocative of local genealogical culture in New Orleans but also show the influence of national and international practices.

A second pivotal local institution remaining from Louisiana's colonial past is civil law, that descendant of Roman law, modeled first in New Orleans on the *coutume de Paris* or "custom of Paris." Genealogists always mentioned the notarial records, unique, they felt to Louisiana, or almost so in the United States (since they can be found in Puerto Rico as well).

Civil law favored the work of notaries (rather than lawyers). The notaries, very different from notary publics known elsewhere in the United States, were skilled and licensed. Notaries in New Orleans dealt with any and everyone buying land, borrowing money, making wills and prenuptial agreements, forming partnerships and corporations, agreeing on building contracts, purchasing large supplies of goods, depositing plans and surveys, and appointing agents to act on their behalf. Before the Civil War, the notaries in New Orleans also documented the purchase, sale, and emancipation of slaves. Today most of the notaries' acts are found in a central repository that holds some forty million pages of signed acts that account for every commercial transaction between 1735 and 1970.[9]

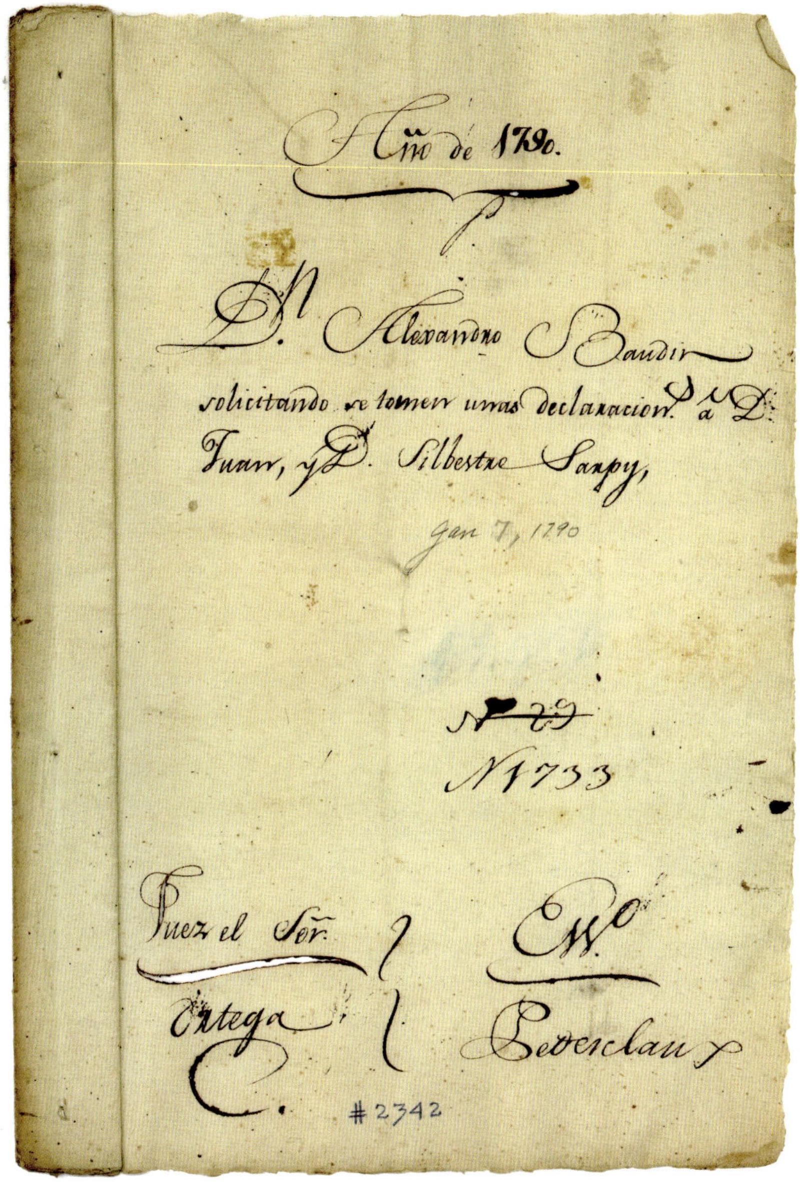

Año de 1790.

D.n Alexandro Baudin solicitando se tomen unas declaraciones a D.n Juan, y D.n Silbestre Sarpy,

Jan 7, 1790

N° 29

N 1733

Juez el Sor. Ortega

Escno. Pedesclaux

#2342

FIGURE 2.4
Declaration. Alexandro Baudin and Juan Silbestre Sarpy. Before Pedro Pedesclaux, No. 1733, January 7, 1790. Judicial Records of the Spanish Superior Council. Courtesy of the Louisiana State Museum and the Louisiana Historical Society.

This Spanish judicial record shows the signature of Pedro Pedesclaux, who is credited with saving most of the French and Spanish judicial records during the fire that burned the city in 1788. He later told of saving these records at the expense of losing his own home, office, and personal belongings.

Genealogists use these records by looking through indexes to find a recognizable name. If lucky, they find the details of such diverse events as an ancestor making a claim for goods lost at sea, an ancestor's involvement in a complaint about the overpricing of flour, a whole gathering of relatives charged with determining guardianship of children after the early death of a father, or any number of other scenarios in which forebears found cause to visit a notary.

One exceptional notary, Pedro Pedesclaux (1760–1816), came to New Orleans from the Basque region of Spain sometime in the 1780s, about the time Père Antoine arrived. By 1784, Pedesclaux had established himself in his profession, handling the businesses of a number of families. By 1788, the year of the fire, he was also clerk, recorder of mortgages, and notary for the Cabildo, the Spanish governing body. In these capacities, he was the archivist of the French records that had been left so that the Spanish might continue governance. Pedesclaux's duty was to guard and preserve these records: to keep them in a chest made of tin or cedar and to lock this chest with three keys. The records were important, in other words. So, on the day of the 1788 fire, alongside the records hurled into the Plaza de Armas by Père Antoine, the good notary saved another part of the city's heritage: its civil and criminal records. The contents of his étude (his "office," for the French language still prevailed, more often than not, over the Spanish) were more important than his family's clothes and furniture, which were lost in the fire.[10] Tossed and saved, these judicial and notarial records form the second pillar of the foundation of the city's history. Added to the similarly saved sacramental records, these records collectively undergird the city's unique genealogical culture.

That said, genealogy is never stationary, never based only on one culture. It is a stream of geographic locations and many kinds of lists, all based on differing bodies of government and church, differing family habits. Migration itself motivates the desire to know why ancestors traveled to North America; migration itself is part of the foundation of American genealogy.

Thus, in the history of American genealogy, one usually looks first to the first thirteen English colonies, the first early migrating ancestors who left written records. Within their eastern seaboard homes, the foundational figure to consider is John Farmer (1789–1838), who formalized family history work in New England and articulated an ideology that genealogy could be an acceptable pastime for a democratic country. He became "the most distinguished Genealogist and Antiquary" of his time.[11] He compiled his book *A Genealogical Register of the First Settlers of New England* using listings of the names of magistrates, the ministers of the Gospel, the graduates of Harvard University, and other groups. He and his colleagues also visited people in their homes and copied information from family records. They did so because they wanted to name a "large portion of the First Settlers, of the most prominent, as well as the more humble." This aspiration was not possible for one individual to complete, Farmer wrote, but he set forth the task for future genealogists. He offered an origin story for New England families that was equal, as he saw it, to English stories of descent from the Normans. The location was important: *New England* would be central to American genealogy, but Farmer's emphasis not on the manor houses but on private institutions and humble homes, and on rules of evidence, was also critical.[12]

The formation of the New England Historic Genealogical Society (NEHGS) in 1845 and the creation of its *Register* two years later confirmed the leadership of New England families in the history of American genealogy.[13] New England nurtured this center of activity around genealogical records. Until the expansion of the Latter-day Saints' Family History Library in the 1960s, the NEHGS Library was the only one of its kind, devoted exclusively to genealogy, in the world.

The "ancestors" of this newer library, the Family History Library, are the other two foundational figures to consider: Joseph Smith (1805–1840), who established the LDS Church; and Susa Young Gates (1856–1933), who established the first classes on genealogical work for church members. As Farmer encouraged genealogical inquiries of all early Americans, so too did Smith and Gates take the next steps that made possible the access genealogists have today to records. Smith articulated the LDS Church's position on "sealing" families for eternity. Sealing required (and still requires) the naming of ancestors, who could then be baptized in proxy into the LDS Church. To find these names, LDS members must compile genealogies. In this way, ancestors who did not have the chance to hear of this new religion are given continued love after death.[14] Gates furthered this policy. She popularized genealogy and united the women of the church in learning and teaching research methods and amassing books for what would become the Family History Library.[15]

Colonial Influences First

All these pillars of genealogy, and of course many other individuals and institutions who made American family history, inherited attitudes and habits that had crossed the Atlantic. The first colonists came with both practices and prejudices toward lineage. They would have known of royal genealogies in Europe (created since the sixth century) and of lineage documentation amassed by the nobility (created since the twelfth century).[16] In Europe, genealogical evidence could prove families' rights to lands surrounding their homes, could mean lower taxes since so promised by an earlier monarch, and could bestow privilege even in the choice of a church pew.[17]

The century before the first European colonists settled in North America, the 1500s, was an especially pivotal one for genealogy. During this time in England, members of the College of Arms began visits to the homes of the nobility to inspect their documents, specifically their suitability for displaying coats of arms. The heralds, already practiced in reading the meaning of decorative displays on the armor and clothing of knights in tournaments, outlined the types of acceptable personal knowledge, records, and customs that could support the claims of family histories.[18] Within less privileged enclaves, other people also found practical reasons to write down their lineages. In northern Italian city-states, merchants took to writing in beautiful volumes that combined the functions of a commonplace book, an account book, a chronicle, and a

FIGURE 2.5
Gravestone of Henry and Jane (Dummer) Sewall, 1700. Photograph by Harriette Merrifield Forbes. Farber Collection. Courtesy of the American Antiquarian Society.

The writing framed by the winged death's heads, copied here exactly as rendered on the gravestone, reads: Mr. HENRY SEWALL (SENT BY Mr. HENRY SEWALL, HIS FATHER IN YE SHIP ELSABETH & DORCAS CAPT. WATTS COMMANDER) ARRIVED AT BOSTON 1634. WINTERD AT IPSWICH. HELPD BEGIN THIS PLANTATION, 1635 FURNISHING ENGLISH SERVANT NEAT. CATTEL, & PROVISIONS. MARRIED MRs. JANE DUMMER MARCH YE 25, 1646. DIED MAY, YE 16, 1700. AETAT. 86. HIS FRUTFULL VINE, BEING THUS DISJOIND FELL TO YE GROUND JANUARY YE 13; FOLLOWING; AETAT 74. PSAL.27.10

Whereas only a small percentage of those who lived have any gravestone at all, cemetery markers and records remain a favored source for genealogists. In addition, genealogists see cemetery records, as all other records, as a chance for self-education. As one said of a similar inscription: "I learned the Latin for age, *aet*." Note that in Henry and Jane Sewall's headstone, age is written *aetat*. Henry Sewall died at age seventy-four, "fell to ye ground." As another genealogist said, "You get a sort of poetry and passion too, in these ways of explaining that our ancestors had."

diary. They sometimes divided their *ricordanze* into two parts, one for accounts and the other for memories.[19] As paper became more plentiful, other European households also "turned account books and books of hours into family records. . . . All these private records associated genealogical consciousness and celebration of social aspiration, ancient roots, and power."[20]

Plentiful paper also made rulers take more notice of the importance of records. Cognizant of the quality of the recordkeeping that she had inherited as head of the relatively new Church of England, in 1597 Elizabeth I ordered the ministers of the Church to write their parish records of births, marriages, and deaths within registers made of parchment paper. They were also to recopy earlier, cheaper registers at least back to the beginning of her reign in 1558 and enter the information they found into the new ledgers. She further mandated that the ministers were to submit a copy of their parchment books to their bishops each year.[21] As if mirroring this monitoring by others, some individuals and families similarly began to write names, births, marriages, and deaths in the blank pages of their own religious books.[22]

Although some North American settlers sought to abandon the rules of recordkeeping maintained by the church and state, others emulated European forms of private recordkeeping.[23] They arrived with and continued practices of recording births, marriages, and burials in the church registries. They arrived also with the names of families on the back pages of Bibles. Moreover, as in Europe, they carved names on gravestones, etched family initials in silverware, painted family likenesses on canvas, printed family names on bookplates, and wrote names in commonplace books.[24]

Colonists also wrote about family heritage in letters sent between the Americas and Europe. Eager with "personal curiosity and desirous of connections to the past," they relied on relatives in England and Ireland to furnish them with genealogical information.[25]

One of the first published American genealogies appeared within an account of an early settler, Roger Clap (1609–1691). In 1731, one of his descendants, James Blake, added a family history to the description of the new American home. Blake considered that information on both family and settlement of the colony might "instruct, counsel, direct and command" his "children and his children's children to the Latest Posterity." Genealogy, Blake saw, allowed some sense of immortality.[26]

A more pivotal publication, in 1771, was the straightforward compilation by Luke Stebbins about his ancestors: *A Genealogy of the Family of Mr. Samuel Stebbins and Mrs. Hannah Stebbins, His Wife*. Luke Stebbins's purpose was to "give Demonstration of the Power, Faithfulness, and Goodness of GOD to their ancestors; excite in their Children and Children's Children, Thankfulness, Hope and Dependence on the GOD of their Fore-Fathers." His record of family would also instruct future generations in knowing "where their Ancestors have led pious and religious Lives, been exemplary in their Conversation." Genealogy to him and others would be a means by which compilers might "excite in their Descendants a laudable Ambition to imitate those Things that were excellent, praiseworthy and amiable in them." Even in his printer's statement, Luke Stebbins's book left a remarkable clue about American genealogy. Ebenezer Watson felt obliged to add, or Stebbins directed him to do so, that the little book was printed "for the Use of Descendants now living." Family history then was proclaimed private, modest, but also generous to others. Stebbins wished to leave something for his family. This would be an American pattern that would continue.[27]

There were, of course, different developments of an American genealogical practice. Virginian colonists were not averse to the old hierarchies

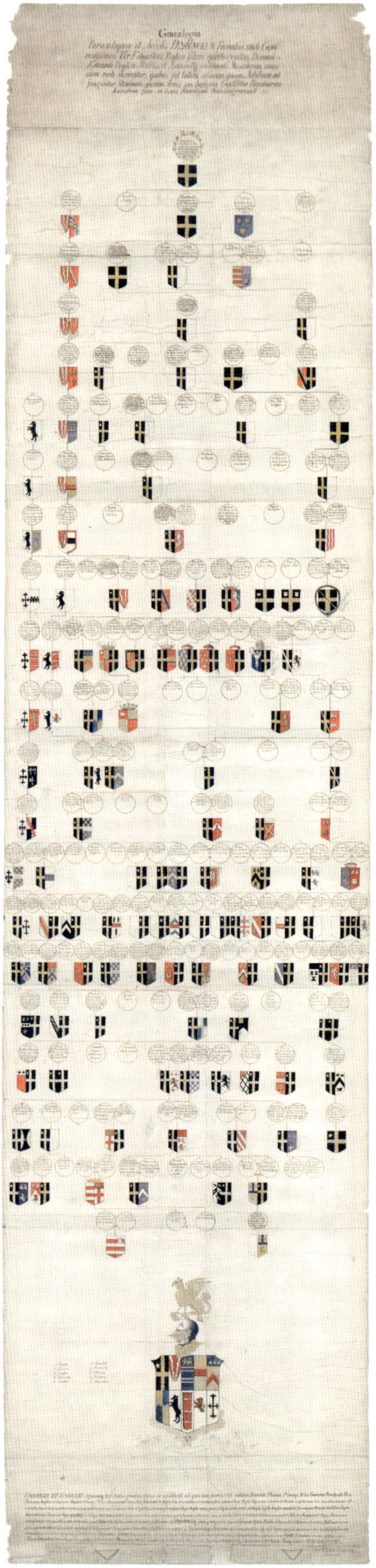

FIGURE 2.6
The Peyton family genealogical chart. Mss 6:2 P4685:2. Courtesy of the Virginia Historical Society and the Peyton Society. This elaborate and illuminated pedigree chart of the Peyton family was prepared first by the English College of Heralds in 1688. The original was discovered some two hundred years later in Florence, Italy, by a branch of the Peyton family still residing in Worcestershire, England. The original was sent to Bernard Peyton of California to be copied. Two copies were made. The copy shown here was one of those two and measures thirteen feet long. A larger chart, over nineteen feet long, extended to include the American branch as it was understood in 1885, and was donated to the Alderman Library at the University of Virginia.

of England in their genealogies. William Byrd II, for example, commissioned a pedigree prepared at the College of Heralds in London, and other Virginian families wrote about their pedigree charts.[28]

Not so differently in New Orleans, Carlos Gayarré (1774–1813), grandfather of the nineteenth-century historian, slept under his family's coat of arms, which depicted "three mountains spanned by a bridge, surmounted by the turbaned head of Abderahaman, the testimonial of the proud day" when his homeland of Spain "defeated the Sultan in the native valley of Roncal, about the year 800." His grandson would name his home across the lake from the city, Roncal.[29]

Thomas Jefferson lived close to such desires for nobility, and to changes that would shape genealogy in the United States. Sometime before 1771, he sought confirmation about his family arms. The colonial Jefferson was diffident when he asked a friend traveling to London for help: "I have what I am told are the family arms but on what authority I know not." There is no indication that he ever heard anything in reply, and it was not until 1786 that he purchased a seal. It is likely that, with many open books before him, he "created" family memory for himself, foregoing the authority of the College of Arms. He wrote his own motto, which, translated from Latin, reads: "He who gives life gives liberty."[30]

Genealogy in the New Nation

With the end of hostilities of the American Revolution, many Americans considered themselves happily free from European customs. New traditions of keeping family history were part of new identities. "Cheaper and more personal visual remembrance[s] of . . . ancestry" came to replace "the old decorated arms and family portraits."[31] New forms (watercolor paintings, samplers, and printed or hand-decorated family registers) eventually exhibited distinct motifs and styles that differed from town to town, as well as differing from those in Europe.[32] As with Stebbins in his book in the late colonial period, many of these artifacts were created not for asserting status but rather as efforts of "straightforward record keeping" and were only displayed within the home.[33] "Pride had to be narrowly local before it could ever be national," Ola Elizabeth Winslow wrote when describing the birth of an American interest in "her own landscape and her own heroes possessively."[34] An American genealogy meant a search for a vision of local participants, local variations in larger national events, the collection of historical materials in private institutions, and a questioning of the place of lineage practiced in any showy way or even of any group based upon family connections.[35]

In 1783, when the former officers of the Continental Army created the Society of the Cincinnati to lobby for veterans' benefits and to join together in an elite group open only to themselves and their descendants, this early patriotic organization worried many new Americans. Had not

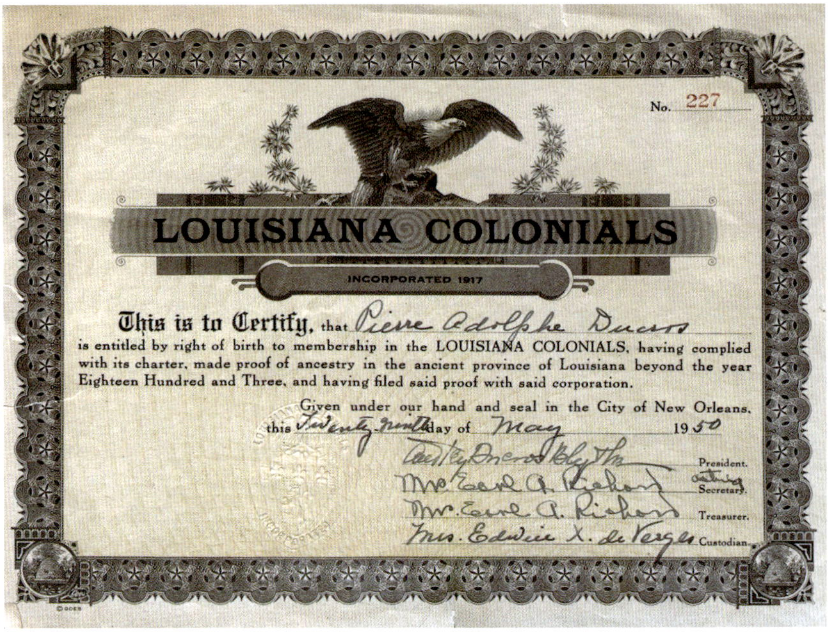
No. 227

LOUISIANA COLONIALS

INCORPORATED 1917

This is to Certify, that Pierre Adolphe Ducros is entitled by right of birth to membership in the LOUISIANA COLONIALS, having complied with its charter, made proof of ancestry in the ancient province of Louisiana beyond the year Eighteen Hundred and Three, and having filed said proof with said corporation.

Given under our hand and seal in the City of New Orleans, this Twenty ninth day of May 1950

President.

acting Secretary.

Treasurer.

Custodian.

FIGURE 2.7
Louisiana Colonials Certificate. Joseph Émile Ducros family papers, Collection 893, Louisiana Research Collection, Tulane University.
Like the Society of the Cincinnati certificates created for the oldest American patriotic society, this document was issued so that some visual presentation might be made of membership. Aspiring members of the Louisiana Colonials had to prove ancestry in the state before 1803.

their new world been designed for better circumstances, for a social structure not based on family lines? They feared that a group such as the Society of the Cincinnati would "breed a new ruling dynasty."[36]

In opposition to the group, Jefferson wrote to George Washington in 1784. This new organization, said Jefferson, went against the "letter of some of our constitutions." American institutions deserved to be built upon "the natural equality of man, the denial of every preeminence but that annexed to legal office, and particularly the denial of a preeminence by birth."[37] While legislation quickly enough solved the need for the Society of the Cincinnati's financial lobbying powers, some of the opponents' arguments set the stage for future predilections to distrust and disparage birthrights, or certainly the display of birthrights.[38]

These evolutions also coincided with other discussions on inheritability. Article 2 of the 1787 Constitution ruled out, for example, the "corruption of blood," the idea that children could be punished for the crimes of their parents. New laws also prohibited other kinds of inherited status for white males.[39] By 1791, throughout the South, primogeniture was abolished in an effort largely led by Jefferson.[40]

On the other hand, Jefferson saw information on the practice of genealogy as important enough to be included in his library and, later, that of the nation. In 1815, when he sold his books to re-create and transform the burned Library of Congress, he included a printed copy of the 1086 *Domesday Book* (1733), Thomas Wotton's *Baronetage of England* (1771), *Peerage of Ireland* (1725), and many other French, Italian, and English imprints on family history.[41] The Library of Congress had been, before the fire, a law library, but Jefferson wanted a larger body of knowledge for the

FIGURE 2.8
"Library for State Historical Society, Madison, Wis.," Print from the *Inland Architect and News Record*, vol. 37, no. 6. (1901). Courtesy of the Library of Congress, American Memory.

Founded in 1846, the Wisconsin Historical Society is one of the oldest and most prestigious repositories in the nation. In the history of New Orleans records, it has a revered place. During the Civil War, documents housed in the Louisiana state capitol were the least of the concerns of the Northern army. Yet one soldier rescued some colonial records there during a fire. The head of the Wisconsin Historical Society, Lyman Draper, later located these documents and sent them back to the Louisiana Historical Society.

country's representatives in Washington; he argued that the nation deserved a broader "understanding of legislation based upon all learning."[42] Some of this education should concern those older customs of power, like genealogy, that had failed as well as prospered.

There was, too, the continuing desire at least on the part of some Americans to be attached to nobility. Writing on the new country of the 1830s, French visitor Alexis de Tocqueville found that "[o]ne hardly ever meets an American who does not want to claim some connection by birth with the first founders of the colonies, and as for offshoots of great English families, I think America is simply full of them."[43] Of course, this was an exaggeration, but it shows some of the desires of the people Tocqueville met and their tenacity in promoting themselves through family lines attached to power.

Documania

Into this mix creating American attitudes toward genealogy, northeastern men and a few women—those interested in history, called antiquarians—took the lead in amassing documents of the early colonies and the republic.[44] These collectors worked together feverishly in what David Van Tassel describes as "documania."[45] The Massachusetts Historical Society (1791), the New York Historical Society (1804), and the American Antiquarian Society (1812) were the three most influential groups, but a number of other state and local societies were critical actors in the formation of repositories where genealogists came to work.

Several events of the early nineteenth century encouraged greater access to, and interest in, family records. These events included the fiftieth anniversary (1826) of the signing of the Declaration of Independence and an 1853 call for printing the records of the Colony of Massachusetts.[46] To celebrate meant looking back, and to do so, one had to have documents. The antiquarians in the historical societies created what has come to be called "the historical manuscript tradition"; the antiquarians amassed primarily private collections of personal papers, but also turned attention to public records and gathered and arranged as much as they could according to library principles.[47]

FIGURE 2.9
John Farmer. Lithograph, ca. 1838. Courtesy of the New England Historic Genealogical Society.
This lithograph of John Farmer is from the first issue of the *New England Historical and Genealogical Register.*

The emphasis on private papers had meaning for family history, and for the developing formulation of American genealogy. John Farmer first molded genealogy as a faction within the collecting efforts, the documania, of the historical societies. In the mid-nineteenth century, another New Englander, James Savage (1784–1873), revised and expanded Farmer's text, taking up the cause of adding settlers "without regard to rank or wealth." Like Farmer, Savage was quite lyrical in his mission and message that American genealogy was different from that of Europe. He sought to make visible "the second or third generation descendants of the most humble," adding in parenthesis, "Thank God we are all equal before the law."[48]

In a similar preoccupation with defining lineage in a way that would not be associated with inherited power, in 1825, the Historical Society of Pennsylvania's first president, William Rawle, boldly suggested a change to that society's constitution by removing all references to hereditary ties, such as the word "native," and replacing them with terms referring to chronological precedence: "predecessors" in the place of "forefathers," and "early periods of our history" instead of "history of our ancestors."[49] By the late 1830s, antiquarians all over the new country were commended not just for gathering records but also for "collecting and preserving the fading memorials of our little democracies." One of these little democracies in which the antiquarians worked would be New Orleans, where the Louisiana Historical Society was founded in 1835.[50]

Widening American Genealogy

We do not know if LDS founder Joseph Smith gave thought to the "little democracies" or the antiquarians. He led a life far from the comfortable status of those people who had leisure enough to go about collecting records. He was born and raised in upstate New York, a hotbed of religious ferment. His family moved many times (usually a sign of struggle, genealogists told me) and was himself the fifth of eleven children. Yet Smith was concerned with inscription as well. Near his home in Manchester, New York, he reported finding buried gold tablets that told of the lost tribes of Israel in the Americas. Based upon these tablets, he created what would become a new denomination within Christianity. He and his followers called themselves Latter-day Saints.[51]

FIGURE 2.10
"The angel Moroni delivering the plates of the Book of Mormon to Joseph Smith," 1886. Print. Courtesy of the Library of Congress, American Memory. Joseph Smith, founder of the Church of Jesus Christ of Latter-day Saints, recalled a number of meetings with the angel Moroni during the 1820s. Moroni gave him the Golden Plates from which to translate the Book of Mormon, first published in 1830.

They sought a home in various midwestern communities, where, more often than not, their practices appeared dangerous to other residents. Moses might have had the Ten Commandments presented on two stone tablets that have never been found in subsequent centuries, but nineteenth-century golden tablets revealed only to Joseph Smith, read by magic glasses that permitted translation and were then lost, along with the practice of polygamy, were not to the taste of mainstream Americans. In 1840, in Illinois, Smith was killed by a mob enraged by his increasing power in their hitherto more homogeneous communities.[52] Yet before he died, Smith received a message in a vision of the Prophet Elijah concerning the necessity of "turning the hearts of the fathers to the children, and the children to the fathers." Elijah gave Smith and another man, Oliver Cowdery (and by extension later leaders of the LDS Church), a specific meaning for this text—namely, the critical imperative to "seal" families throughout time, a sealing that would necessitate locating names from previous generations, that would direct all LDS members on a search for ancestors.[53]

The 1894 creation of the Genealogical Society of Utah formalized the initial work of missionaries to gather these names of ancestors.[54] Much of this effort revolved around Susa Young Gates.[55] She organized the women of the LDS Church to complete family histories and to serve as models for the way their sons should take over this work. In 1911 and 1912, she wrote some of the first lessons on genealogical methods.[56] Then she pushed for adequate funding for the Genealogical Society's library in Salt Lake City and for its more efficient management. Their goal, she said, should be "to purchase every genealogical book now published or to be published."[57] A copy of her book, *Surname Book and Racial History* (1918), was sent to every known historical library in America and Europe.

FIGURE 2.11
Susa Young Gates with daughters, ca. 1890. Studio print. Joseph F. Smith Personal Photographs (Ph 2016). Courtesy of the Church History Library and the Church of Jesus Christ of Latter-day Saints.
Gates was intrepid in every area of her life. In 1915, she helped organize attendance for LDS women at the International Congress on Genealogy held in San Francisco. Some 215 women reserved places on fourteen train cars and arrived in time to attend both a preconference and the congress.

Names, locality, and kinship were the cornerstones of her methodology, an approach that required the verification of data. More so than the genealogical methodology practiced in the Northeast by John Farmer and others who followed him, Gates's methods acknowledged wider spheres of interest, the need to return to sources in other places that were, for LDS members and of course for later Americans, geographically remote and not often associated with prosperous families with private records. Although she understood that she had to carefully cement all her innovations by getting the full support of the male leaders of the LDS Church, she assiduously brought genealogy not only to those in her immediate area but also to many others who would eventually come to use the cards and other tools of research in the library in Salt Lake City. These are the tools from which databases such as FamilySearch would initially grow.

Moreover, as a key figure in this history of genealogy, she represented legions of women who promoted the practice of genealogy through patriotic societies in the late nineteenth and early twentieth centuries. Gates herself was a founding member of the Utah Chapter of the Daughters of the American Revolution.[58]

Efforts across Boundaries

Today, the LDS Church is central to a national culture of genealogy, and ultimately an international one, because it has allowed access to large collections of records. As many as two thousand persons routinely visit the LDS's Family History Library on any given day.[59] Researchers come in tour groups, they come as families, they come alone, and they come electronically. They may draw, free of charge, on the records collected there. Legions of volunteers—seven hundred alone at the Family History Library and more at distant locations, all duplicating records—make these resources accessible. Some one hundred full-time and part-time employees oversee the work of volunteers and answer the questions of researchers. The building itself is 142,000 square feet on five stories.[60] The more records one finds within the huge collection that LDS members have amassed, the more amazing the library appears. It is a daring feat, a continuing and seemingly always advancing act of genealogical imperialism.

The LDS Church houses all the retrieved records within a vault created in one side of Granite Mountain, not far from Salt Lake City; this is today "the world's largest storage facility for temperature-sensitive historical data"—namely, microfilm and electronic forms of data storage. Historian Donald Harman Akenson called it a "palace to the eternal."[61] At least one "gentile" (as non-LDS people are called), journalist Alex Shoumatoff, visited this vault in the early 1980s and found it even then to be "the closest there is, and the closest there will be, to a 'catalogue of catalogues' for the human race . . . [employing] some of the most sophisticated records-processing technologies in existence."[62] By 2014, Granite Mountain Vault preserved even more, of course, more "than 3.5 billion images on microfilm, microfiche, and digital media."[63]

The timeline of these efforts itself is impressive, for in less than a century, the LDS Church and its members became leaders in almost all of American genealogy. In 1924, the LDS Church had begun the conversion of a huge collection of names onto standardized cards, first begun under the direction of Susa Young Gates; by the late 1930s, they had begun experimenting with microfilm; and by 1942, they had standardized the creation of family group sheets that contained the names of ancestors retrieved from records around the world. Continuing into the twenty-first century, they began other initiatives that enabled individuals to submit their genealogical work to databases maintained in Utah.[64] The push for

FIGURE 2.12
The Eternal Family through Christ, Judith Mehr, 1988. Oil and gold leaf mural painting. Courtesy of the Church of Jesus Christ of Latter-day Saints. This mural occupies a space of seven by twenty-three feet above the information desk at the entrance to the Family History Library in Salt Lake City. The mural is often called by its shortened name, *Families Are Forever*. LDS official commentary notes that the mural beckons viewers to come to Christ through genealogical and temple work.

the creation of the library and other LDS member initiatives, outside the church but concerned with genealogy, have created an unprecedented achievement of a connected world of records.

Migration and Other Contexts for Understanding Genealogy's History

I visited Salt Lake City in the early winter of 2011. I came because a New Orleans genealogist, Doris Ann Gormon (b. 1941), told me to do so. "The library's shelves—just walking through them—explain how far we have come, even in New Orleans, where, once," she said, "genealogy was only for social climbers." I, like so many other researchers, found books there that I could find nowhere else, but I was also reminded that microfilm especially could be sent to me in New Orleans. The LDS Family History Library has made genealogy acceptable and possible across many social and economic boundaries precisely because it also, in the 1960s, established Family History Service Centers, branch libraries to which such microfilm could be sent for use by anyone who was registered as a researcher. Genealogy once required leisure time and money for travel—in other words, it required wealth—but now the practice requires only a computer or even just a trip to one of the 4,600 LDS Family History Centers located in most major cities and towns.

FIGURE 2.12
This image represents the preservation and transmission of family history materials in books, photographs, and other writings, as well as in the lives of ancestors grouped with descendants.

Yet, for serious genealogists, the library in Salt Lake City still warrants a pilgrimage. For me, this pilgrimage involved seeing how the city manifested the presence of genealogy and genealogists in its public landscape. Less often visited than the Family History Library is the headquarters of the Daughters of Utah Pioneers. Susa Young Gates was one of the organization's founders. Filled with artifacts and clothed mannequins, the Daughters' rooms contain the portraits of the wives of the founders and their many children. Here is Gates in the large group that was her family. Born to Lucy Bigelow, Brigham Young's twenty-second wife (or forty-second, by other counts), she was one of his fifty-eight children. Gates herself had fifteen children by two husbands, divorcing her first husband in the 1870s. She was also a novelist and a musician.[65]

In sharp contrast to the crowded rooms inside and to the huge families in portraits on the walls, a statue stands on the grounds of the building. It is the representation of a lone woman with one child in her arms and another clinging to her long skirt. She symbolizes the difficult crossing of the plains to Utah, a crossing that was one step in the passage that would, over time, make the LDS a part of mainstream America and would make, too, American genealogy.[66]

The woman and her children are LDS *and* national motifs about migration. They are reminders that most Americans search for records about their ancestors in order to answer two overriding questions that are part and parcel of almost every American life: Where did we come from? And why did we come to North America?

These questions concern our "*crossing ancestors*—that is . . . those who migrated to the New World." As one writer describes it: "It's the story of the way we became Americans. In African-American family history, the crossing is a nightmare of oppression, and for many other families it is a story of hardship and persecution. But it is also a source of pride, because it's the start of a kind of spiritual pedigree." Such stories are rarely written down but are embodied in the form of a quilt, a chest, or a small kernel of hope. "They usually exist in the oral legends that families tell about how they got here, in which truth often yields to a good story and an illustrious forebear."[67]

Barack Obama evoked these similar origin stories in his 2009 inaugural address as the forty-fourth president of the United States:

> For us, they packed up their few worldly possessions and traveled across oceans in search of a new life. For us, they toiled in sweatshops and settled the West, endured the lash of the whip and plowed the hard earth.[68]

The closer a society is to the time of its founding, the more important are the genealogies of those who migrated, who began the new home.[69] These crossings now are re-created to help shape the most popular manifestation of information technology, to make genealogy "the most public of all history."[70] Cyndi's List of Genealogy Sites on the Internet includes more than 332,885 links. By January 2014, more than 2.7 million people had joined Ancestry.com, a Utah-based firm. Over time, the website has added more than 12 billion records to its database and more than 55 million family trees containing more than 5 billion profiles. The performance of Ancestry.com and other sites over the past twenty years confirms the steady growth of genealogy online.[71]

At the heart of these inquiries into the past are intellectual and emotional inquiries. As one searches for an ancestor who came here or went there, one is also learning about one's self, about leaps, geographic or otherwise, one has taken or not taken, explorations in the present, considerations of what kind of life anyone gets to live on earth. These travels away from the self and then back to it are at the root of the appeal of family history.

What an itinerary Père Antoine and the other foundational leaders have created, what a message they have enabled, from the dead to the living. That raises another question a genealogist told me to consider: *Did my ancestors consider that we might come searching, that we would want to know them?*

CHAPTER THREE

The Journey to a Populist Culture of Searching

By 1850, New Orleans had become one of the United States' largest cities, and one of five principal ports where European immigrants first set foot on American soil.[1] Many of these people stayed in the city for a short period of time and then left for other places. But their names appeared on records in the city, and their descendants often "return" to these records. Figuratively, then, New Orleans and other ports of debarkation play a role in the family stories of many more people than those who have remained in their first American homes. There is always this movement of people to consider, genealogists told me.

One early family historian, Joseph William Cruzat (1858–1913), collected materials that represent the influx of people into the nineteenth-century city. Cruzat came from a Francophone family, but his grandfather had married an American who had come to the city just after 1803. Cruzat, then, as many others would have done, did not rely solely on sacramental registers or notarial records but on many private records from the East. He was the beneficiary of a large collection of family letters. Among this correspondence, his father and his great-great-grandfather especially had written to one another and to others about family lineage, saving papers from the 1600s onward, a trove of records that had begun in England. Cruzat inherited among other records the 1686 holographic will of his first English ancestor to have settled in New York. Cruzat also inherited letters written among cousins, such as one from 1832 in which his great-uncle wrote to a cousin and asked her to bring him the family pedigree so that information could be entered into the family Bible. "There is sometimes great advantage in these records," he wrote, and "every distinguished family . . . ought to keep them up."[2]

Cruzat's circle of correspondents extended to Europe; to them, he wrote in French and Spanish.[3] His wife, Heloise Hulse Cruzat (1862–1931), was also a prominent collector as well as a translator and archivist. She donated materials to the other repositories, especially in the city but also in other locations.[4]

Their network of genealogy proved both solitary and social. They lived and worked among Francophones in neighborhoods near Rampart and Esplanade, and they were very active in their church, where most members spoke French. Joseph Cruzat used his bookkeeping skills for some

FIGURE 3.1
Monument to the Immigrants, Franco Alessandrini, 1997. Statue in white marble, New Orleans. Photograph courtesy of the artist and Margaret Alessandrini.
Looking toward the city, the immigrant family looks determined as they face their future. Sculptor Alessandrini, himself an immigrant, chose faces and clothing from photographs of nineteenth-century immigrants in deciding how he would carve the people in the statue. He also used marble that came from his hometown of Sansepolcro, Italy, and so the statue embodies two cultures in many ways. The statue stands in Woldenberg Park near where earlier immigrants first stepped onto American soil. New Orleans was a busy port of entry, at times second only to New York in number of debarkations.

FIGURE 3.2
Monument to the Immigrants, Franco Alessandrini, 1997. Statue in white marble, New Orleans. Photograph courtesy of the artist and Margaret Alessandrini.

The angel here, facing the Mississippi, represents gratitude for safe passage. Similar monuments are located in New York, Philadelphia, Boston, and Baltimore, as well as a few inland locations such as Buffalo, New York. However, most such memorials do not incorporate figure work.

FIGURE 3.3
Biagio Badolato and Victorina Zuppardo, 1903. Gelatin silver print with pigment added. Courtesy of Salvadore J. "Sal" Serio.

This portrait was given to Giuseppa Badolato by her parents to take with her as she left Sicily in 1903 to come to New Orleans. "Take this because you'll never see us alive again," they told her. The family always remembered these words, and the gift of the photograph remains part of a continuing legacy.

Women in Sicily retain their maiden names, Badolato's great-grandson wanted me to know, and when she arrived in the United States she had to adjust to the custom of being called by the French/English version of her name, Josephine, and by a combined form of her maiden and married name: Badolato Lodato.

FIGURE 3.4
Will of John Mapes, 1684, from New York. Cruzat family papers, Collection 249, Louisiana Research Collection, Tulane University.

This will was passed on to Joseph William Cruzat from his "American" side of the family, as Francophones in New Orleans called cousins who came from other parts of the country and sometimes even other parts of the city outside the French Quarter and adjacent neighborhoods.

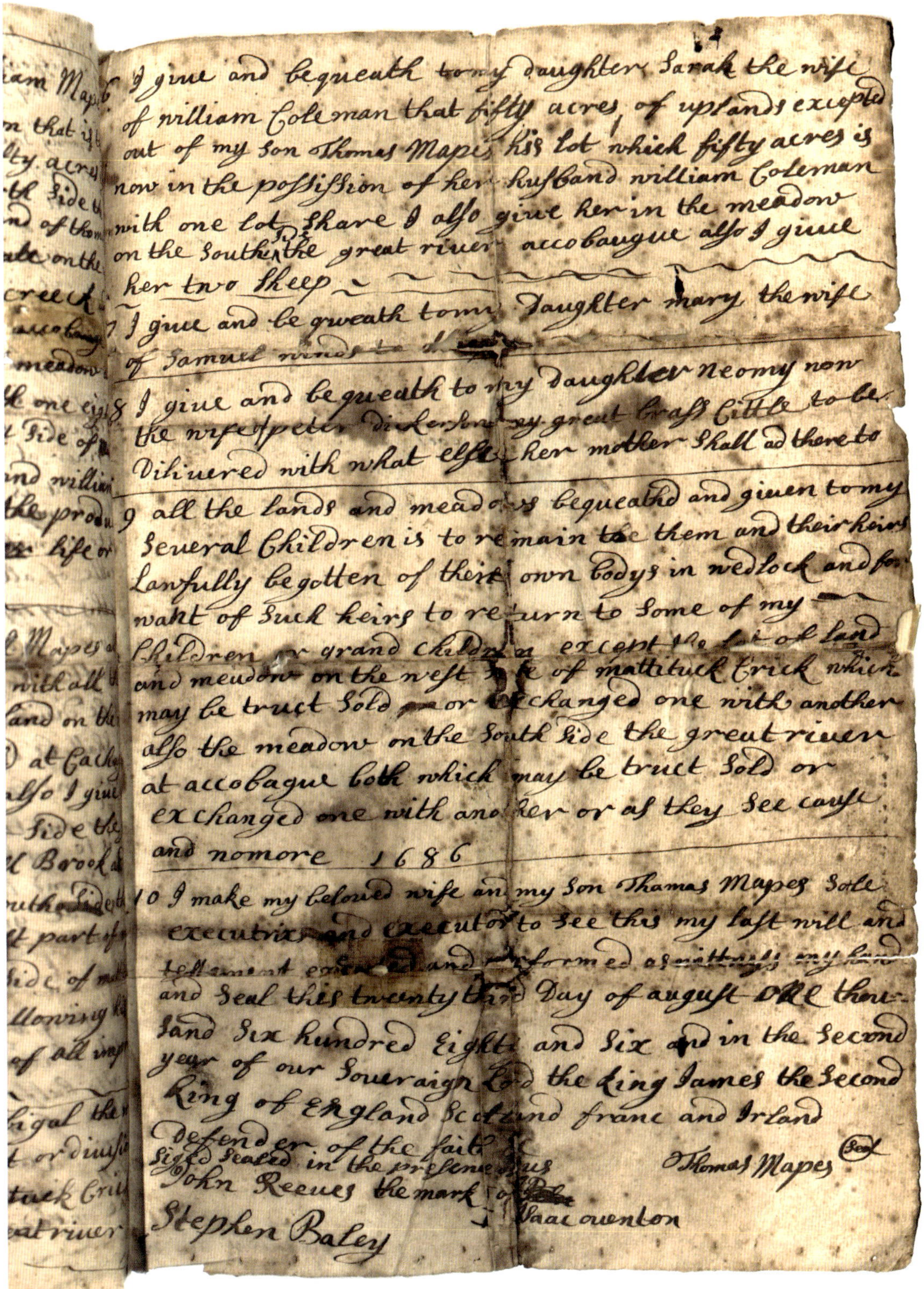
6 I give and bequeath to my daughter Sarah the wife
of william Coleman that fifty acres of uplands excepted
out of my Son Thomas Mapes his lot which fifty acres is
now in the possission of her husband william Coleman
with one lot share I also give her in the meadow
on the South side the great river accobaugue also I give
her two Sheep
7 I give and be queath to my daughter mary the wife
of Samuel wines [illegible]
8 I give and bequeath to my daughter Neomy now
the wife of peter dickerson my great brass kittle to be
Dilivered with what else her mother shall ad there to
9 all the lands and meadows bequeathd and given to my
Several Children is to remain to them and their heirs
Lawfully begotten of their own bodys in wedlock and for
want of Such heirs to return to Some of my
Children or grand children except the lot of land
and meadow on the west side of mattituck Crick which
may be truct Sold or exchanged one with another
also the meadow on the South side the great river
at accobague both which may be truct Sold or
exchanged one with another or as they See cause
and nomore 1686
10 I make my beloved wife an my Son Thomas Mapes Sole
executrix and executor to See this my last will and
testament [illegible] and performed as witness my hand
and Seal this twenty third Day of august one thou-
sand Six hundred Eighty and Six and in the Second
year of our Soveraign Lord the king James the Second
king of England Scotland france and Irland
defender of the faith
Thomas Mapes (Seal)
Signed Sealed in the presence of us
John Reeves the mark of [illegible]
Isaac ovenlon
Stephen Baley

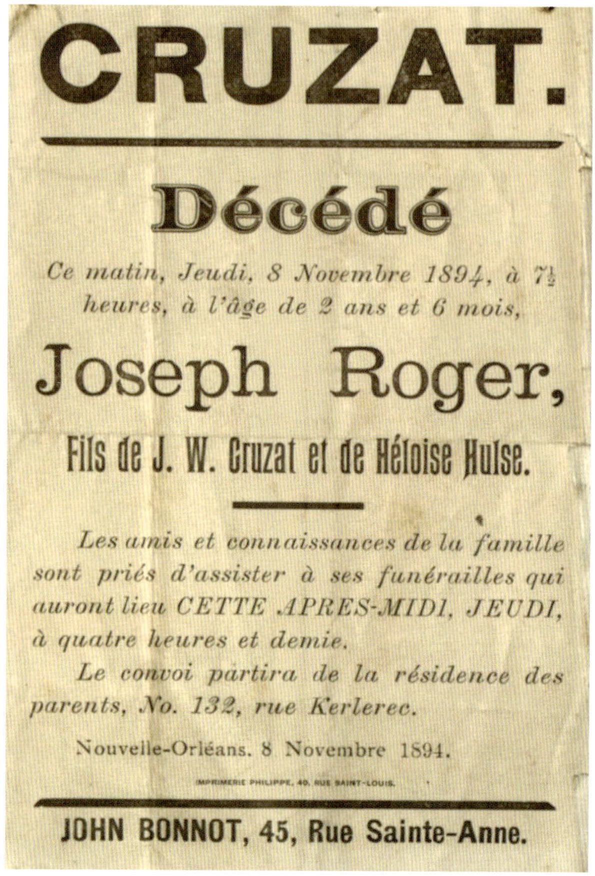

CRUZAT.

Décédé

Ce matin, Jeudi, 8 Novembre 1894, à 7½ heures, à l'âge de 2 ans et 6 mois,

Joseph Roger,

Fils de J. W. Cruzat et de Héloise Hulse.

Les amis et connaissances de la famille sont priés d'assister à ses funérailles qui auront lieu CETTE APRES-MIDI, JEUDI, à quatre heures et demie.

Le convoi partira de la résidence des parents, No. 132, rue Kerlerec.

Nouvelle-Orléans. 8 Novembre 1894.

IMPRIMERIE PHILIPPE, 40, RUE SAINT-LOUIS.

JOHN BONNOT, 45, Rue Sainte-Anne.

FIGURE 3.5
Death Notice, Joseph Roger Cruzat, 1894. Cruzat family papers, Collection 249, Louisiana Research Center, Tulane University.
Commentator Edward Tinker (1881–1968) believed that the French language was a "sentimental addiction" for most late nineteenth-century people in New Orleans. The Cruzat family's preference for using French for the formalities of life appears most poignantly in the death notices of three of their six children. The death notices were saved among genealogical papers, projecting into the future the research of others.

ten years as treasurer of the Louisiana Historical Society, where most spoke English. Yet he was equally known for his retiring personality.[5] In her book of family histories called *Creole Families of New Orleans* (1921), Grace King (1852–1932) described him as "a recluse" who had nevertheless left a legacy in family history records.[6] Genealogists in the city spoke of a similar propensity to work alone yet connect to the universe of family members who are unable to speak except through words or artifacts they left behind.

Almost one generation younger, another New Orleanian, Joseph Émile Ducros (1871–1946), led a collecting life that shows an even broader reach of genealogy, but also evolving complications. Ducros went to work almost every day of his adult life as a railroad clerk but spent all his free time gathering material about family history and going to meetings with others interested in local history and genealogy. He worked in the mode of the antiquarians, of John Farmer even.

In the 1990s, Ducros's granddaughter gave his letters to Tulane University's Special Collection. The archivists valued the words of his brothers as they found work in Nicaragua, China, the Philippines, and various American cities. What is not apparent from the current library descrip-

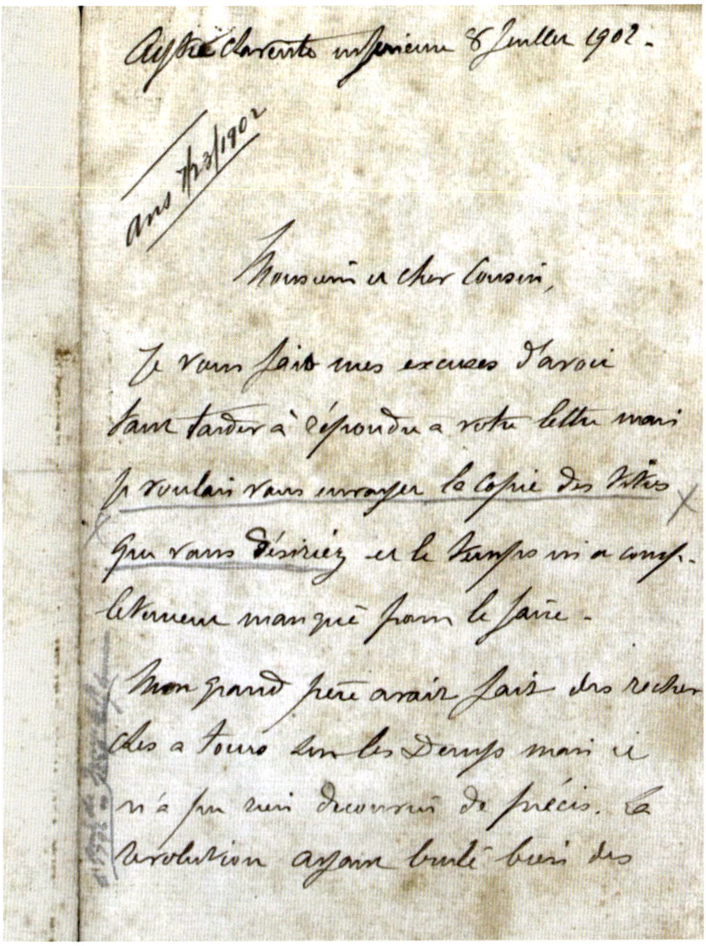

Charente inférieure 8 Juillet 1902.

Monsieur et cher Cousin,

Je vous fais mes excuses d'avoir tant tardé à répondre à votre lettre mais je voulais vous envoyer la copie des titres que vous désiriez et le temps m'a complètement manqué pour le faire.

Mon grand père avait fait des recherches à Tours dans le temps mais il n'a pu rien découvrir de précis. La révolution ayant brûlé bien des

FIGURE 3.6
"Monsieur mon cher cousin," 1902, Letter to Joseph Ducros in reply to his genealogical inquiries to cousins in Honfleur, France. Joseph Émile Ducros family papers, Louisiana Research Collection, Tulane University.
Genealogy before the Internet age relied completely on correspondence such as this, along with networking at meetings and "want ads" that family historians could place in newspapers and specialty magazines such as *Everton's Genealogical Helper* (1947–2006).

tion of this collection is that Ducros had been donating genealogical material since 1899. Some of these family history materials had been bound and shelved as books; some were kept in a file under the letter M, to designate single-page manuscript items. In the older schema, history was biography, and local history was genealogy. But trickling-in donations such as those by Ducros (letters to Canadian and French archivists, marriage contracts, family correspondence, deeds, pensions, notarial and school records, and many other records, as well as other single page materials), what were they? Not really unique, so not archival and not really printed, so not bibliographic. Tulane's librarians then united the single page materials with similar items from other local families and placed them within two general collections called "personal documents" and "genealogical paper series." Similar solutions were made all over the US to accommodate the simultaneous growth in the print and paper worlds, the genealogical community, and the prejudice towards family history. Under the new arrangements, librarians would offer some genealogical materials; on the other hand, they would also place these documents to the side, without the same benefit of attention to provenance (or funding involved to provide such) that other collections might receive.[7]

Since the end of the nineteenth century, genealogy in general has experienced this sort of displacement. While earlier attitudes held that genealogy was an undemocratic pursuit of only the socially climbing middle classes and the elite, from the 1870s forward family history found even more disfavor. This shift was part of a national trend that had to do, in part, with the professionalization of history. As in all new endeavors, the newcomers had to assert their authority. The antiquarians and, especially among them the genealogists, could no longer assume leadership of many of the libraries and historical societies where they had previously guided the collection of materials. If the antiquarians did remain in control, they still did so under the assumption that the historians were the true experts, and with nearly constant reminders that historians saw them as dilettantes. For example, in 1897, John Franklin Jameson, the first American PhD in history (Johns Hopkins University, 1882), officially dictated that no historical society had the right "to use its research and publications in furthering" genealogy.[8] Nationwide, some librarians wrote in their collection policies that they would not accept work of a genealogical nature at all.[9]

This schism between history and genealogy in some ways has persisted in American society, and it certainly persists in some archives where historians remain the preferred users.[10] Even in the early 2000s, Laura Graham, writing about the Library of Congress's digital American Memory Project, conceded that she and others had no idea that "the flow of content and information back to the Library of Congress from people who have local history, genealogical, or other specialized information to offer" would be so beneficial in "enhancing descriptions of items in the institution's collections."[11] Most likely, she had no idea because she had never been encouraged to know about genealogists and their ways of practice.[12]

The Spread of Interest in Family History

Despite such evolving and persistent negative attitudes toward genealogists, Ducros represented something unrelenting in another way, something more hopeful and inclusive of various forms of learning: he would not stop, no matter what the academicians thought of his pursuit. He was a member of various lineage groups and historical societies, and he learned much from these groups. In New Orleans, he witnessed the founding of the Louisiana State Museum around colonial records in 1906. Nationwide, he witnessed and benefited from the printing of early censuses, the indexing of passenger lists, and the creation of hundreds of other access points to records.

These steps toward greater access to records coincided with the bad press generated by historians about family history. More often than not, advancements came about through the efforts of the New England Historic Genealogical Society and other emerging historical and patriotic societies. There was so much work to do—records were scattered across so many different locations (families, organizations, churches, cities, states, and nations), and only a huge corps of volunteers could make these disparate whereabouts known in an environment intent on local authority. Church records and those of the local governments of the early republic were the only public records available to most citizens in the late eighteenth and most of the nineteenth centuries, the only records from which they could easily or not so easily find the names of their ancestors. Among these records, each denomination, sometimes each ethnic group within a denomination, and each government office followed a different practice. Each town or city might keep a book listing all the records together—probate alongside arrests, and so forth.[13]

In addition, there was little access to what we call today vital records. The systematic registration of births and deaths would not come to a handful of states until the mid- to late nineteenth century, and not to all states until the twentieth century. There were exceptions: as a Spanish colony in 1790, New Orleans had begun civil registration of the various passages of life of its citizens. Boston began civil registration in 1848, Philadelphia in 1860, Pittsburgh in 1870, and Baltimore in 1875.[14] No wonder then that even as these first public registrations of vital statistics occurred, an emphasis on private papers persisted. Antiquarians penned county histories, which often included accounts of early community leaders and their descendants. Various catalogs and dictionaries of New England and Virginia were the prototypes of these volumes. By 1862, when William Whitmore compiled *A Handbook of American Genealogy, Being a Catalogue of Family Histories and Publications Containing Genealogical Information*, his chosen 108 genealogies were supplemented by sixty-two local histories.[15]

None of these were from New Orleans, which remained somewhat outside the mainstream of genealogical practices, in part until the end of the nineteenth century, in full until the 1970s. This may have been because the few practicing genealogists in New Orleans, even those like Cruzat who collected records from around the United States, revered first ancestry in France and Spain, not England, so did not seem to conform to the path shaped by the NEHGS and other local history organizations on the East Coast. New Orleanians preferred their French or Spanish or at least Creole ancestors. Even the term "American" among some genealogists still means a newcomer, someone "outside the world where most of my ancestors lived." In New Orleans, family historians placed their origin stories not in the New World, as many from the Northeast did, but in Europe. Even New Orleanians who were descended from those who first came from French Canada wished to prove allegiance to France. In ad-

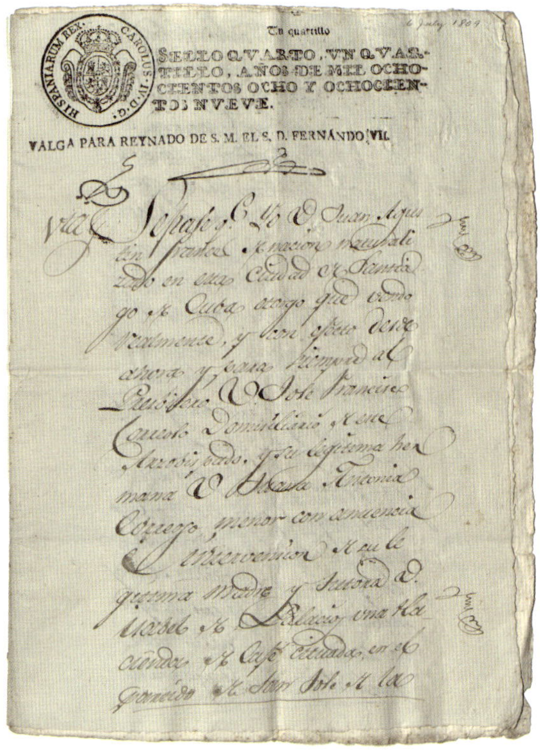

FIGURE 3.7
Spanish document about the sale of a coffee plantation in Cuba, ca. 1808. Augustin, Wogan, and Labranche Families Papers, Collection 223, Louisiana Research Center, Tulane University.
The Augustin family brought a number of records with them as they fled Saint-Domingue during the Haitian Revolution in the early 1800s and later emigrated from Cuba to New Orleans. Two documents concerned a coffee plantation, and another a property claim in "Santo Domingo."

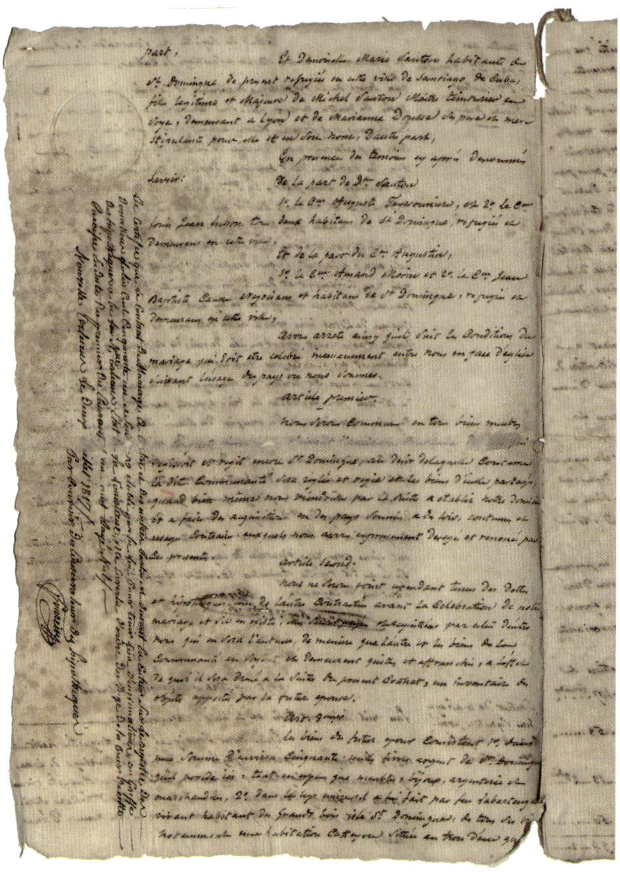

FIGURE 3.8
Deposition of Citizen Augustin and Marie Sauton. Created in Santiago de Cuba, October 1, 1803. Augustin, Wogan, and Labranche Families Papers, Louisiana Research Center, Tulane University.
This document shows a marriage contract created once the French government set up an office in Cuba to help refugees from Saint-Domingue. Since there was no civil French authority in Cuba when Jean Augustin and Marie Sauton first arrived and were married, they had to wait to execute this contract, hence a deposition. This document then was joined with their certificate of marriage from the Catholic Church. Marriage contracts were common in French colonies and continue to be a favored document for genealogists in New Orleans.

FIGURE 3.9
"Mrs. Harding and Daughters of 1812, April 26, 1921." Photograph. Courtesy of the Library of Congress, American Memory.
The Daughters of the War of 1812 was one patriotic group especially valued in New Orleans, because one of the final battles of that war was fought in the city. The Daughters sponsored yearly trips to Washington, DC, and the chance to travel there and meet with national leaders was especially appealing to local women.

dition, their ancestors' sacramental records and notarial acts were most often written in French and Spanish. Even late into the nineteenth century and early into the twentieth century, some records continued to be written in French.[16] These differences coincided with residents' desires to save their distinctive culture from encroaching American habits.

This tendency was reinforced by the fact that many who arrived in the city from 1800 to 1880 continued to be French-speaking immigrants. Early nineteenth-century refugees from Saint-Domingue brought some of the first traditions of genealogy, since notarial acts and other documents would be needed if they were to ever find compensation for their losses.[17] Other later immigrants (who came during and after the Napoleonic wars and various revolutions) also brought papers in French, and these became valued as sentiments of attachment as much as evidence. The first published compilations of family histories all emphasize strong attachments to a French heritage, followed by attention to Spanish and finally American ties. One sees this in Charles Patton Dimitry's columns for the New Orleans *Times-Democrat* in 1892 and 1893 (considered the first published genealogies in the city); in Grace King's *Creole Families of New Orleans* (1921); and even in Stanley Clisby Arthur and George Campbell Huchet de Kernion's *Old Families of Louisiana* (1931), a book that sought purposively to include some families with Protestant origins.[18]

Nevertheless, to some extent, the city also followed the agenda being framed in New England for American genealogy, a practice that called for finding, accumulating, and especially prizing private family records.

The founders of the Louisiana Historical Society (LHS, 1835) came from widely dispersed families: from New England and other East Coast cities, from Saint-Domingue and white Saint-Dominguean families, from France, and from New Orleans–born backgrounds. But they were homogeneous in being white men whose education and training had made them familiar with practices elsewhere, and who were aligned with the elite elsewhere.[19]

Besides the leadership of John Farmer and the New England Historic Genealogical Society, northeastern genealogists could lead the nation because they were backed by many more active antiquarians than could be found in Louisiana and other southern states. Later, northeastern records were also safe from the ravages of the Civil War. On the other hand, genealogy was being promoted nationwide, since the postbellum era witnessed a national "imperative" to heal "sectional scars and political wounds."[20] One way this might be achieved was through the realignment of Americans who could proclaim themselves descendants of the oldest settlers. Increasing immigration from southern and eastern Europe

FIGURE 3.10
Collective Tomb of the Contessa Entellina Society, Lakelawn Cemetery, Metairie, Louisiana. Photograph by Yuka Petz. Immigrant societies offered newcomers assistance adjusting to their new homes, including the possibility of financial help to families for burials and interment in collective tombs. Later generations looked to the societies for genealogical information as well as celebrations of their ethnic origins. The Contessa Entellina Society continues to celebrate a number of holidays together, and members remain interested in the Sicilian village from which they emigrated in the late nineteenth and early twentieth centuries. On some occasions, they even celebrate their much earlier migration to this village from Albania in the 1400s and 1500s.

made some of these alliances all the stronger. A nativist sentiment arose all over the United States: those whites with ties to Europe going back more than one generation boasted of a more rightful place in American genealogy. Society as a whole became consumed by theories of eugenics and "the ideology of race in its broadest sense."[21] Many patriotic societies emerged at this time, in part to emphasize this preference for finding genealogical connections to first settlers and excluding newer arrivals.

New immigrants responded in two ways: either by distancing themselves from such impulses or, more often, by forming their own ethnically based groups, many of which also had an interest in genealogy. These groups understood that part of the process of becoming a US citizen involved both a knowledge of one's ancestry and the ability to subsume one's ethnic identity under one's new role as an American. New Orleans, home to many immigrants, experienced this same national trend, more so than did other southern cities.[22]

Also in this late nineteenth-century, migration within the country and new printing technologies began to influence and encourage other forms of genealogical pursuit. For those who had left the Northeast to settle the Midwest, reunions came to represent "a kind of mini-social movement, a voluntaristic and moral crusade among middle-class white Protestants, who, caught in the anomalies of rapid social change, sought to comprehend their situation and control their future." These reunions led to "collective genealogical efforts" in the form of albums and family history books made possible by cheaper paper and printing equipment. Expanding on the resolutions that came from the 1876 Centennial, local historians began to discuss how more genealogies could be compiled. They became conscious of county clerks in courthouses and the records kept there. They began to create "glory albums" featuring business or professional people in flattering photographs.[23]

The proliferation of public and university libraries at the end of the nineteenth century and beginning of the twentieth century also meant a central place for genealogical sources. Privately written family histories came to be housed in local repositories, the beginnings of those departments called "special collections," some of which also held records. A few of the new libraries also developed reader services, especially for family historians.[24] Here was an important passage from the private historical societies to the public sphere set within traditions encouraged by democracy and technology.

Historians and archivists also began to understand that the work of their professions demanded more attention to public records than had hitherto been given. They saw that public records were neglected within the historical manuscript tradition; that, for many researchers, public records were less accessible than family papers. To remedy this problem, to standardize care of public records, archivists looked to European practices, especially to the codification of Dutch (and to some extent Ger-

FIGURE 3.11
"Puck: What Fools These Mortals Be; America's Proud 'Four Hundred' and Europe's Haughty 'Nobility.'" Centerfold illustration (chromolithograph from drawing by Frederick Burr Opper), *Puck* 34, no. 865 (October 4, 1893). Courtesy of the Library of Congress, American Memory.
This chromolithograph shows the American upper class on the left and the European nobility on the right beneath their family trees with such American ancestors as "Skin Trader, Money Lender, Slave Trader, Squatter, [and] Tavern Keeper" and such European ancestors as "Marauding Knight, Robber Baron, King's Favorite, Plundering Viking, [and] Rapacious Seigneur."

man and Italian) archival methods. These methods had to do with provenance, *respect des fonds*, and the context of record creation rather than the creation of subject access as in the historical manuscript tradition.[25] A Dutch archivist, Arnold Johan Ferdinand van Laer, was among the first to make these practices known in America when he reorganized the New York State Archives in 1899. In the early 1900s, the American Historical Association, drawing on these same European traditions, pushed for legislation to save records, create public repositories, and survey existing collections. Their Public Archives Commission facilitated the founding of the first state archives in the country (Alabama in 1901 and Mississippi in 1902).[26]

American genealogy everywhere fell between the two varying collecting cultures, one being the public archives tradition and the other, the historical manuscript tradition. This duality was especially prominent in Louisiana, where European conventions were long practiced in the Saint Louis Cathedral Archives, in New Orleans's City Archives, and in notarial practices (all since the 1700s), but where the early twentieth-century collections in the universities and the Louisiana State Museum were formed in the historical societies model.[27]

Communities United and Divided around Genealogies

Just as Tocqueville had noted, there was also a continuing belief that people interested in genealogy had dreams of themselves as members of

Celebration
of the
127th Anniversary
of the
BATTLE OF NEW ORLEANS
and the
50th ANNIVERSARY
OF THE NATIONAL SOCIETY
OF THE U. S. DAUGHTERS OF 1812

IN JACKSON SQUARE, NEW ORLEANS
THURSDAY, JANUARY 8, 1942
Under Auspices of
Chalmette Chapter U. S. Daughters of 1812

TIMES-PICAYUNE NEW ORLEANS STATES, SUNDAY, JANUARY 18, 1942

CATHOLIC ACTION of the SOUTH

Thursday, January 15, 1942

Wins Contest

Mary Patricia Hebert

Mary Hebert Wins Contest

Mary Patricia Hebert, 11-year-old pupil of Redemptorist school, School Sisters of Notre Dame, won the award in an essay contest conducted by the Chalmette chapter and the Louisiana Society of the United States Daughters of 1812, and received presentation of the prize during the ceremonies marking the Battle of New Orleans anniversary last Thursday in Jackson Square.

The award was presented by Mrs. W. W. Willson, state chairman of patriotic education on behalf of the Chalmette chapter and the Louisiana group. Mrs. Willson lauded the winner for her time, effort and research and for her American spirit of achievement.

The essay subject was "Commodore Perry and His Brilliant Victory on Lake Erie." Miss Hebert in her essay graphically depicted the preparations made by young Commodore Perry to meet the British, and the actual battle with its ultimate victory that elicited his famous message: "We have met the enemy and they are ours." Pupils of all schools were entered in the contest.

Miss Hebert is a pupil of the seventh grade at Redemptorist parochial school, Constance near Josephine street, which is staffed by the School Sisters of Notre Dame.

During the ceremonies in Jackson square, Major General Allison Owen was master of ceremonies, and the benediction was given by Rev. Francis A. Duffy, O. M. I.

FIGURE 3.12
Scrapbook page from the Chalmette Chapter, Daughters of the War of 1812. Daughters of the War of 1812 papers, Collection 656, Louisiana Research Collection, Tulane University.

The Daughters sponsored essay contests, especially promoting leadership and academic skills among girls.

European nobility, or as products of America's leading families, or better yet as descendants of both types of elites. The 1883 publication of Charles Browning's *Americans of Royal Descent* and other similar projects fed the idea that genealogy was not quite to be believed.[28] Precisely because of such ideas, some felt that an interest in genealogy should be hidden. Mark Twain made clear this sentiment in his posthumously published autobiography when he wrote of his mother, Jane Lampton Clemens, who would never "refer in any way to her gilded ancestry when any person not a member of the family was present, for she had good American sense." She nevertheless believed "with all her heart" that "the family descended from" great lords with castles. Twain also spoke of one of his cousins, "the colonel," who always recalled

> "the head of our line," flung off with painful casualness that . . . compelled inquiry. . . . Then followed the whole disastrous history of how the Lambton [eventually Lampton] heir came to this country a hundred and fifty years or so ago . . . while at home in England he was given up as dead and his titles and estates turned over to his younger brother. . . . And the colonel always spoke with studied and courtly defense of the claimant of his day—a second cousin of his—and referred to him with entire seriousness as "the earl."[29]

FIGURE 3.13
Scrapbook page from 1915, Chalmette Chapter, Daughters of the War of 1812. Daughters of the War of 1812 papers, Collection 656, Louisiana Research Collection, Tulane University.
The Daughters of the War of 1812 oversaw, and indeed still oversee, yearly enactments of the Battle of New Orleans as well as many other celebrations about the battle. In the early 1900s, they undertook the preservation and continued care of the battlefield. These clipping pages from their scrapbook tells of two actual daughters (as opposed to daughters by virtue of membership), then in their very old age, whose fathers had fought in the battle. Note that the two women use different conventions of namings: one is identified by her married name (Mrs. L. M. Harper) and the other uses her given name along with her husband's surname (Mrs. Felicité Gayoso Tennent). Genealogists contend that women of French and Spanish descent are more apt to use their given names than women of other backgrounds.

The stereotype of the genealogist was, then, at the end of the nineteenth century and the beginning of the twentieth, someone like this colonel, someone rather silly and certainly elitist. The stereotype was also increasingly a woman. The Colonial Dames of America (1890), the Daughters of the American Revolution (1890), the National Society of the Colonial Dames of America (1891), and other such groups recognized themselves as forming an elite defined around their male ancestors. They used records to find these ancestors, and they became actors in the field of public history, participants in national culture, and part of how genealogy served to heal wounds left by the Civil War. Through genealogy, they changed their role as private recordkeepers, a noted role for women since medieval times, into public ones, into visible intellectual pursuits. Women in patriotic societies took positions not unlike that held by Susa

Young Gates that made genealogy and public history popular and visible across the nation.[30]

Such women, for example, played a major role in erecting monuments to commemorate the Civil War dead and in the establishment of Memorial Day as a national holiday. They organized public displays of records in smaller libraries and erected their own headquarters—for example, the mammoth Washington, DC, headquarters of the Daughters of the American Revolution. Women's patriotic societies led book groups and provided prizes and scholarships to countless students. For years, DAR chapters across the United States compiled and published "lineage books" and multivolume sets of members' contributions of family Bible entries.[31] In addition, "[s]ince the early 1900s local DAR units donated one copy of each of their publications to the public libraries in their jurisdiction."[32] In short, these and other women's organizations moved family history out of homes and into the public realm.

Women then challenged the position of the antiquarians as *the* "men of letters," which returns us to the discrimination that Joseph Émile Ducros likely felt in his genealogical work. Since the first generation of mainly male professional historians had emerged, great numbers of women engaged in the practice of family history only made more painful the demotion of male antiquarians.[33] At the same time, the early twentieth century saw efforts to achieve a balance such that genealogy could remain within the fold of respectable and useful historical practices.[34] The *William and Mary Quarterly*, hailed today as one of the first scholarly journals in the United States, was founded in large part to address equally genealogy, biography, and history within a tradition that demanded documentation.[35] In the 1920s and 1930s, an eminent genealogist, Don-

FIGURE 3.14
Works Progress Administration project typists' office, third floor of the Presbytère, Louisiana State Museum, 1940. Courtesy of the Louisiana State Museum.

WPA workers typed many of the materials associated with the museum's archival projects, such as indexes and catalog cards to the judicial records later used by genealogists.

FIGURE 3.15
Works Progress Administrative bookbinder and letterer, 1940. Courtesy of the Louisiana State Museum.
The department was officially called the Lettering and Sign Printing Office. The worker here holds a book with a common binder used for family histories often submitted as typed or handwritten manuscripts.

ald Lines Jacobus, worked to establish the first professional standards for genealogists. He and his colleagues published their evidence-backed findings in the *New Haven Genealogical Magazine* (1922); ten years later, this journal would become the *American Genealogist*. If I could have, in chapter 2, chosen one other foundational figure, it would be him. From his work grew the professionalization of genealogy, notably the Board for Certification of Genealogists. From his work also grew other legacies that would become current online projects devoted to explanations of record types and sources as well as rules of evidence.[36]

Jacobus anticipated the growth of the universe of records and, within it, access to genealogical sources, an environment in which more and more people could go to their local libraries and find genealogical sources. The Works Progress Administration added workers to museums, libraries, and archives who transcribed records, assessed preservation needs, and created card catalogs and finding aids for collections. The genealogical ephemera and copies of records amassed by Ducros, for example, were bound into books by WPA workers.[37]

World War II and the affluence of the postwar years provided a climate in which yet other new technologies, new archives, and new uses for social history changed the conventional paths for the work of genealogists. At the New Orleans Public Library in the late 1940s, administrators wrote monthly reports that attested to an ever-increasing number of archival visitors asking for family records. The librarians also mentioned more and more requests for documents concerned with voter registration, Social Security, and other government programs. This reflected an active use of records for practical purposes, not strictly for genealogy, but it indicated that more people knew that access to such records was available. They used this knowledge when needed to reconstruct family history.[38] The founding of the Louisiana Genealogical and Historical Society in 1953 and the Genealogical Research Society of New Orleans in 1960 also created a setting favorable to the preservation and use of records.[39]

The 1960s and 1970s witnessed more and more such groups springing up everywhere. Returning to Jacobus's influence, there emerged a small group of professional genealogists who codified standards and established the means to achieve and test professional status from 1964 onward, within the Board for Certification of Genealogists. There emerged also a much larger group of avocational family historians for whom standards are also urged through books, workshops, and online courses.

Two other significant events of the twentieth century shaped genealo-

FIGURE 3.16
Microfilm volunteers from the Church of Jesus Christ of Latter-day Saints, ca. 1982. Courtesy of the Louisiana Division/City Archives, New Orleans Public Library.
Volunteers from the LDS Church undertook microfilming in New Orleans in the 1980s and 1990s. The first experiments with microfilm began at the Louisiana State Museum in 1941, with the assistance of WPA workers.

gy locally, nationally, and internationally. The first was the LDS Church's microfilming project, which began in the late 1930s in Connecticut, Delaware, Maryland, and North Carolina.[40] Halted by World War II, LDS microfilmers expanded their efforts in the 1950s and, to the present day, these mostly volunteer efforts have continued to increase. All over the Americas and Europe, the LDS teams are well known. Their efforts also made genealogists even more aware of the importance of records—not just those that had been filmed but others that could be used in conjunction with those filmed.[41] "Take the census records," one genealogist told me; "then I could go to other records: probate, those were some the Mormons filmed. Ship manifests, another sort. You had a bigger world. Who could have traveled to all the places where the Mormons filmed and found the originals? One person in a hundred."[42]

Or, as another astutely noted, the LDS Church noticed the disparate projects copying records in thousands of localities. They made these hundreds of thousands of records and indexes and lists accessible from one place; they brought names across the continent and made discoveries more possible. "The Mormons took the small little projects done all over the world and merged them," one family historian said to me. For example, she said,

> they even connected what the Catholics had divided. New Orleans was once part of the Province of Quebec, under the Bishop of Quebec. There is, in my family, always a "Marie Elodie." But you know, I thought it was a name from the way past, from *Acadie*, from *le grand dérangement*. I had that in a baptism certificate from the Church. Not the real record, mind you. But as soon as Ancestry.com put the Drouin Collection online, their notary records [Quebec Notarial Records, 1647–1952], I found that she called herself something different. The marriage contract there showed her signature: "Chaumont Elisabeth Marie E." She wrote as I have found they did by custom: last name first, like that. "E," not even "Elodie." Maybe Elodie was one of her other names, one she didn't use. Maybe not. Still, I liked that surprise. The dead can surprise. It was moving, I can tell you.[43]

The second event to revolutionize American genealogy came with the publication of Alex Haley's novel *Roots* and its televised series (1976–1977).[44] The Civil Rights era (1956–1968), the Civil War centennial (1961–1965), a World Conference on Records held in Salt Lake City in 1969, and the American bicentennial (1976) had all set the stage for an increased interest in learning about families and signaled an expanded inquiry into ancestors' lives. *Roots* rendered vigorously alive the desire to find ancestors, no matter how remote this quest might seem. Moreover, *Roots* addressed the problem of American slavery within the context of national and international history, something not even the academics could ignore.

Mass Appeal

Although most genealogists and historians continue to stress that *Roots* is a novel, almost everyone agrees that Haley broadened, and continues to broaden, the appeal of genealogy.[45] Immediately after the television series, librarians began a long, continuing leap to keep up with demand for genealogical services. They could finally justify costs for such services and acknowledge that genealogists were deserving of respect.[46] Academicians, too, responded and began to include genealogy as a part of social history, and to use genealogy as a part of public education, especially public history.[47] Twenty-first-century examples are such programs as *African American Lives* (2006) and *Finding Your Roots* (2012), both moderated by Harvard professor Henry Louis Gates Jr. and always featuring the work of genealogists.

Genealogists often criticized these and other programs as making their work seem too easy, as not revealing the complications of genetic testing, and, in general, as lacking in evidence, but all the same they also conceded that the shows illustrated the continuously widening appeal of family history, especially as a legacy of *Roots*. In essence, Haley made the time spent looking for ancestors part of an acceptable endeavor involving a large community of people who crossed boundaries of race, class, and even, yes, lineage.

Yet perhaps Americans like Joseph Cruzat and Joseph Émile Ducros always were conscious of an American nation of ancestor seekers and of genealogy as beneficial to, even explanatory of, an ever more diverse nation. The same granddaughter who donated Ducros's letters, Coralie

FIGURE 3.17
Coralie Guarino Davis, with spoon collection, ca. 1959. Coralie Davis Collection. Newcomb Archives and Vorhoff Library Special Collections, Newcomb College Institute, Tulane University.
Silver and other metal utensils last much longer than do other materials often passed down in families.

Guarino Davis, left her own papers to the Newcomb Archives at Tulane. Within them, Davis included diaries from 1944 to 2004 and correspondence and reports of the Daughters of the War of 1812. She is representative of another legacy that Joseph Ducros and others like him left in family history. From him and an uncle who also collected family history, Davis learned that documentation in itself was especially important, and collecting, joyful. These activities gave her connections to others, presented her with more and more visions of families, and put her own problems into a different perspective. She drew upon her knowledge of ancestors as she was excluded from, and included in, various groups based upon different parts of her family lineage: a Sicilian father, a mother who did not have enough money to attend college but could educate herself through work for the patriotic societies, and too, her grandfather, who persisted in family history work to the end of his life even though many looked down on him for this passion. She learned to see her family as American in these inclusions and exclusions, however painful the latter were.[48]

At the end of Davis's life, the Daughters of the War of 1812 were debating whether to accept a woman born of an unknown male sperm donor, whose mother's family had male ancestors in the War of 1812. In this discussion, Davis witnessed another twenty-first-century way in which family history challenged assumptions about inheritance.[49] "It often makes you really think, to ask," said Cheryl (b. 1961), "[t]here are so many stories about the past and so many you find out just weren't so, or were different than you could imagine them."

Family history does challenge practitioners to think of what it means to be both an individual and part of a larger group, part of a family as well as a nation. Historian Francesca Morgan studied the workings of "lineage as capital," of genealogy's allowance of connections to the elite in New England (sometime by those not as elite). But the connections could work in other directions too, some unwanted. She found that leader John Farmer advocated at least once that undesirable kin could be ignored.[50]

Something happened between the time he presented that option and the late twentieth century. More confident American family historians began to include their black sheep, or even their slightly eccentric cousins, their marriages across color lines, in their family lineage charts. They could do so because they had enough other greatness in the promise of an individual being awarded merit on his or her own terms. Family historians proclaimed that one could also always find somewhere a counterbalance to some less than wanted trait in the family. With more accessible records, one had the names of more ancestors upon whom to place one's understanding of identity.

This stance implies a choice, an acknowledgment of all but a focus on those one "likes." There is still some "cutting and pasting," but now this is done in best practice to frame the black sheep within the fold. This evolution has to do with a trust in the records, a belief that they allow not only interpretation but also reinterpretation. In archival terminology, genealogists are part of a "community of records," a phrase given to mark how written documentation or knowledge of written documentation is central to how people understand and represent the past.[51] A community of records means that records live as actors in history, and this was certainly true for the genealogists in New Orleans.

For the people introduced in this book and for countless others in the American tradition, genealogy is also ultimately about being more than an observer. Genealogy is about the journeys involved in moving between the ideals and the reality of social classes and other divisions that are still so much a part of America, especially the documentation of these journeys, as both observer and observed.

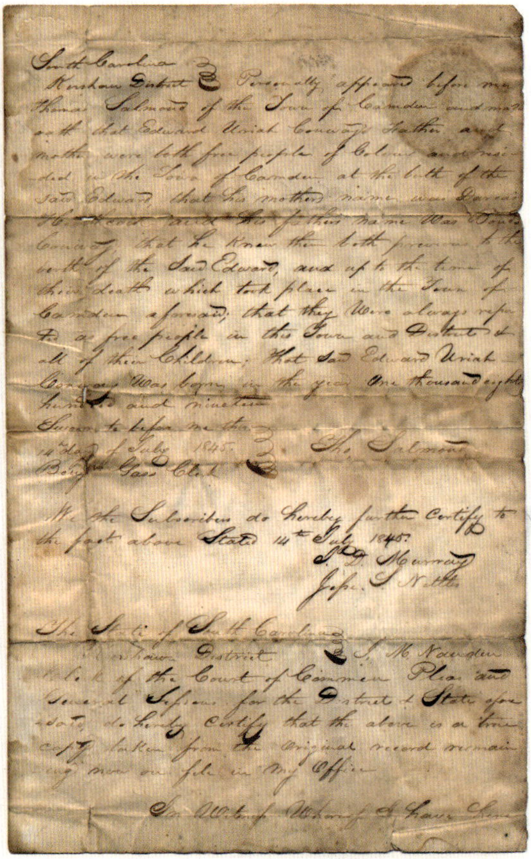

FIGURES 4.1, 4.2, 4.3
Freedom papers of Edward Uriah Bonds, 1845, South Carolina. Harrietta Harris papers. Courtesy of the Amistad Research Center, New Orleans. Genealogist Harrietta Harris was given this paper by a relative about their shared ancestor, Bonds Conway, purported to be the first African American in South Carolina to purchase his freedom. Conway and his wife, Dorcas Heathcock, had one son, Edward Uriah Bonds, born in 1819 in Kershaw District, South Carolina. This son was born free, but he carried this document to prove his status.

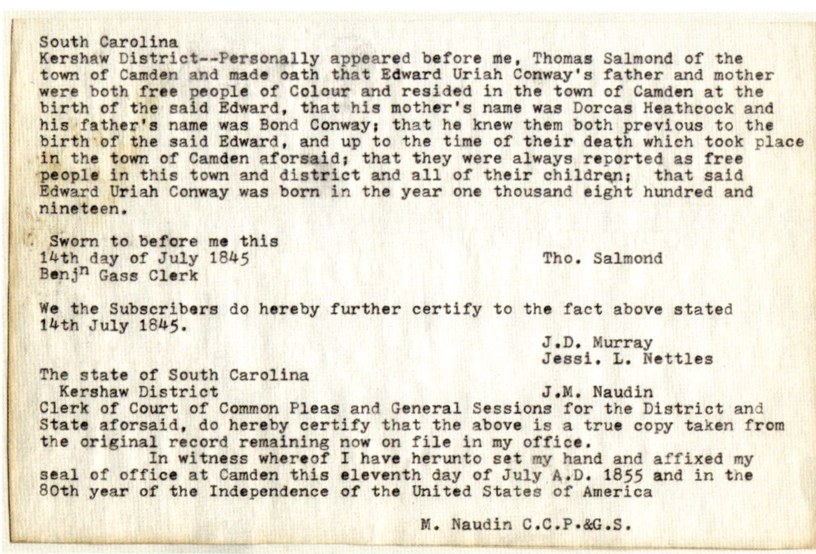

South Carolina
Kershaw District--Personally appeared before me, Thomas Salmond of the town of Camden and made oath that Edward Uriah Conway's father and mother were both free people of Colour and resided in the town of Camden at the birth of the said Edward, that his mother's name was Dorcas Heathcock and his father's name was Bond Conway; that he knew them both previous to the birth of the said Edward, and up to the time of their death which took place in the town of Camden aforsaid; that they were always reported as free people in this town and district and all of their children; that said Edward Uriah Conway was born in the year one thousand eight hundred and nineteen.

Sworn to before me this
14th day of July 1845   Tho. Salmond
Benjn Gass Clerk

We the Subscribers do hereby further certify to the fact above stated 14th July 1845.

J.D. Murray
Jessi. L. Nettles

The state of South Carolina
Kershaw District   J.M. Naudin
Clerk of Court of Common Pleas and General Sessions for the District and State aforsaid, do hereby certify that the above is a true copy taken from the original record remaining now on file in my office.
In witness whereof I have herunto set my hand and affixed my seal of office at Camden this eleventh day of July A.D. 1855 and in the 80th year of the Independence of the United States of America

M. Naudin C.C.P.&G.S.

CHAPTER FOUR

Public Genealogies around Creole and Other Ethnic Identities

With genealogy's spreading popularity, with changes that grew from the Civil Rights movement, the 1960s through the 1980s witnessed a turn to thoughts on one of the most persistent of all genealogically based practices: the classification of people by their race, or when that race is not apparent, by the race of their mother, or some percentage of their ancestry. Family historians in New Orleans all discussed some aspect of race and felt that learning about race and ethnicity was a consistent part of their work. Look at what's written by names, genealogists said. Look at how citizens and residents, and ancestors, were labeled, and even included or excluded, on records. Listen to the word on the street, they said; you will hear about family histories that are only about race.

Of course, this discourse was not unique to New Orleans. One persistent example of a family story involving inquiries into race is the life of Thomas Jefferson and his complex home, where, for at least forty years, a mixed-race slave named Sally Hemings also lived. Together, the two had many children. Although today we most often think of their union as coming to light in the late twentieth century, historians have shown recurring bouts of notice to the liaison, beginning as early as 1799.[1]

Jefferson himself always struggled with the part the enslaved played in his world and the world beyond. Sally Hemings, their children, and other Hemings relatives were part of his Virginian history, of his family history, of the legacy of mixed races in the Americas, and especially of his genealogy and that of his children. Sally Hemings and Jefferson's wife, Martha Wayles Jefferson, were half-sisters. In addition, as a slave Sally Hemings and a number of the Hemingses were the property first of the Wayles family, and later the property of Martha and her husband, Thomas Jefferson. Many Hemings family members lived in the area of Jefferson's beloved Monticello, which was then connected to their own family homes. Some from the Hemings family departed and "passed" as white.[2] They became other families, but the two names of Hemings and Jefferson remained entwined over time. As one Hemings-Jefferson descendant recalled, she had learned of this heritage from "lips to ears, down through the generations."[3] This remarkable lineage has continued to bring a na-

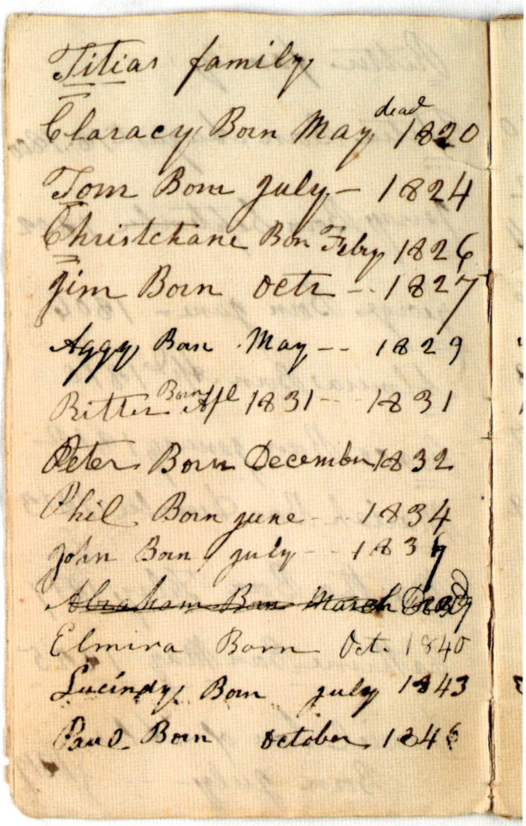

Titias family
Claracy Born May 1820 dead
Tom Born July 1824
Christchane Born Febry 1826
Jim Born Octr 1827
Aggy Born May 1829
Ritter Born Apl 1831 1831
Peter Born December 1832
Phil Born June 1834
John Born July 1837
~~Abraham Born March~~
Elmira Born Oct 1840
Lucindy Born July 1843
Paul Born October 1846

FIGURE 4.4

"Titia's Family," page from commonplace book, George Hannah family papers, Mss 1.H1956a193_004. Courtesy of the Virginia Historical Society, Richmond.

Pages like this one don't disclose much information about slave families; because of this dearth of information, the novel *Roots* was very popular, and other indexes to transports and sometimes names of early Africans and African Americans, enormously valued. To recapture information on the ancestors and descendants of people like Titia and her children turned out to be an American dream.

tional focus on concepts of family, on what it means to be the descendant both of slaves and of those who enslaved them.[4] Today, publicity brochures of the Thomas Jefferson Foundation, which maintains Monticello, state simply that they "and most historians believe that, years after his wife's death, Thomas Jefferson was the father of the six children of Sally Hemings mentioned in Jefferson's records, including Beverly, Harriet, Madison, and Eston Hemings."[5]

In New Orleans, family historians believed that they had more to talk about various degrees of mixed-race people, of their genealogies, than did others in the United States. In the city, genealogists had their own stories to tell to reinforce this belief that talk of race is prevalent and usually concerns families. There are the often told episodes in which a mixed-race person "passing for white" could not greet her darker family members on the street. There existed a code among family members to keep silent about those passing. Even as I was editing this book, a friend called to tell me that she always remembered a funeral home director who told of people "passing for white in all areas of their lives" who had to "sneak in" under the cover of night, after closing hours, to see their deceased family members who were Creoles of color. A person passing as white could not be seen at the funeral of a Creole of color. One genealogist told of finding vital and census records that went in the other direction, in which her great-great-uncle had declared himself a descendants of Africans so that he could legally marry a person of color. Genealogists thought about these types of accounts as commonplace. To them, this was part of the conversation of family history in the city.

One can place the written historical trajectory, something of the beginning of this conversation, by looking to the founder of the city, Jean Baptiste le Moyne Bienville, who, in his modifications of the code of 1724, the Code Noir, provided rules for the circumstances of alliances between slaves and colonial "white subjects" as well as for children born to slaves and free persons of color. Over the following centuries, legal experts also had to work out definitions of various degrees of mixing, creating categories that told of their own prejudicial attitudes and perplexities (mulatto, griffe, quadroon, octoroon, and others). All the while, mixed-race people stood up for their rights and the rights of others of African descent, interpreting their family histories in doing so. They were leaders among the *gens du couleur libre*, the free people of color, who made up

FIGURE 4.5
Page from childhood scrapbook of Nell Pomeroy O'Brien, ca. 1908. Genealogical Materials (120-50), John A. and Nell Pomeroy O'Brien Collection (Mss 120), Earl K. Long Library, University of New Orleans. This blank page, where once something appeared, suggests both the indignity of slavery and the decisions required to place or not place slaves among white family history records. The document was likely moved by an archivist, placed now, for protection, among a folder called Documents (120-45) in the same collection.

FIGURE 4.6
New Orleans Militia Officer, Alfred R. Waud, ca. 1864. Drawing. Courtesy of the Library of Congress, American Memory. An artist and correspondent for a number of newspapers during the Civil War, Waud drew this portrait sketch of one of the First Louisiana Native Guards, the first non-white regiment officially a part of the Union Army.

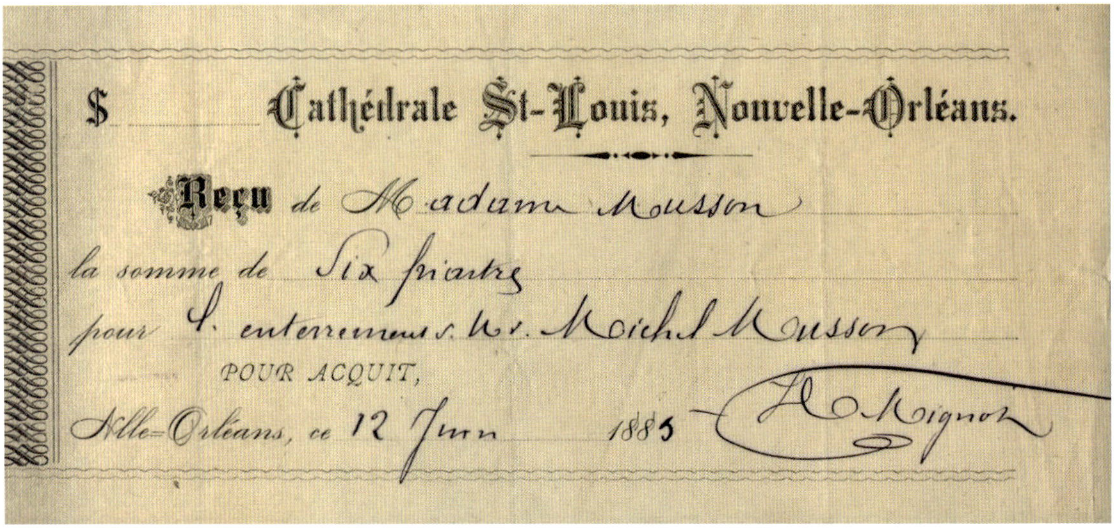

$ Cathédrale St-Louis, Nouvelle-Orléans.

Reçu de Madame Musson

la somme de Six piastres

pour l'enterrement de Mr. Michel Musson

POUR ACQUIT,

Nlle-Orléans, ce 12 Juin 1885

FIGURE 4.7

Receipt for burial, Saint Louis Cathedral, 1885. Degas and Musson Families Papers, Collection 226, Louisiana Research Collection, Tulane University.

This receipt for the 1885 burial of Michel Musson comes from the collection of papers maintained by the Degas-Musson family in the city. Michel Musson was the uncle of the painter Edgar Degas. Saint Louis Cathedral continued to use the French language in its official dealings with parishioners until 1910.

a sizable segment of the population—one-third of the Saint-Domingue immigrants, for example, in the early nineteenth century. In addition, journalists wrote about legal cases involving attempts to define how different degrees of race figured in the lives of particular people, and academics too later analyzed these public lawsuits to understand race and family in the city and state.[6]

More often than not, mixed-race people in New Orleans called themselves Creoles of color, or simply, Creoles. The word *creole* comes from the Latin *creare*, and then from the Portuguese word *crioulo*, meaning a slave of African descent born in the New World. The Spaniards called all Africans and Europeans born in the colonies some variant of *criollo*, as did the French, using *créole* as the French version of the word. In general, in all languages the word means "locally born" or "born here." Some people remember growing up with this definition of "born here." As genealogist Winston De Ville (b. 1937) said, "*Creole* was *anything made in, anything grown in, anyone born in* the colony. Has *nothing* at all to do with race. And their descendants." As an aside, he added a telling comment about not the city, but the rural Acadiana countryside: "I wasn't aware that I was really American until I registered as a freshman: Nationality: French. I was so reared."[7]

Someone born here is certainly the simplest definition, yet "Creole" *has* been hotly contested as a categorizing name for people.[8] By the late nineteenth century in New Orleans, white descendants of the French and Spanish wanted Creole to be "their" name, not that of the Creoles of color. They wanted this with the passion of those excluded in other ways. Having been on the side that lost the Civil War, the white Creoles strove to demonstrate their similarities to the ruling classes in other US cities.

In other parts of the United States, there was no clearly delineated three-tiered society, including substantial numbers of mixed-race peo-

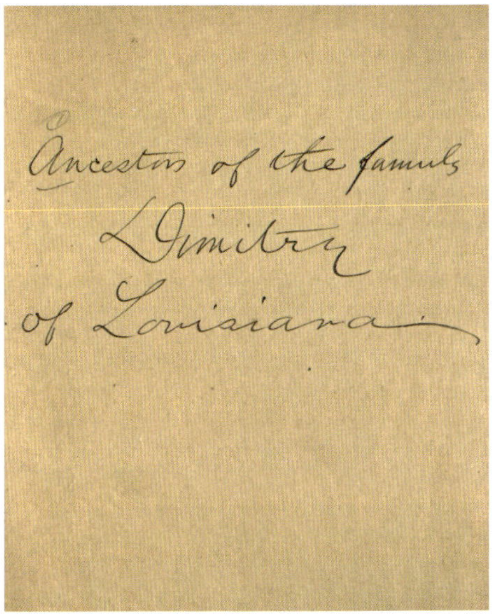

Ancestors of the family
Dimitry
of Louisiana

FIGURE 4.8

Title page of *Ancestors of the Dimitry Family*, Genealogical Paper Series, Collection 504 (24), Louisiana Research Center, Tulane University.

The Dimitry family was one New Orleans family who faced legal challenges for being considered "nonwhite." Four notebooks show extensive notes on the family's heritage in Greece, France, Canada, and other parts of the United States.

FIGURE 4.9

Marianne Celeste Dragon. Attributed to the School of Salazar, ca. 1796. Collection of the Louisiana State Museum.

It was Marianne Celeste Dragon Dimitry (1777–1856) and her daughter Euphrosine Dragon Pandelly (1802–1873) whose appearances were questioned in an 1855 trial in which George Pandelly petitioned the court to rule that he had been slandered when he was called "nonwhite." The trial involved notarial and sacramental records as well as testimony by residents of the city.

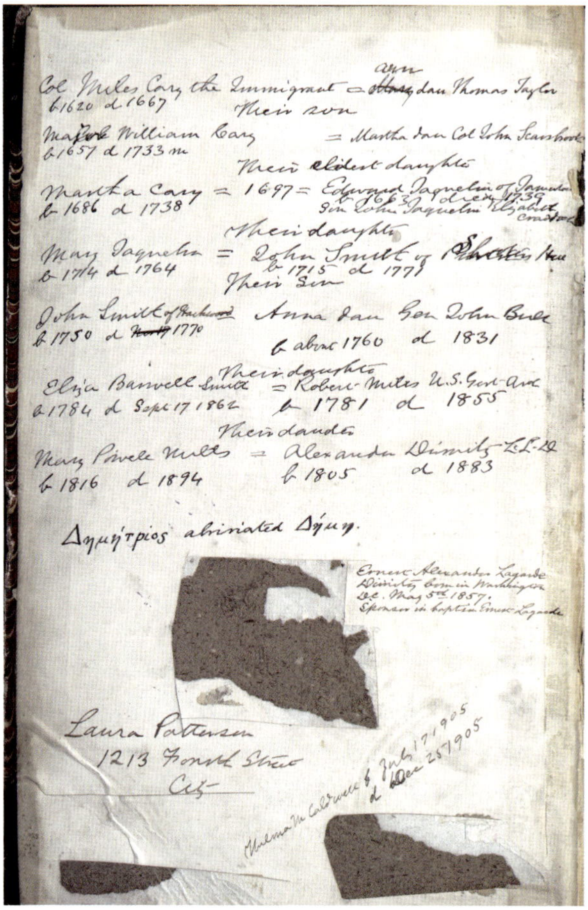

FIGURE 4.10
End papers of the genealogical notebook on the Dimitry family, Genealogical Paper Series, Collection 504 (24), Louisiana Research Center, Tulane University.
This paste-down end paper shows the origins of one member of the family, Alexander Dimitry (1775–1852), presented in the Greek alphabetic spelling of his name. Other portions of the book give attention to his son, another Alexander Dimitry (1805–1883) and his wife, Mary Powell Mills (1816–1894).

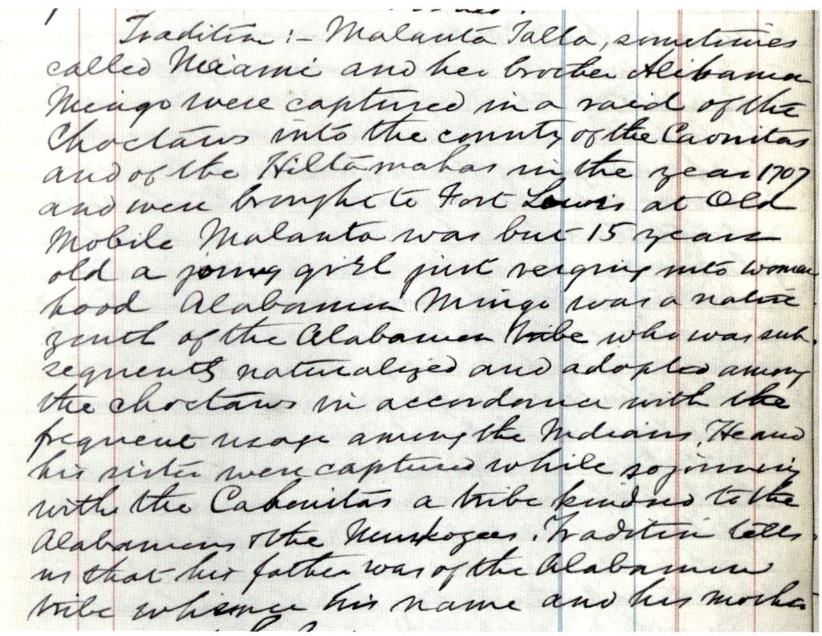
Tradition :- Malanta Talla, sometimes called Miami and her brother Alibama Mingo were captured in a raid of the Choctaws into the county of the Caonitas and of the Hiltamahas in the year 1707 and were brought to Fort Louis at Old Mobile Malanta was but 15 years old a young girl just verging into womanhood Alabama Mingo was a native youth of the Alabama tribe who was subsequently naturalized and adopted among the Choctaws in accordance with the frequent usage among the Indians, He and his sister were captured while sojourning with the Cabonitas a tribe kindred to the Alabamas & the Muskogees. Tradition tells us that her father was of the Alabama tribe whose name and his mother

FIGURE 4.11
Page from the genealogical notebook on the Dimitry family, Genealogical Paper Series, Collection 504 (24), Louisiana Research Center, Tulane University.
Theodore Dimitry (1871–1950?) was said to have been the family genealogist, although his older cousin, Charles Patton Dimitry, also wrote genealogical columns for the *Times-Democrat.* Theodore Dimity here writes about family "tradition" as he tells the story of descent from an Alabama Indian princess, Malanta Talla. As early as 1912, genealogists were recommending this method of marking what one found in records versus what one heard from family members.

ple. Outside of Louisiana, except in scattered pockets, most Americans had never had, in such a visible way, "cousins" across degrees of racial mixing.

A Connection Extending to Today

Jari Honora (b. 1991) researches Creoles of color and other family lines within Catholic and Protestant families of European, African, and Native American ethnicities. Asked to identify one of his favorite resources in genealogical research, he recalled an archives outside New Orleans, one that shows much about overall Louisianan Catholic recordkeeping. Genealogists from Louisiana and other places with an affluence of records, as we have seen, are appreciative of their good fortune in this regard.

> The Baton Rouge Diocesan Archives stands out so much because of the red books they've published. It's a series of books that are red in color. And it's all the sacramental records they have for the 1700s all the way up until about 1900. And it's for, I guess maybe all twelve . . . maybe fourteen parishes that they cover. And my ancestors are all from parishes within those books. However, before 1865, the only information on slaves and perhaps on Native Americans that you'll find in the books are [for] those who used surnames, which were far and few between. Therefore, I have to go up there . . . sit there and go through the huge slave books of baptisms, which aren't indexed, aren't organized. It's just chronologically as a slave was baptized or confirmed or something. . . . But it's always so fun, because it's one of the few times, other than at the courthouses, that I get to use the original records. And it's so interesting because you find an ancestor who was a slave. It's been preserved. There in writing. We are lucky.

Honora talked passionately about his use of these Baton Rouge sacramental records, supplemented with other records, for context. In several inquiries, he mapped the social milieu of his ancestors found via the signatures of the godmothers, godfathers, and people who "stood" in the weddings (through baptismal and marriage records), and the addresses of these people (through census listings and city directories). From these sources, he learned about his ancestors' circles of support and affection. He learned how they earned their living, how they could have walked to public markets, caught the streetcar, and traveled to church. He plotted the settings of their lives. This process, he said, "rounds out the picture."

Honora is rare among family historians in that he is a young person. In New Orleans, most genealogical groups are predominantly made up of persons forty years or older.[9] A round face makes him seem even younger than he is, but he has a mature composure, likely because he is used to being around much older people. He has been their peer in libraries since he was eleven. He is a Tulane University history major graduate, but he says that genealogy more than formal studies has defined his life. "Genealogy has made my world bigger."

Besides the tactile excitement of the actual records, human interaction is important to Honora. One of the groups that offered him the most help in beginning was the Creole Heritage Education Research Society. Their goal is to assist "Creoles of Color in researching their ancestry," to educate "the general public about Creole culture," and to celebrate "the contributions and legacy of a unique, sometimes forgotten people."[10] The people in that group have become his best friends, regardless of their age.

Honora once researched a relative who was in the state legislature during Reconstruction, and he remains especially interested in this period. He tries to understand how it would have been to say you were Creole at that time, a Creole of color or a white Creole. He mentions that it was the historian Charles Gayarré (1805–1895) who had prominently emphasized the registration of slaves, free people of color, and mulattoes. In his four-volume work on the history of Louisiana (1866), Gayarré commented on a bishop in 1799 who despaired that Spanish military officers "with colored concubines . . . do not blush at carrying the illegitimate issue . . . to be recorded in the parochial registries as their *natural children*."[11]

Becoming an American City

Despite Honora's extensive network of fellow family historians today, and despite the contention that race has made genealogy always something that at least some New Orleanians attended to, others suggested that genealogy in general was slow to gain popularity in the city. They contended that there was a lack of interest in genealogy in New Orleans prior to the twentieth century. They spoke of a connection between the ubiquity of Church records and the lack of interest in other forms of knowing about ancestors. The availability of such good records maintained by the Catholic Church seemed reason enough to not worry over family history, to rest assured that one could find what one wanted, should one need to do so.[12]

At least one earlier writer posited that genealogy was not popular in the city for another reason: the Creoles were modest, unwilling to make much ado over their ancestors. "The old Creole families, due to their high sense of modesty and horror of anything pretentious, neglected their genealogies," an unnamed author wrote in a 1917 article in the *Louisiana Historical Quarterly*.[13] Or could it have been that genealogy was neglected in privately written documents *and* acknowledged in routine conversations precisely because of the city's prominent mixed-race population? Was genealogy too dangerous to write about, but too much a part of everyday life to avoid altogether? Could it be that public genealogies about race always ran as background noise, sub rosa to the published accounts, and that these discussions of race could be considered the city's first widely known discussions of records and family history?

Although the earliest published writings that specifically referred to "family history" or genealogy completely ignored Creoles of color, their absence does not mean that attention was not paid to their family lines. Throughout the nineteenth and twentieth centuries, their genealogies were openly part of any interpretation of the rules of a segregated society. Their birth certificates and those of their ancestors were the evidence called in court proceedings. Certainly, these efforts also gave warning and promoted a reluctance to probe too publicly, too deliberately into family histories.[14]

As Honora suggested, one oddity is the degree to which Gayarré emphasized the Church registries of slaves and free people of color while at the same time pointing out that at least one person (the bishop) had found this to be a cause for despair. This story becomes all the more complicated when one learns more about Gayarré, a "Creole among Creoles" as he is often called, active in writing both in French and English about the state's history. Gayarré founded the State Library and spearheaded other efforts promoting Louisiana history.[15] But by 1892–1893, when Charles Patton Dimitry (1837–1910) was writing his columns on genealogy, the first works published on ancestors in the city, Gayarré and others like him had also seen almost a whole century of erosion or bolstering, if one wants to see it from a different direction, of their white Creole and Southern identities.

Gayarré's adversary was another type of spokesperson for Louisiana, George Washington Cable (1844–1925). Nationally known to readers of literary magazines and, at the time, the literary peer of Mark Twain, Cable had written essays in favor of racial equality and fictional portrayals of New Orleans's triracial and caste society.

One argument between the two men centered on Gayarré's belief that Cable had used Alexander Dimitry, the father of genealogist Charles Patton Dimitry, as an inspiration for stories about mixed-race characters. For the historian, "private feelings of sacred character" were violated by this insinuation. Dimitry *père* was his cousin and peer.[16]

Historian Lawrence Powell unraveled part of this fight between the great men, showing that Cable never suggested that Alexander Dimitry was his model but rather that he had furnished him with "The Dirge of St. Malo," a song of a slave insurrection that Cable later used in creating a character in *The Grandissimes: A Story of Creole Life* (1880). Gayarré didn't have this insight. His argument with Cable culminated in a series of lectures on the Creoles of "romance" and of "fact." Gayarré's thoughts were also influenced by the perceived notion of family histories, of genealogies.[17]

The Dimitry family was always proud of their Greek ancestors, but Alexander Dimitry was also prominent in the city and beyond. He spoke eleven languages and had worked in Washington, DC, as a translator. He had served as US ambassador to Costa Rica and Nicaragua and had

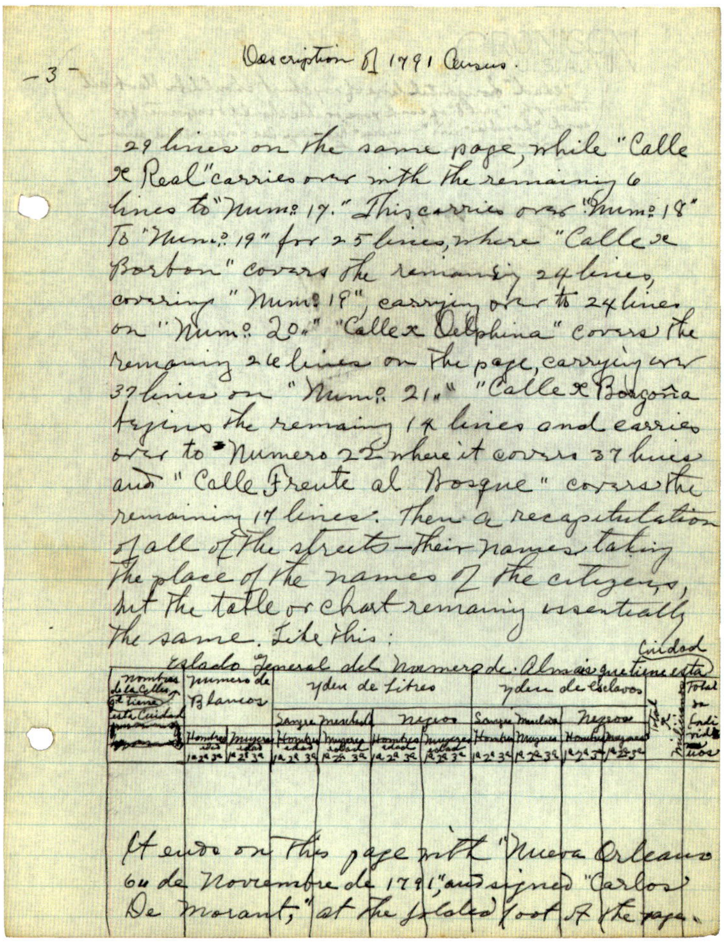

-3-

Description of 1791 Census.

29 lines on the same page, while "Calle x Real" carries over with the remaining 6 lines to "Num.º 17." This carries over "Num.º 18" To "Num.º 19" for 25 lines, where "Calle x Borbon" covers the remaining 24 lines, covering "Num.º 18", carrying over to 24 lines on "Num.º 20." "Calle x Delphina" covers the remaining 26 lines on the page, carrying over 37 lines on "Num.º 21." "Calle x Borgoña begins the remaining 14 lines and carries over to "Numero 22 where it covers 37 lines and "Calle Frente al Bosque" covers the remaining 17 lines. Then a recapitulation of all of the streets—their names taking the place of the names of the citizens, but the table or chart remaining essentially the same. Like this:

Estado General del Numero de Almas que tiene esta Cuidad

Nombres de la Calles que tiene esta Cuidad | Numero de Blancos | ydem de Libres | ydem de Esclavos | Total | Militares | Total de Individuos

Sangre mesclada | Negros | Sangre mesclada | Negros

Hombres edad | Mugeres edad | Hombres edad | Mugeres edad | Hombres edad | Mugeres edad | Hombres | Mugeres | Hombres | Mugeres

1a 2a 3a | 1a 2a 3a | 1a 2a 3a | 1a 2a 3a | 1a 2a 3a | 1a 2a 3a | 1a 2a 3a | 1a 2a 3a | 1a 2a 3a | 1a 2a 3a

It ends on this page with "Nueva Orleans 6 de Noviembre de 1791," and signed "Carlos De Morant," at the isolated foot of the page.

FIGURES 4. 12, 4.13
Cover of Portfolio Notebook and Notes kept by Marcus Christian, ca. 1947. Marcus Christian Collection (Mss 11, Boxes 3, 12), Louisiana and Special Collections Department, Earl K. Long Library, University of New Orleans. This notebook includes a number of handwritten notes such as one on the 1791 census. Christian collected materials for a proposed article on race, segregation, and movement between its divisions. He looked to a number of genealogical and journalistic sources to discuss the practice of passing as white, or "passe pour blanc" as he called it, especially in New Orleans. He intended to publish a history of Creoles of color and began with notes for a proposed but never completed article for *Ebony* magazine.

acted as a school reformer in New Orleans. His wife, too, brought prominence from her family. Mary Powell Mills Dimitry was the daughter of Robert Mills, architect of the Washington Monument in Washington, DC.[18] But such is the strength of interest in persons who "pass for white," in genealogical stories of mixed-race people, that today Alexander Dimitry is remembered mainly for his place in the old arguments about race, especially in the argument between Gayarré and Cable over the meaning of Creole. This may be all the more so because his son, Charles Patton Dimitry, was interested in genealogy.

Charles Patton Dimitry's columns in the *Times-Democrat* appear to be similar to writing about genealogy across the nation in the 1890s. He referenced conversations with families and family portraits as his sources, so bringing genealogical pursuit in the city for the first time to private records and away from the records of the Church and notaries. He also exhibited the worst feature of American genealogy at that time: the desire to find only noble ancestors.[19]

On the other hand, precisely because he did not write about his own family, surely at least some contemporary readers would have thought of this family when they saw his articles, and of the debate between Cable and Gayarré. The Dimitry family had been involved in two trials concerning race and genealogical evidence in the 1830s and 1850s. In 1833–1834, two free women of color, Pauline and Josephine Forstall, sued to have property returned that had been left by their family to Maria Anna Dragon Dimitry. Her identity in the notarial records about this legacy had specified her status as a free person of color. Yet, by 1833, the Forstall sisters noted, Mrs. Dimitry claimed that she was white. The two then could not be the same woman, and Mrs. Dimitry, the white woman, should return her property to the Forstall sisters. The court let her keep both the property and her status as white, ruling that her family long had been "in possession" of the right to be categorized as persons "not born of Negro extraction."[20]

The other case involving the Dimitry family occurred in 1854, when Charles Dimitry's first cousin and Alexander Dimitry's nephew, George Pandelly, had gone to trial to collect damages against a man who had accused him of being "nonwhite." The bilingual newspaper *L'Abeille* and other newspapers covered the trial in detail. The voice of these journalists remains today very compelling. As historian Shirley Elizabeth Thompson notes, "The *Louisiana Courier* recognized as peculiar the extent to which dim recollections attained the status of fact. . . . Genealogy, then, was not merely a matter of establishing the factual details of family lineage; it also involved describing how the broader public had perceived those family relationships over time." She aptly called the trial and its coverage an episode of "public genealogy," part of the "archives of our history" based on records about race. There had been earlier such cases but none involving a public office (that which George Pandelly could

FIGURE 4.14
Assitha Dubuclet Grandjean, Lucia Chesse Dubuclet, and Veturia Dubuclet, ca. 1940. Photograph. René Grandjean Collection (Mss 85-126), Earl K. Long Library, University of New Orleans.
Assitha Dubuclet Grandjean is here pictured with members of her family, Creoles of color in New Orleans. In 1913, Assitha and Frenchman René Grandjean traveled to Saint Andrew, Jamaica, to marry there because Louisiana law forbade interracial marriages. Today, one can find Assitha Dubuclet Grandjean's later naturalization papers online at Ancestry.com. To marry a Frenchman, she gave up American citizenship, but regained it at some point through her own initiative.

hold only as a "white man"), and none so explicit in newspaper coverage of pieces of evidence. The trial lawyers used the very tools of genealogy: baptismal records, marriage certificates, notarial records (among them a slave sale), and other archival documents. Alexander Dimitry was likely one person mentioned in this coverage. One witness called to testify reported on the "Mediterranean" and "Indian" elements of one of Pandelly's uncles' appearance.[21]

Like the earlier trial, this one had a favorable but not perfect outcome for the Dimitry family, specifically for Pandelly. The court deemed that he was "white," based on family beliefs that they had an ancestor who was Indian rather than African, but he was not awarded the $20,000 in damages he sought. There would always be such cases, the court seemed to say, if damages were awarded. Thompson noted that the Dimitry family in this way "continued to affirm their white identity publicly" and that Charles Patton Dimitry's columns were part of these assertions. When Thompson was researching the topic, it seemed still current. As an archivist said to her: "We all know the Dimitrys are black."[22]

One year before Dimitry's *Times-Democrat* columns on elite families, another public local genealogical case, although it was never referred to as such, began. This case would influence segregation throughout the nation. In June 1891, Creole of color Homer J. Plessy boarded the white-only car of a train bound out of the city. He was quickly removed because the train conductor argued that Plessy should have been riding, by law, in the "colored car." His removal was preplanned via prior arrangement with the conductor specifically to engineer a test case for segregation.

Plessy filed suit, saying that the state's Separate Car Act violated his constitutional rights. The case would take five years to reach the national Supreme Court; his statement and arguments all along remained consistent. In essence, how could people with authority know for sure where he fit in the taxonomy of race? How could they know his genealogy? What qualifications did the conductor of the streetcar have to determine the lineages carried within a person? Plessy "looked white" because he was seven-eighths white and thus was able to enter the white-only section without being noticed.[23] Following the 1896 ruling in *Plessy v. Ferguson*, in which Plessy did not prevail, states could maintain "separate but equal" public facilities, "separate cars" but also schools and other institutions. States could segregate, in other words, on the basis of genealogy.

FIGURE 4.15
Stella Brown, ca. 1920. Studio print. René Grandjean Collection (Mss 85-126), Earl K. Long Library, University of New Orleans.

Other Influences on Public Genealogies in New Orleans

Over the course of the latter half of the nineteenth century and the beginning of the twentieth, other influences were added to this mix of public and private family lineages. New Orleans itself was changing, and new immigrants brought new traditions that had to do with families, identity, and searches for family records. In the early 1800s, men and women from New England, other parts of the Northeast, and the frontier of the Midwest were seen as "the Americans." The Creoles did not want to work with them, did not want to lose their place as leaders. So the city itself was divided into municipalities largely accommodating these different, older settlers, immigrants, and newcomers from 1836 to 1852.

But there were other immigrants too, from even more "different" backgrounds. The New Orleans Deutsche Gesellschaft, still active today but whose origin dates to 1848, was one significant association of these new immigrants. Later, Sicilian groups organized similar and equally long-lasting mutual aid societies around the villages from which they came: the Contessa Entellina Society (1886) and Società Italiana di Mutua Beneficenza Cefalutana (1891) being two such groups. These and other immigrant societies had their own forms of recordkeeping. Their collective tombs and monuments and those of other German, Portuguese, Italian, Sicilian, Irish, and Dalmatian groups changed the physical landscape of

FIGURE 4.16
Eugenie Darensbourg, ca. 1920. Studio print. René Grandjean Collection (Mss 85-126), Earl K. Long Library, University of New Orleans.

FIGURE 4.17
Raoul Decuir, ca. 1920. Studio print. René Grandjean Collection (Mss 85-126), Earl K. Long Library, University of New Orleans.

These studio prints show some of the images collected by the Grandjeans. Most of the people pictured were descendants of Reconstruction state treasurer Antoine Dubuclet. Assitha and René Grandjean gathered the photos and other family information into a scrapbook they called *Livre d'Or*. René Grandjean also collected the records of a group of Creole of color spiritualists.

the city, adding reminders of new families in the mix of New Orleans ethnic divisions and unions.

Creoles of color had to jostle for a place in the city, as they were increasingly marginalized, funneled legally into black or white by Jim Crow laws that began after Reconstruction ended. One way to combat this erasure of their mixed heritage was through knowledge of families and their genealogies. Rodolphe Desdunes's compilation *Nos Hommes et Notre Histoire* (1911) was one example of this effort. Less well known were various individual attempts to use Creole heritage as leverage against the social and economic oppression of all African Americans. During and shortly after Reconstruction, Creoles of color and some of their white allies, for example, could look to written documents to expose the genealogies of certain white families who dismissed their African ancestors. This strategy was used in a case that involved the persecution of an African American teacher then teaching in a white school. Marcus Christian (1900–1976), African American writer and poet, found this and other examples where mingled European and African heritages, documented in the public records, could be used in later struggles between the "white" and "colored" descendants of the pirate Jean Lafitte and the philanthropist Thomy Lafon.[24]

The French in the city were not unilateral in their heritage either and, from the early twentieth century on, publicly created genealogies that told, more and more often, distinctive stories of origin in specific parts of France, Canada, and Saint-Domingue. For example, Anna (b. 1924) spoke about always being told about ancestors who were mixed French, German, and Irish. She later learned of one line of the family whom she called "African relatives." But she remembered too that her grandfather had emphasized not the "unspeakable background" but another one: he wanted her to be sure to separate their heritage from the Acadians, to make sure she knew that she was from "the true French."

This grandfather had made New Orleans his home in the mid-nineteenth century. He came in one of the waves of immigrants who kept the city "French." He fled France in the 1870s, arriving, of course, with his own stories, traditions, and prejudices about being French. In his particular case, this meant thinking of French heritage coming directly from France as better than French heritage from Acadia, Saint-Domingue, or elsewhere. In a bigger picture, the Creoles welcomed all French-speaking people and let these "Foreign French" be counted as allies.

Some of the new patriotic societies cut across these regional and ethnic divisions. Those women who arrived from the east coast and had male ancestors who had fought in the War of 1812, for example, could join New Orleans women in the Chalmette Chapter of the Daughters of the War of 1812, created in 1892, just after Dimitry's works appeared. White Creole women especially became involved in this group, the Daughters' second chapter in the nation. As one elderly genealogist

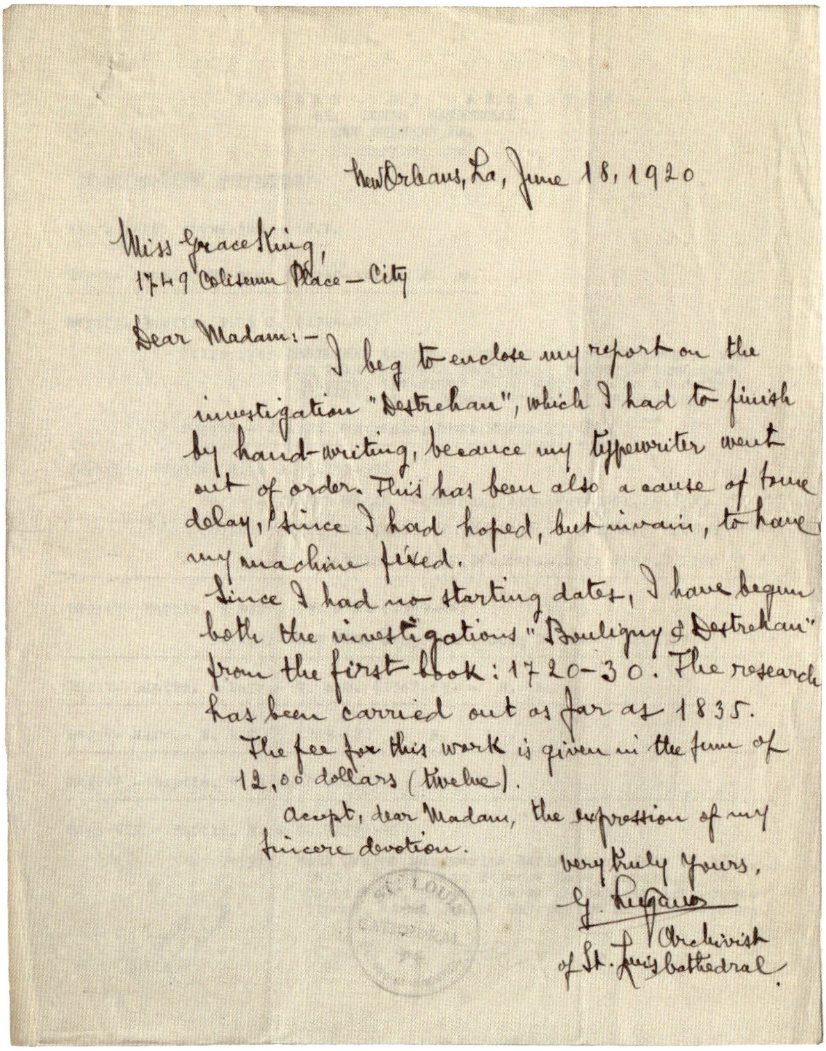
New Orleans, La, June 18, 1920

Miss Grace King,
1749 Coliseum Place — City

Dear Madam: — I beg to enclose my report on the investigation "Destrehan", which I had to finish by hand-writing, because my typewriter went out of order. This has been also a cause of some delay, since I had hoped, but in vain, to have my machine fixed.

Since I had no starting dates, I have begun both the investigations "Bouligny & Destrehan" from the first book: 1720-30. The research has been carried out as far as 1835.

The fee for this work is given in the sum of 12,00 dollars (twelve).

Accept, dear Madam, the expression of my sincere devotion.

Very truly yours,
G. Lugano
Archivist
of St. Louis Cathedral.

FIGURE 4.18
Letter to Grace King from Gaspare Lugano, August 16, 1930, Grace King Papers, Collection 564, Louisiana Research Collection, Tulane University.
Father Gaspare Lugano of Saint Louis Cathedral signed all his letters "Archivist of St. Louis Cathedral." His seal and letterhead reinforce this professional status. The seal reads "St. Louis Cathedral Bureau of Records"; his stationery displays the words "Bureau of Archives" on its letterhead. The cathedral archivist was thought of as an expert on records and their history in the city.

said to me, it was the Daughters of the War of 1812 who represented the heart of the city, its ties to both the colonial past and its early American period, especially the Battle of New Orleans. Throughout the first half of the twentieth century, the New Orleans members tended their headquarters in the Jackson House, a building adjoining the Cabildo. Here they commanded a symbolic as well as a literal placement in the old city. The group also maintained monuments and graves in the city's oldest cemeteries and held a yearly reenactment of the Battle of New Orleans.[25] In 1917, a number of Creole women active in the Daughters of the War of 1812 also helped form the Louisiana Colonials, a group whose membership required descent from the first colonial families, "here before 1803," thus, more often than not, Creole.[26]

New Orleans author and historian Grace King was a pivotal figure in all matters concerned with genealogy and records, a bridge between some of these various groups and the Louisiana Historical Society (LHS), for which she served as a leader from the 1890s on. In 1921, she published a series of genealogies in her *Creole Families of New Orleans* (1921). Her mentor was Charles Gayarré, and, like Dimitry, she was touched by the old arguments with George Washington Cable, although less personally. She was not a Creole, but she had been educated as a Francophone, and her work was influenced heavily by this education. In addition, she first found her public voice when she persuaded New York editors that she could produce accounts to rival Cable's.[27]

Although a number of genealogists were quick to point out that they would never use King's work, it does form part of the history of genealogy in the city. She told readers that she began as "a humble student" who wanted "to go back to the printed names in the pages of Gayarré and Martin," to show the early New Orleanians their "good blood, their *maintenances de noblesse*" in the "time between Bienville and Claiborne."[28] In her written conception of this time, Creoles of color were not present at all.

Like Gayarré, King both protected records and encouraged others to study them. More so than Charles Patton Dimitry, she used archives and libraries. She wrote that she located her sources for *Creole Families* with the help of librarians and archivists, people who, as we know today, knew of the records on Creoles of color.[29] She also corresponded extensively with Father Gaspare Lugano, archivist of Saint Louis Cathedral.[30] She credited "the kind permission of Mrs. J. W. Cruzat, from the compilation made by her late husband from the authentic documents in the family archives of the Marquis de Feria, all of which have been legally attested"; in another case, she mentions that "the family notes [were] kindly furnished by Alfred Grima, Esq."[31]

Yet she also ascribed some mystical quality to such work, as well as what can be called a nod to the way genealogy was practiced in other parts of the United States, to a reliance on family Bibles, letters, and so forth. She wanted to bring New Orleans in line with this national culture of private documents. In her preface and acknowledgments, she names *not* the public records she was fighting to save via the LHS, but scattered "[b]its of old furniture, jewelry, glass, old miniatures, portraits, scraps of silk and brocade, flimsy fragments of lace."[32] She wanted to demonstrate the depressed economy of New Orleanians, white martyrs of the Civil War, and their bond with greatness through genealogy.

The third published genealogical work about New Orleans families appeared in 1931. Stanley Clisby Arthur (1881–1963) and George Campbell la Bédoyère Huchet de Kernion (1878–1953) called their book *Old Families of Louisiana*—"old" as opposed to only to Creole families, and representative of the entire state. Yet they began their work focusing on the same families that Charles Patton Dimitry had. Indeed, they only slightly revised twenty-one of his *Times-Democrat* sketches before adding fifty-three other families. Still, in the new mix were "English, Scottish, and Irish lineages whose representatives now form an integral part of the present day population," uptown Protestant families who became part of a New Orleans white genealogical project.[33] Among the new families also was Dimitry's family. In this family history, Arthur and Kernion omit altogether the conflated identity of a woman who was said to be either "the '*mulatresse* slave of a M. Lallande' or Marianne '*La Sauvagesse*,' an 'Alabama Indian woman,' . . . born in 1707," discussed in the Pandelly trial.[34]

George Kernion was a working genealogist. For his work on *Old Louisiana Families*, he acknowledges "the eminent Canadian genealogists, l'Abbé Tanguay and Mr. Pierre George Roy." Both men were well known for their pioneering work on the French in the New World, especially in Canada.[35] Yet, Arthur and Kernion more or less carried forward undocumented stories of the city's families.

A Living History

Genealogists today regard the works of Dimitry, King, and Arthur and Kernion with great skepticism. Such works reflected family history methods and attitudes before many public records were accessible, in times when there was a desire to show that white Creoles were not so different from other colonial ancestors in other parts of the United States, certainly to make clear by omission that Creoles of color were not part of the picture of the city. When genealogists founded the Louisiana Genealogical and Historical Society and the Genealogical Research Society of New Orleans in 1953 and 1960, respectively, they continued to build on the infrastructure established by Dimitry, King, and Arthur and Kernion, focusing on whites only among ancestors and especially searching for and favoring stories of noble birth. Membership too was restricted to whites, usually excluding Jews and "most Italians." As Bruce (b. 1940), a member of both groups, stated: "They used to have this very elaborate membership application process which basically was trying to see if these people were black or Jewish . . . [the guidelines] weren't written down anyplace they were just sort of an unwritten policy that was in place."

Change in written genealogies did come, as well, in response to access to records and to new social attitudes. Bruce noted that "some of the early people would probably turn over in their graves, as the local phrase goes, if they would realize we have black people coming to meetings." Genealogist Charles Maduell compiled histories of families based on records and thus on evidence in the Notarial Archives.[36] Winston De Ville, another leader of this new era of evidence, published works in which records, rather than stories, were printed. His work was used by family historians and scholars alike. Notably, he was made a Fellow of the American Society of Genealogists in 1970, an honor limited to fifty members worldwide. He was also instrumental in saving countless records of the state and in starting an effort to create a formalized state archives, founded in Baton Rouge in 1956.[37]

Still, asked about public genealogies concerning race, De Ville recalled that much of his paying work up through the 1980s frequently came from testifying about records in various court proceedings in which genealogical evidence was needed to "prove" race, to verify the percentages of different family lines.[38] Genealogy upheld the categories assigned legally.

On the other hand, another family historian claimed that genealogical work "always had the potential to disturb segregation, to upset the strict categories of racial designations, the 1/32 rule, since one could find so many families who passed for white for generations and so it [the system] seemed unfair." People then began to question the status quo. "Crossovers," the family historian continued, were "in a way, protected by the Catholic Church." This protection came in the form of a policy not allowing genealogists entry into the Archives to see the registries. Powerful and also "secretive," the Church could be the "disturbing party . . . actually . . . kinder to those who sought to have their mixed-race background hidden."[39] The Church never designated the category of "octoroon" in their records; by that stage of mixing, a person was considered white.[40] At the same time, the word "mulatre" was used to designate not just half and half but other percentages of mixing, and this too could make the genealogical record, the certificate granted by the archdiocese, "incorrect." But on the whole, the interviewee continued, he didn't disrespect the Church and its recordkeeping habits. Instead, he disrespected those people who oversaw state vital statistics records: "The people there operated to 'out' families who had passed for white, no matter how long this might have been [taking place]."[41]

It was this "outing" that seemed to suggest something was amiss in the manner in which family history was discussed in the city. Was one race really better than another? Or more simply, why was one race preferred or thought to be preferred over another? Surely, if genealogy showed anything, it was that ethnic and racial groups could not easily fit into only two groups, "white" and "colored." In the 1960s, public genealogical discussions of these two designations on records centered on the New Orleans office for the State Board of Health. Supervisor Naomi Drake (1907–1987) determined the racial status of many individuals, eventually so alarming citizens and officials with her dictatorial decision making that she was fired. In her Civil Service Commission hearing, her power to maintain lists of persons she thought to be "colored" was questioned. So, too, was her decision making as she changed the race on various initial and subsequent requests for birth certificates. At the hearing, she spoke of the Genealogical Research Society's praise of her work. Officials dismissed her in 1965, charging her with holding up some 4,700 birth certificates and 1,100 death certificates. They had been left in a queue pending her research into "proper" racial categorizations.[42]

Not everything changed on her departure; the rule of "1/32 part African descent" marking one as "Negro" remained in place until 1983. Another much discussed case involving genealogy arose in 1981 when Susie Guillory Phipps sued to have the racial designation on her birth certificate changed from Negro to white. Reports of her efforts riveted the public for weeks. She had hoped that she was white and the public discussed these hopes, embodied in family lineage. Oddly, or perhaps not oddly, when Louisiana abolished the practice of classifying race by percentages, it would be the last state to do so.[43]

New Orleans is not the only place, of course, where complexity about race figures in conversations about genealogy. Although a number of people claimed that New Orleans was more fixated on race than other places, Elizabeth Shown Mills, one of America's leading genealogists, argued that racial crossover was far less common among Louisiana's elite than in other American societies, contrary to the general opinion in New Orleans among family historians. Why? She noted that this had to do with the city's nineteenth-century consciousness of evidence. Because of their Catholic habit of always registering their children—Catholics knew that some record would be kept of their entire community, person by person—New Orleanians were less apt to choose to have a mixed-race child. "The Fairfaxes of Virginia, the Woodwards of South Carolina, and countless other elite families in the Anglo colonies had their ethnic secrets that they knew could not be exposed by sacramental records," said Mills.[44]

But at the same time, not everyone, not even most people, are elite. More importantly, many New Orleanians, as the court cases and the stories told, were conscious of Creole designations involving triracial societies: people descended only from Europeans, those descended only from Africans, and those whose descent was mixed. One had only to look at the various shades of skin color to know that genealogies between whites and African Americans were combined. In addition, because many in the large population of free persons of color could educate themselves about the legal constraints that touched them, they and their descendants would be interested in records and how to read the categories to which they were assigned. Again, one turns to the importance of records to public discourse about race and the idea that this centrality had also to do with the recordkeeping culture, in Louisiana especially. As historian Gwendolyn Midlo Hall notes in the preface to her online slave database made from Louisiana records, the "richness of this information is certainly unique for any documents which describe slaves who became part of the population of the United States."[45] Or, as Bliss Broyard writes in her memoir of her father and the painful realization of his shame and secrecy about passing for white, "the constant shuffling of the Creoles

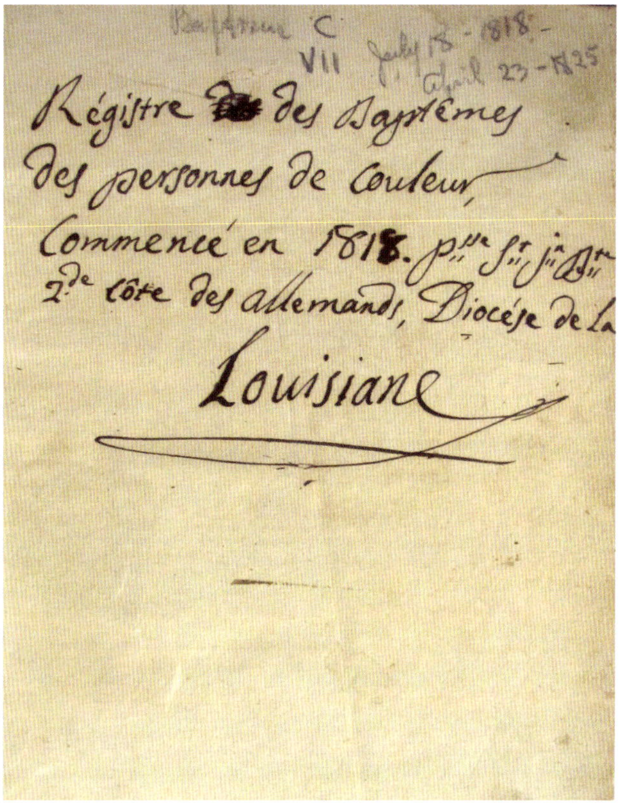

Baptêmes C
VII July 18 - 1818 -
April 23 - 1825

Régistre des Baptêmes
des personnes de couleur,
Commencé en 1818. p.r le S.t J.n B.te
2.e côte des allemands, Diocèse de la
Louisiane

FIGURE 4.19
Saint John the Baptist, Edgard, Baptisms, PC, vol. 7, 1818–1825. Courtesy of the Office of Archives and Records, Archdiocese of New Orleans. Genealogists are not allowed into the Archdiocese Archives. In other words, this Registre des Baptêmes des personnes de couleur (PC), from the German Coast Saint John the Baptist Church, cannot be seen in its original form by genealogists.

of Color between the categories of mixed, black, and white made it hard to believe in any racial labels. It was in New Orleans that I finally understood the dilemma that history had created for my father."[46]

This shared heritage came to be something that could be celebrated rather than feared only after the publication of *Roots*. This novel brought more people to the local archives, and in turn better funding was given for care of civil records in general. Scholars themselves, changed by a more representative community in academia, began to focus on Creoles of color.[47] The family historians took notice. As one recalled, "Not only had I just read an article about something called 'the little races,' people who were neither white nor black in the South, but there sitting next to me at the library was a black woman and she and I were interested in the same records and I know it sounds not so good now but it was as if for the first time I felt this is what America can really be, a democracy of information and we were there helping each other."[48]

Another project to document the city's architecture also influenced how people came to know the mélange of cultures in New Orleans. As part of their inventory and description of houses, the authors of the Friends of the Cabildo series (1971–1997) told the histories of families who had built, renovated, purchased, sold, and in some cases abandoned homes. These histories came from notarial records and other land records—that is, from public records, from archives.[49] Creoles of color, slaves, and everyone else were in these records. This popular series told about both the records and the people aligned with the beautiful houses, small and large, of the city.

Established genealogists adapted to, and sometimes initiated, similar projects. Many genealogists, for example, were involved in the formation of new organizations such as the Louisiana Creole Research Organization. For Jari Honora, the huge popularity of this new group reinforced the feeling that "genealogy and history are disciplines in other places. Here they are a part of the way of life."

As if to confirm this statement, Anna (b. 1924) spoke about the division of her family history endeavors; she worked daily sorting, labeling, and filing photocopied pages of handwritten registers and Bible entries, small textile pieces and photos of embroidered samplers, receipts of family businesses, marriage licenses, and photographs of first communions. She also chose the pattern of her chintz curtains to imitate those of a seamstress aunt; she cooked recipes handed down by her grandmother; and she made holiday decorations similar to those told about in letters.

Pierre Nora's assertion that "modern memory is first of all archival," something not known except through study, does not hold for these genealogists. Rather, study coincides with, and challenges, what they know from their families—about landmarks, even street names and "what was once on this corner."[50]

Besides the traditions of civil law and the Catholic Church, an abiding interest in being French, a racialized genealogy, and the fact that the city welcomed many immigrants starting on their journeys to becoming Americans, New Orleans genealogists spoke about their continuing fascination with the city. Why would they ever want to live elsewhere? New Orleans has a high nativity rate, meaning that persons born in the city tend to remain in the city, even today. According to one source, only New York City has an equally large proportion of its population as native-born residents.[51] In turn, longevity of family in one place means that both memories and records are more readily called to mind, more easily reached. Consider, as one family historian told me, that the daughter or son who inherits the house also inherits the records, however many or few they may be. If a family moves, such records are more apt to be thrown away.[52]

Still Living Stories

Charles Gayarré was one person who understood a living archival record, living on paper and in the minds of people, and living also after the deaths of the creators and subjects. The birth record of his own Creole of color son was at the center of a public response he made in 1859 in a printed pamphlet. Here he told this son to quit, in essence, saying that he was his son.[53]

But Gayarré the father also imparted a longer message, one about families, records, and race. The text in the eight-page pamphlet reads as if he cannot help himself from telling a long, hidden tale. He was a storyteller, after all.

He begins with the 1826 birth registration of this son, Carlos Nicolas Arthur Gayarré, of errors in the registry made in naming the child's mother, and also the mistake, later corrected, in placing the birth in the register for whites. Charles Gayarré had never really known this son; he addressed him in the pamphlet: "Not long after your baptism, in this same month of May 1826, in which I publically recognized your status (which certainly wasn't an act of ill will regarding you, and even less an omen of the hostility without reason that you assume I have toward you), I ended the relations that had given way to your birth, and I went to study law in Philadelphia." After that, Charles Gayarré went to Europe for seven years.[54]

In the pamphlet, he mentioned the dishonor his son had brought to his mother's family by calling himself the son of a white man. Charles Gayarré wanted him to stop. He wanted his son to "take the role in society that belongs to you truly; be honest, hardworking, and most of all humble. That is how you will make yourself esteemed and respected by everyone. Do not blush to avow yourself to be what you are—a colored man. I know many truly respectable ones in this class that you despise, and whom I recommend you take as role models."[55]

The story as told in the pamphlet is worthy of any soap opera. As Charles Gayarré admitted: "The confession of a fault, Sir, is always distressing, particularly when pressing circumstances can require that the confession become public."[56]

Could the pamphlet have been published by a third party to harm the public man, the politician as well as the historian? We know only that the pamphlet still exists and that someone valued it enough to deposit it in the archives at the Louisiana State Museum. We know that the son lived. He is listed in census records of the city in 1850, 1880, and 1900, always identified as white.[57] Yet, as genealogists say, sacramental records very often tell the truth, but mistakes, especially of spelling, are not uncommon. The author, likely Gayarré the father, wrote of such errors. We know too that whoever wrote it told about race in the city, and about race within genealogy.

The museum acquired this pamphlet in 1930, and one of the people who worked there at the time was librarian Josie Cerf (1878–1968). Cerf was acknowledged by many who worked with other records, notably Grace King, Stanley Arthur, George Campbell Huchet de Kernion, and later Earl Noland Saucier, a biographer of Gayarré. Sometime before 1935, Cerf had told Saucier that her father had brought the mother of Charles Gayarré's son, called Le Maitre, to Mississippi. There, Le Maitre had burned down the white family's plantation. Cerf also told Saucier

FIGURE 4.20
"Á Monsieur C.A.N. Gayarré, homme de couleur libre," 1859. Pamphlet. George Smith Collection, Historical Center, Louisiana State Museum. In this pamphlet, Charles Gayarré first printed two letters, one from his son and one from another person about this son, and then replied with his own much longer letter. He explained how Père Antoine of the Saint Louis Cathedral, a friend of the family, had incorrectly placed this son's name in the book "Registre des Blancs."

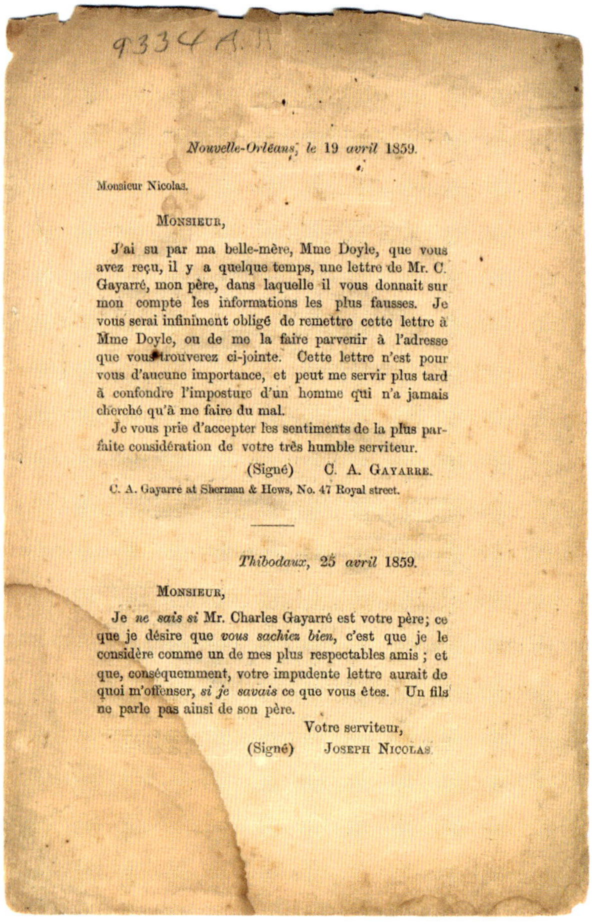
9334 A.H

Nouvelle-Orléans, *le* 19 *avril* 1859.

Monsieur Nicolas.

MONSIEUR,

J'ai su par ma belle-mère, Mme Doyle, que vous avez reçu, il y a quelque temps, une lettre de Mr. C. Gayarré, mon père, dans laquelle il vous donnait sur mon compte les informations les plus fausses. Je vous serai infiniment obligé de remettre cette lettre à Mme Doyle, ou de me la faire parvenir à l'adresse que vous trouverez ci-jointe. Cette lettre n'est pour vous d'aucune importance, et peut me servir plus tard à confondre l'imposture d'un homme qui n'a jamais cherché qu'à me faire du mal.

Je vous prie d'accepter les sentiments de la plus parfaite considération de votre très humble serviteur.

(Signé) C. A. GAYARRE.

C. A. Gayarré at Sherman & Hews, No. 47 Royal street.

Thibodaux, 25 *avril* 1859.

MONSIEUR,

Je *ne sais si* Mr. Charles Gayarré est votre père; ce que je désire que *vous sachiez bien*, c'est que je le considère comme un de mes plus respectables amis ; et que, conséquemment, votre impudente lettre aurait de quoi m'offenser, *si je savais* ce que vous êtes. Un fils ne parle pas ainsi de son père.

Votre serviteur,

(Signé) JOSEPH NICOLAS.

how, in the 1920s, "a woman negroid in features" had called on her, "seeking information about her great-grandfather, Charles Gayarré, the historian."[58]

Jari Honora first led me to the pamphlet in which Gayarré told his Creole of color son to stop bothering him. I was working as a consultant in the same archives where Josie Cerf had worked, now called the Louisiana Historical Center of the State Museum. Before Honora's inquiry, I had looked online for Gayarré's genealogy and found a listing showing no descendants, but that day, right in the card catalog (one likely created by Cerf, and edited or re-created by WPA workers and then completed by volunteer genealogists), I found the title and location of Gayarré's acknowledgment of his son.

What is significant here is that often it is a genealogist who extends the whole of the record of history. Honora made visible the context he so often sought, another example of the generosity he and other genealogists so value, and another example of the Creole complexity found in New Orleans records and family history.

CHAPTER FIVE

Treasures: Memory Objects, Private Records, Science, and Art

The closet at the top of the stairs, one family historian told me, was what I should see before we began our conversation. From here she pulled barely visible images of ancestors in daguerreotypes, a jacket of a soldier from the First World War, a telegram about this soldier missing in action, a piece of a quilt, and many other objects and papers. The closet couldn't hold it all. She also had an office in a detached room off a patio where she filed and shelved her work. "I don't know what one would do without this type of space," she said. "If you collect family history, others send you what they cannot keep. But I do feel that each little item . . . well, I return to it. It might begin my search of a particular ancestor, but it also tells me something when I learn more." Genealogy cannot be practiced without accumulations, every family historian said in one fashion or another. There are "all the records," but there are also these treasures "one cannot let go of."[1]

Books on genealogy call these materials "home sources." Handled by ancestors, used by them, or created for or by them, these materials remain viscerally evocative of the past. Family historians wanted me to see these sources, to understand them as their *most* important personal documents.

Any discussion of such forms concerns big pictures of the past but also small, intimate ones. National and international access to records permits both and changes the framework of our visions of past lives today. Clearly census, church, court, land, tax, military, institutional, business, employment, vital records, and many other records are pivotal. Family historians today also draw from a range of other sources: city directories, newspapers, local histories, and generations of indexes, biographies, and other kinds of compilations. Science, especially DNA testing, makes possible an even longer stretch of family across time and space. New Orleans genealogists considered then not only the world of personal and local settings as they looked to remember the past, but also the world beyond the city.

They thought of mentioning a difference between what they collected that seemed associated with the city and what was more universal to ge-

FIGURE 5.1
China pipe belonging to Anton Schüle (1849–1919), dated "March 1, 1865, Constanz." Now in the family collection of his great-grandson. Courtesy of Jack Belsom, New Orleans.

nealogy elsewhere. The family historian with the closet and extra room for her artifacts held up her hand in a gesture of stopping and asked if I had "really" compared New Orleans records to those "away." Before I could answer, she continued: "We do not have the great collections of private family papers, the chests of letters, or even the decorative arts. We don't even seem to have the same sort of German records that they had in Pennsylvania, and yet we had all these Germans in the nineteenth century." She showed me confirmation certificates and photographs of generations of girls dressed in white for this ceremony. "Each one, you see, thought of themselves as stepping toward adulthood in this ritual. I don't mean to say consciously 'thought.' They participated and knew that the white dress their mother or grandmother made was part of the Catholic world. I so love these photos, the line in the huge, huge histories of Europe and America."[2]

Do New Orleanians lack the sort of genealogical artifacts that others in other parts of the country have? I did not compare, but it seems certain and obvious that New Orleans artifacts can, like those in other places, have great meaning for their owners. Artifacts shown to me suggested the story of the memory items themselves, their history as a form of remembering. Family historians told about such materials in ways that seem characteristic of memory items everywhere. Still, the specificity of forms and items, and their pasts, are worth exploring.

New Orleanian Jack Belsom (b. 1933) was another to orient me both to the local setting and to the objects that had traveled across distances to him. First, he brought out a pipe.

The story of the pipe began during the ten to twenty years that he spent searching for the place where his great-grandfather on his mother's side had been born. "Somewhere in the Black Forest of Germany" was the most precise answer he had been given by his mother and his great-uncle. There were no church records, not even those of the man's children. There were no census, ship, or military records associated with his name.

"One day I was cleaning. My grandparents had an old country house over in Covington [across the lake from New Orleans]. After my grandmother died, I was over there one day and we were looking through things in her bedroom . . . and here was the pipe."

And, on the pipe in red lettering, Belsom found the information that had eluded him for two decades:

> [The] date on this is 1865, and this was my great-great-grandfather's–my mother's great-grandfather's. This is the only way that I ever found out where he was from. Apparently, he got this when he went into the Prussian Army. It has his name and then it says, "from Steinach, the Greater Steinach Grenadiers Infantry regiment to Constance in 1865." That's what the German says: "the departure of the first of March, 1865." So on the first of March, 1865, he left a little town, Steinach, which is where he is from, and went into the German military in Constance, on Lake Constance, in 1865. And in 1869 he immigrated to New Orleans. He came here. No one in the family knew where he was from. But sure enough, when I went back using the records from the Latter-day Saints to Steinach . . . I found his baptism.

He paused again to make sure the whole of the story was apparent. "When I went back looking through the church record, there's his baptism which gave me then the name of his parents. . . . And it is all because this [pipe] was saved."

Family Bibles and Other Religious Books

Belsom began his genealogy research with family names and dates inscribed in the back pages of a small prayer book belonging to his father's grandfather—a type of record recognized over all the United States and in Europe. People from the sixteenth century on kept their family history in such books.[3]

Holdings in libraries reveal that a number of English colonial families brought Bibles with inclusions about lineage to their new homes in North America. The Samuel Andrews family of New England passed down a Bible published in London in 1599 but listing family history from 1625 to 1790. Members of the James Richards family documented their names and dates in a similarly old Bible carried across the ocean in the late 1600s. Their fourteen-page genealogy began with a daughter's birth in 1661 in England and then showed later births, marriages, and deaths recorded in Hartford, Connecticut (1663–1714).[4]

As cheaper printing methods were invented, publishers saw the chance to expand the sales of Bibles by including specific pages set aside for genealogical entries. Beginning in the 1860s, they went one step further to

FIGURE 5.2
Andachtsbuch zum Troste der armen Seelen (Baltimore, 1868). Original owner, Richard Felder (1832–1916). Courtesy of Jack Belsom, New Orleans.
Published in 1868 in Baltimore, this Catholic prayer book was oriented toward German immigrants. The title's translation is evocative of the loss associated, in part, with emigration: *A Book of Remembrance, for the Consolation of Poor Souls*. Now in the family collection of Felder's great-grandson, the book includes annotations on marriages, births, and deaths of family members.

FIGURE 5.3
Bible record for the Jonathan Snow family, 1755–1884 (Mss C 2583). R. Stanton Avery Special Collections Department, New England Historic Genealogical Society.
Note the very small notation at the top that tells us that this page had been removed from the Snow Bible. Space almost always has necessitated the separation of genealogical information from Bibles themselves.

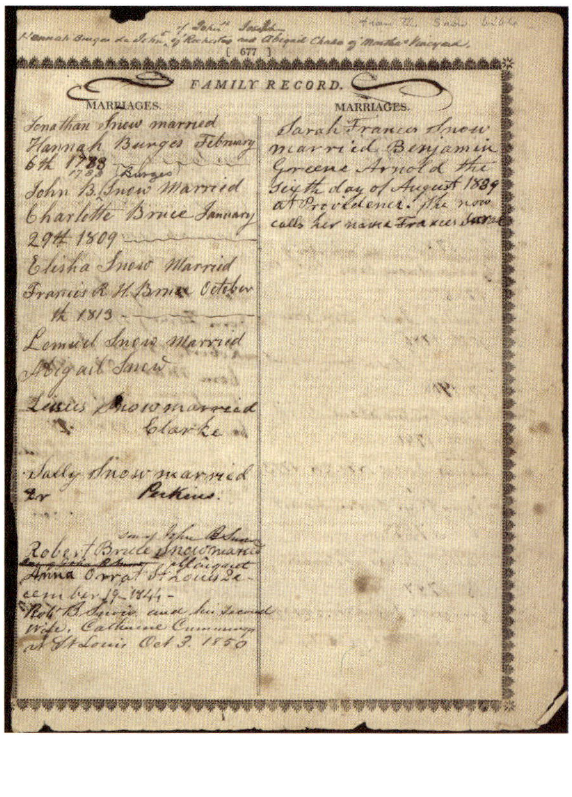
from the Snow Bible

[677]

FAMILY RECORD.

MARRIAGES.	MARRIAGES.
Jonathan Snow married Hannah Burges February 6th 1783	Sarah Frances Snow married Benjamin Greene Arnold the sixth day of August 1884 at Providence. She now calls her name Frances [illegible]
John B. Snow Married Charlotte Bruce January 29th 1809	
Elisha Snow Married Frances R. H. Bruce October [illegible] 1813	
Lemuel Snow Married Abigail Snow	
Lucius Snow married Clarke	
Sally Snow married Perkins	
Robert Bruce Snow married Margaret Anna Orr at St Louis December 19 1844	
Rob B. Snow and his second wife, Catherine Cummings at St Louis Oct 3. 1850	

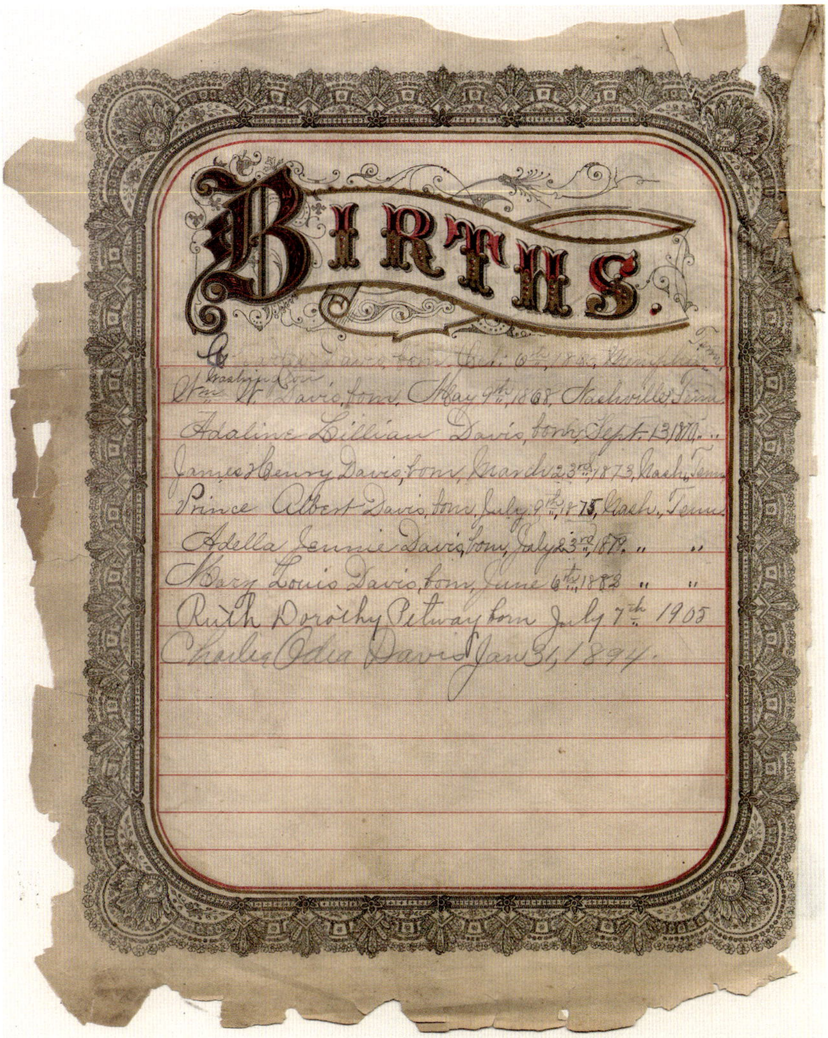

FIGURE 5.4
Birth page from the Proctor family Bible, late nineteenth century. Henry Hugh and Adeline L. Davis Proctor Family Papers. Courtesy of the Amistad Research Center, New Orleans.
As chromolithography and other printing technologies were perfected, Bibles could offer more elaborate designs for adding family information.

provide spaces for *carte-de-visite* photographs. C. F. Short of Saint Louis printed one hybrid Bible/album with spaces for ten photographs. Kurz and Allison of Chicago issued another and added the additional benefit of designated spaces for the photographs of parents and children. Other publishers of Bibles with blank pages headed "Marriages," "Births," and "Deaths" were Isaiah Thomas, Holbrook and Fessenden, B. and J. Collins, Gay Brothers and Company, and the American Bible Society. New Orleans's Hansell Brothers and other stationers and printers would bind on demand Bibles with extra pages for genealogical notes and photographs.[5]

Bible entries of marriages, births, and deaths have long functioned as private and public recordkeeping forms. A widow, for example, would take her Bible pages as documentary evidence to supplement a Revolutionary War pension application, handing the pages over to the War Department. The same pages taken by a widow to the War Department in 1820 are now online. This project involved successive generations of records that have been indexed over time. A host of volunteers began in the 1980s "to abstract the birth, marriage, and death records from the pension applications" into book form. They were microfilmed as well and have now been scanned.[6]

Another use of Bible entries is found in the application processes of lineage and patriotic societies. For example, since the late 1910s, prospective members of the Daughters of the American Revolution have submitted Bible records along with cemetery, county, town, state, church, and military records with their applications for membership. In recent years, the Genealogical Society of Utah has photographed those DAR records created before 1972 on nearly three thousand microfilm rolls.[7]

The movement to make other such Bible pages accessible has been in progress for almost forty years now and has especially gained momentum in the early twenty-first century. A name index to Bible records held by the National Genealogical Society is available as a membership benefit. Another resource is Bible Records Online, a website of the transcribed pages of some 1,158 Bibles, some of which have also been scanned. Large-scale digitization projects such as this—often funded by donations—is the type of volunteer effort that reveals the passion of genealogists. A similar project is based at the Library of Virginia, which over the years has acquired some 6,800 Bible records that are slowly being scanned and indexed. Ancestry.com has a feature that enables users to search for information included on Bible pages, mixing vital statistics and Bible pages together in the same way that they were once utilized in the preparation of applications for benefits from the government or membership in organizations.[8]

Other European Antecedents; Other Evolving Formats for American Genealogy

The third genealogist to orient me to the journey and history of personal family treasures lives in a small house whose first room, once an open room, has now been divided into four separate alcoves for different family branches. "This," he said, "is the family tree and how it had grown."

The most commonly associated visual depiction of family lineage is the family tree. Yet, as in the example of the family-branch "rooms," the "family tree" is a figure of speech more than a reality, more than one artifact or document. All the family historians with whom I spoke had various types of "trees," but most of these were pages in files and notebooks, or electronic documents in cloud spaces. Family historians told of beginning the trees' bare outlines in pencil and adding names within a hierarchical arrangement on branches, some adding names in round circles. In New Orleans, these were often traced from a doubloon left over from Carnival. But the families quickly grew too large for one tree.

FIGURE 5.5
Genealogy. *Lee Family of Virginia and Maryland*, 1886. Print. Courtesy of the Library of Congress, American Memory. Published family trees became a specialty of nineteenth-century printers.

The family tree's similarity across time does suggest the consistency and potency of the tree as a symbol of the family.[9] For the artist and the creative genealogist, the tree evokes the practicality of a movement of lines that can expand to cover different dates as well as the image of a long-lived force of nature.[10]

However, the form of the family tree is illustrative of change as well as stasis. Before the 1700s, the writing on and around the tree could vary from the types of family trees we see today: sometimes in the older trees, for example, the head of the family is at the top of the tree, not the bottom. The current shape of the family tree suggests the accommodation of new forms of transmission, of hierarchies in which the ground is seen as the logical starting point. Later variations in trees used in illustrations also reflect the purpose of their creators in visualizing the family in branches (some branches more tenuous than others) or simply as lines across pages and pages (with some lines added as addendums, not in the main sequence).[11]

Family trees cover literal as well as symbolic distance. The "longest family tree" is said to contain more than two million members of eighty generations, and more than 2,500 years of data. This would be the family tree of Confucius (551–479 BC), compiled in a project that has progressed intermittently from the time of his life to the present.[12] Robert Peril, who created woodcuts to represent the tree of the House of Hapsburg, configured the family tree as a long scroll. His work showed the lineage beginning in the 300s with King Pharamond der Merovingen and ending with Charles V, Holy Roman Emperor from 1500 to 1558.[13] The family tree of Joseph and Emma Hale Smith, Latter-day Saint Church founder and his first wife, can be obtained in different sizes from the family association. Hanging in the Family History Library in Salt Lake City, one of these family trees measures seventeen feet in length and three feet in height and codes family members by different family groups, adjusting for polygamous marriages and generations, temple baptisms, and living baptisms. Creator Michael Kennedy recalled the challenge of using software to create such a huge document of color-coded rectangles for first descendants and cylindrical columns for later generations, with different shades of colors framing each space. Kennedy regularly updates the tree, adding new family members as well as dates and information about newly found ancestors. At the Family History Library, the expanse of the framed sheet represents at once a testament to the quick growth of the first family of the LDS Church and by extension the Church itself (even its baptisms of the dead), the complications of the forms for charting family, and the innovations of LDS members like Kennedy in making such a visual statement for others.[14]

Scholar Sigrid Weigel provides one of the most erudite explorations of the family tree. She examined artists' renderings of biblical paradise, where the tree of knowledge and the tree of life grew. Experience was the only constant element in nature, the lesson learned when Eve ate from the tree of knowledge and the family gave up immortality. It is not just family we are researching here, not the *genus* of genealogy, but rather the story or philosophy, the *logos*, the discourse that we want to portray in visual terms. Weigel theorized that "the history of genealogical knowledge can only be described in the context of its mediation and representational modes."[15] Clearly, twenty-first century computer software, as applied in creating the Smith tree, enables a more complex representation. The New Orleans family historian's warren of rooms also embodied this visual philosophy of genealogical complexity, of abundance of sources overflowing.

Or is family history, in all its enormity and complexity, actually expressive of something much more fundamental and simple? Displayed in another genealogist's library I found this passage that clearly articulates the sentiments underlying the need for a record of family:

> Oh that my words were written!
> Oh that they were inscribed in a book!
> Oh that with an iron pen and lead
> they were engraved in the rock forever! (Job 19:23–24)

FIGURE 5.6
Book cover, Joseph Bryan commonplace book and genealogical notes, Bryan Family Papers, Mss 1 B8408a. Courtesy of the Virginia Historical Society, Richmond.

Like many records that stand for the family tree, this statement tells of the reassuring quality of tangible documents passed on to future generations.

We can now access online a number of predecessors of the formats of material memory. One example is called the Harlestone Register, created between 1289 and 1340. Here, Henry de Bray self-consciously wrote: "In the year 1322, the fifty-second year of Henry de Bray, who with his own hand writes this book, the same Henry arranged this present brief as evidence to his heirs; that is transcriptions to charters and memoranda arising from the time of said Henry."[16] Included were "copies and extracts from deeds and Exchequer records, lists of the lands in [his] mother's dowry, and lists of tenants, interspersed with notes on the history of the village of Harlestone and genealogical data on [his] family." In the emerging archival world of de Bray's time, the English also called their collections "muniments" and their record books "cartularies"—a term that encompassed collections of charters, titles, grants of privileges, and other documents, especially copies in bound volumes.[17]

Commonplace Books and Registers

It is likely that de Bray wrote on whatever was at hand. Later printing technologies permitted more specific books, one called a commonplace book and the other a register. In France, the commonplace book was called a *livre de raison*, and in Italy, a *ricordanze*. In New Orleans I found only one such book, produced in the 1870s in a village in the southwest of France, a small blank book in which different family members had recorded births, marriages, deaths, recipes, and events.

Registers in book form grew in popularity when families took blank books, often ledgers, and wrote in births, marriages, and deaths. They sometimes added art, taking as models the designs on other family keepsakes such as samplers, watercolors, and bed coverings.

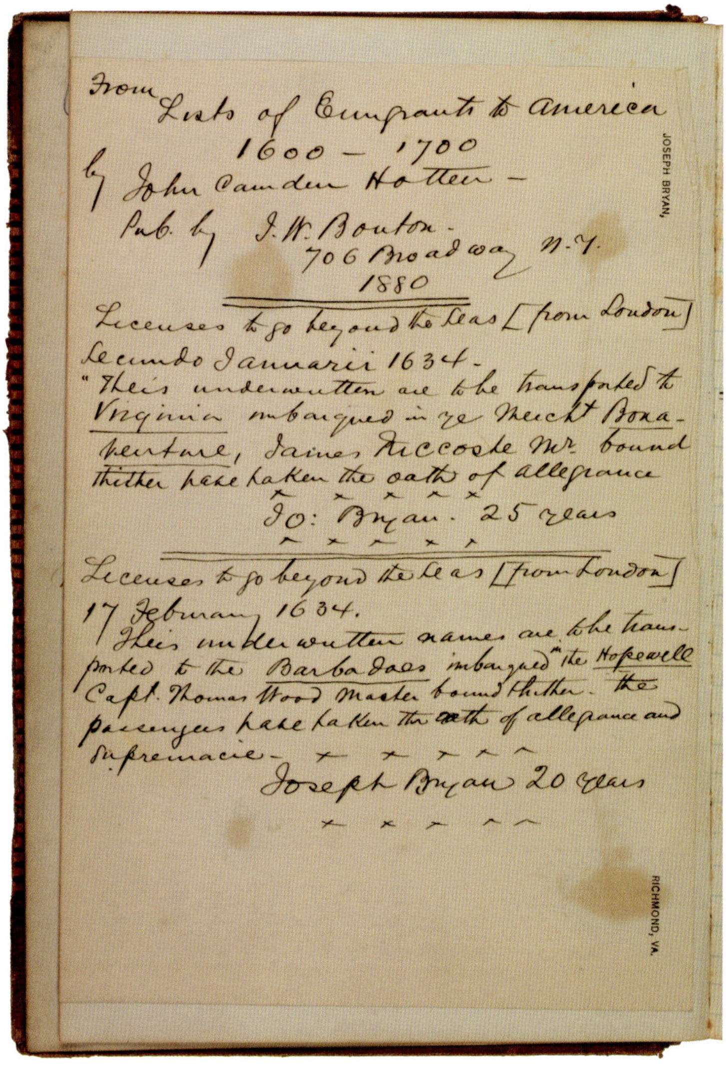

From
Lists of Emigrants to America
1600 – 1700
by John Camden Hotten –
Pub. by J. W. Bouton –
706 Broadway N.Y.
1880

Licenses to go beyond the Seas [from London]
Secundo Januarii 1634.
"Theis underwritten are to be transported to Virginia imbarqued in ye Merchant Bonaventure, James Luccocke Mr bound thither have taken the oath of allegiance
Jo: Bryan. 25 years

Licenses to go beyond the Seas [from London]
17 February 1634.
Theis under written names are to be transported to the Barbadoes imbarqued in the Hopewell Capt. Thomas Wood Master bound thither. the passengers have taken the oath of allegiance and supremacie –
Joseph Bryan 20 years

FIGURE 5.7
Reverse of cover, Joseph Bryan commonplace book and genealogical notes, Bryan Family Papers, Mss 1 B8408a. Courtesy of the Virginia Historical Society, Richmond.
Commonplace books often contain contextual information such as songs, poems, and speeches. Indeed, the definition of a commonplace book centers on such inclusions of learning, but genealogists also used them to record family history. Any type of book might function as a commonplace book, and this is an example of a ledger doing so.
Here, someone has transcribed notes about two ancestors from the 1600s, transported to Virginia and Barbados, with "licenses to go beyond the seas [from London]." The writer is careful to note his or her source at the top of the page, a book from the 1880s that listed America's first immigrants.

FIGURE 5.8
Detail, Ellen Carter Bruce Baylor commonplace book, Bruce Family Papers, Mss 1 B8306a1. Virginia Historical Society, Richmond.
Ellen Carter Bruce Baylor (1858–1899) gathered information on her family from 1752 until the time of her death in this 1899 book.

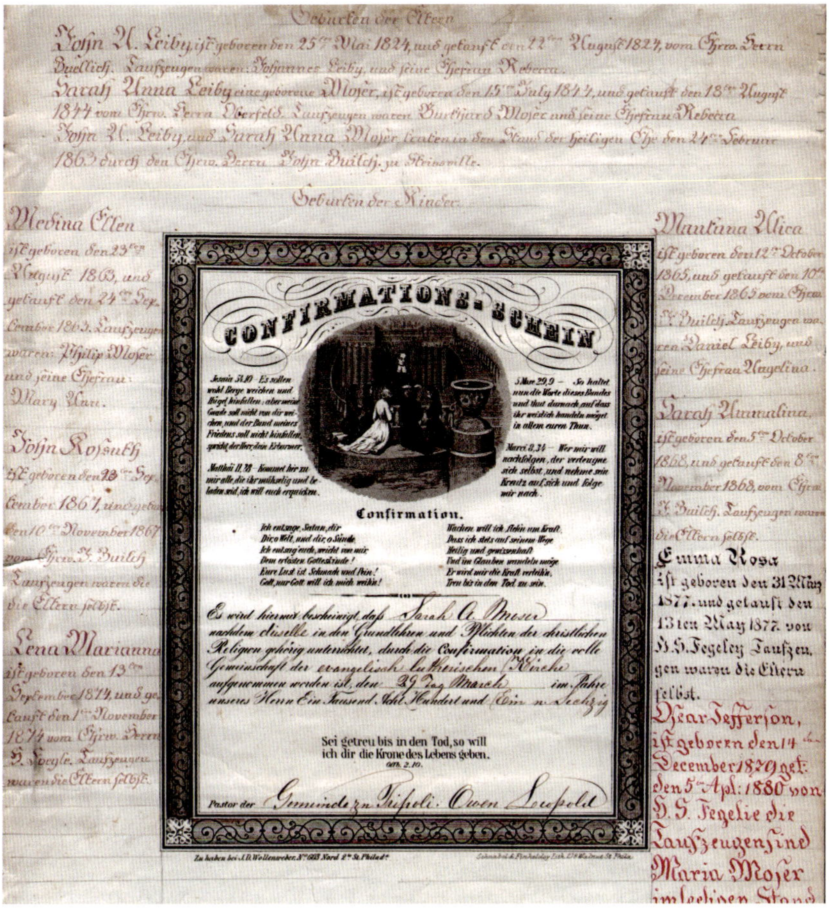

FIGURE 5.9
Leiby/Moser Family Register, ca. 1861–1880. Ink on wove paper. Courtesy, Earnest Archives and Library, Clayton, Delaware.
Most family registers are not created around such certificates, but this one shows the purposeful handwork of a professional scrivener. These scribes allowed the continuation of a tradition of writing with German frakturs, or fractured letters. The lineage document was a private one, here assuredly so, but beautiful in its humble combination of different pens and the retention of the German language.

Registers could also be one-page decorative forms. German-speaking families in Pennsylvania created perhaps the earliest one-page American registers that told family history. The history of their format, as well as the registers themselves, especially their beauty, are prized today. Creators used a style of lettering that imitated a Gothic handwriting called fraktur, "fractured" letters that had originated in the Middle Ages, and they also called their creations frakturs. Inherited from traditions of Alsace, Switzerland, and southern regions of what would become Germany, a register made with this type of calligraphy could be printed, handwritten and drawn, or a combination of print and individual additions. Pennsylvania Dutch artists and printers also made preprinted registers to be bound into Bibles, or printed templates on the blank papers of Bibles and other books.

More so than the custom of writing in Bibles, the fraktur tradition took a distinct style, and although locally specific to Pennsylvania it was considered "American." The frakturs' lineages usually begin in the New World and, unlike the Bibles that came with some colonists, did not usually document older generations in Europe. The fraktur also presented

FIGURE 5.10
Family register of Jacob Ritter and his wife, Catharina, born Langenecker. Water color and ink on wove paper, ca. 1835. Attributed to fraktur artist Samuel Bentz (1792–1850), formerly known as the Mount Pleasant Artist. Courtesy, Earnest Archives and Library, Clayton, Delaware.
Many schoolteachers took up the creation of family registers, and Samuel Bentz was one such person. Bentz came from Lancaster County, Pennsylvania, near the Ephrata community that was so instrumental in nurturing a group of scriveners and artists.

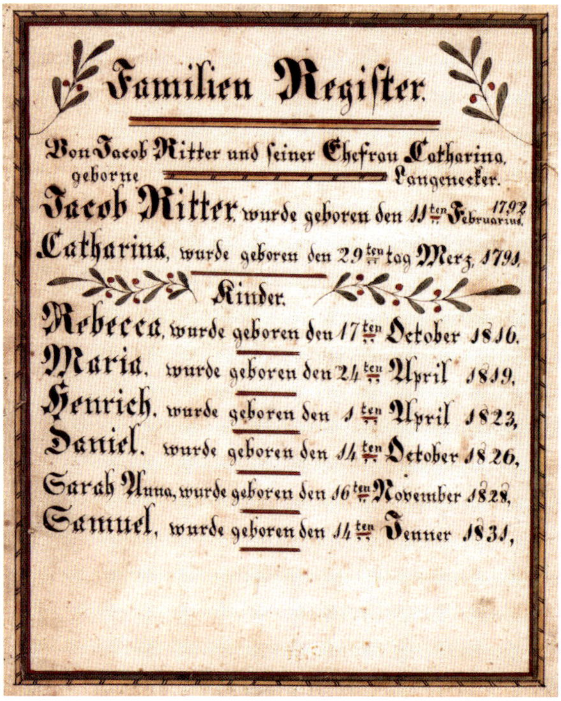

Familien Register.

Von Jacob Ritter und seiner Ehefrau Catharina, geborne Langenecker.

Jacob Ritter wurde geboren den 11ten Februarius 1792

Catharina, wurde geboren den 29ten tag Merz, 1791.

Kinder.

Rebecca, wurde geboren den 17ten October 1816.

Maria. wurde geboren den 24ten April 1819.

Henrich. wurde geboren den 1ten April 1823,

Daniel. wurde geboren den 14ten October 1826.

Sarah Anna, wurde geboren den 16ten November 1828,

Samuel, wurde geboren den 14ten Jenner 1831,

FIGURE 5.11
A Record of the Marriages, Births and Deaths in the Family of Capt. Jonathan Woodbury and Hannah his Wife of the State of Massachusetts County of Worcester and Town of Sutton, 1740–1855. Mss 607, R. Stanton Avery Special Collections, New England Historic Genealogical Society.
Handwritten, hand-painted, and colored registers such as this one are especially valued as unique documents. Note the pride of place shown in the title. Nineteen of the entries are in the same hand with its last date being 1807. The remaining thirteen entries are in a different hand and range from 1814 to 1853.

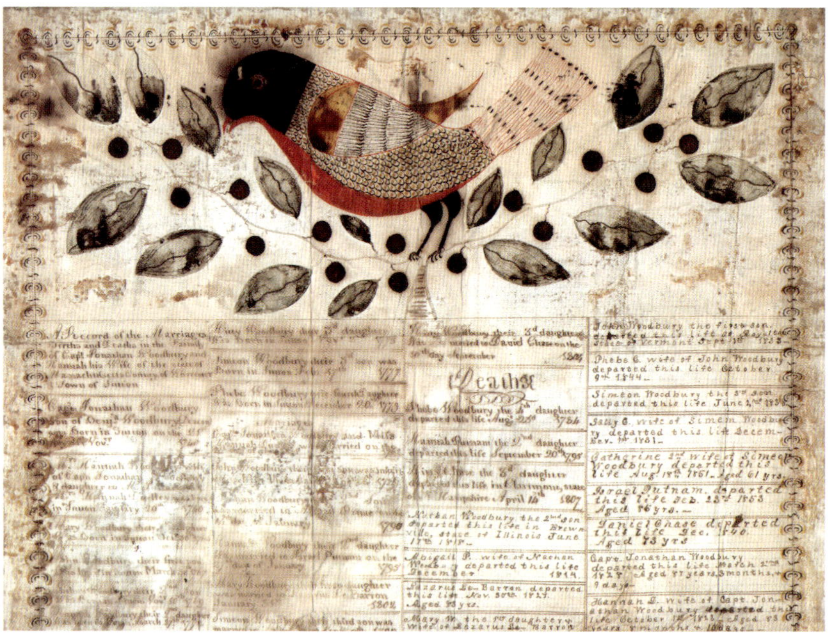

private recordkeeping within a piece of art that could be displayed in the home.[18] The Bollinger family broadside was created in this tradition, and, since its publication in 1763, has been considered, along with the genealogical works of Roger Clap and Luke Stebbins (introduced in chapter 2), one of the first printed American genealogies.[19]

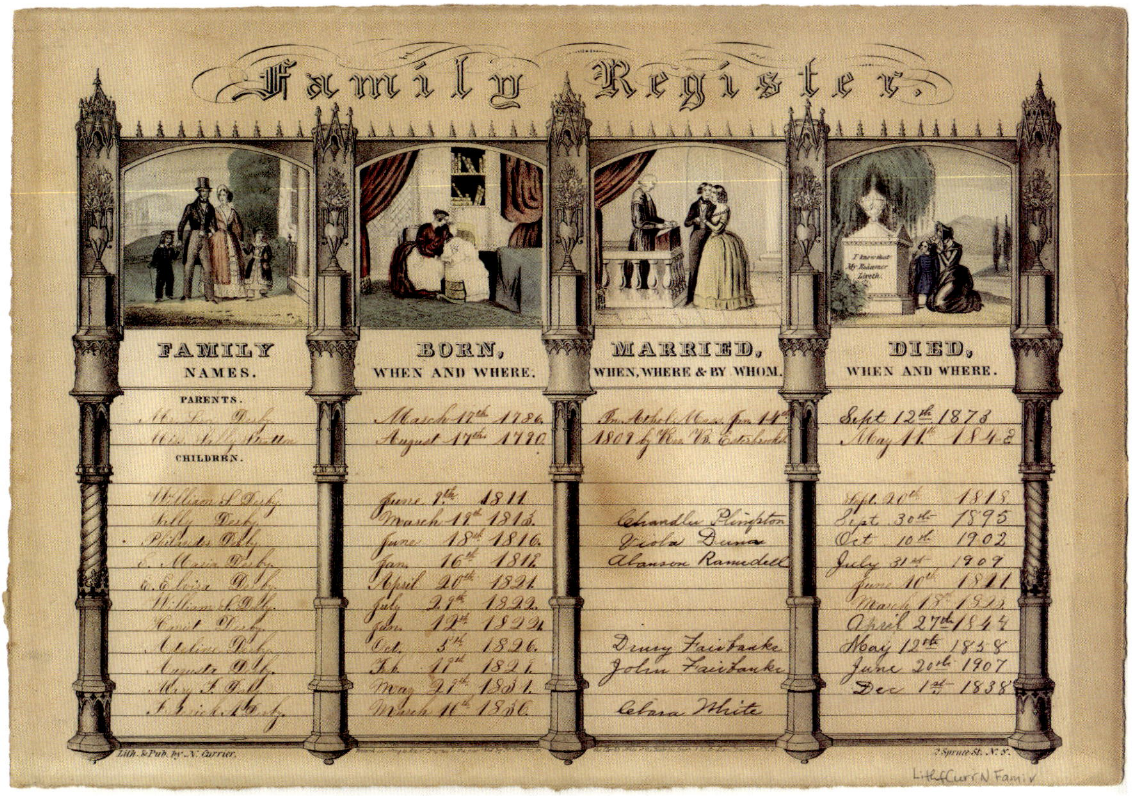

Figure 5.12
Family register, with information added on the Leon and Sally Stratton Derby Family, 1845. Lithograph, hand-colored. Nathaniel Currier, New York. Courtesy, American Antiquarian Society.

Printed family registers such as this one offered a place to display as well as preserve family history information. They remain quite popular today among collectors and are often offered for sale on eBay.

In the Northeast and Midwest, and to a lesser extent in New Orleans, those interested in recording family history created other forms of the single-paged "family register." These creators also printed or inscribed family names and symbols in beautiful calligraphy. They employed the muted colors of the eighteenth- and nineteenth-century palette and the flora and fauna of their new homes: swaths of grays, gray-blues, rusty reds, olive greens to render houses, trees, birds, flowers, and other motifs, set within rectangular frames, sometimes with illustrated columns and blanks for names. Some register makers cast mourning figures beside the tombstones of early New England, with their haunting angel or soul effigies (winged heads), or skulls and bones. Others displayed symbols of journeys, such as ships in full mast or the terrain of a new country. Others wrote out the migratory story: "The family comes out of Altena in Germany from thence went to the Netherlands out of the province of Mary V. Boskirk." The names listed gave generations of descent.

Single-paged family records remained popular throughout the nineteenth and into the early twentieth century. Printers such as Currier and Ives and Auguste Gast quickly saw that a register could also hold images, and later photographs. In the 1840s, Currier and Ives entitled their new product the *Family Photograph Register* and provided spaces for photographs or printed color illustrations.

FIGURE 5.13
Family Record before the War and since the War, ca. 1880. Chromolithograph. Krebs Lithographing Company, Cincinnati. Courtesy of the Library of Congress, American Memory.
This chromolithographed register bears the following information on its reverse side: "Designed for the colored people of America by W. H. Cowell, Martin, Tennessee."

FIGURE 5.14
Mr. Emmanuel B. Christian and Miss Rebecca Harris, ca. 1885. Printed template of marriage certificate. Marcus Christian Collection (Mss 11, Series 2). Louisiana and Special Collections Department, Earl K. Long Library, University of New Orleans.
This register documents the marriage of the parents of Marcus Christian, a writer, poet, teacher, and head of the "Colored Project" of the Louisiana Federal Writers' Project. Note the inclusion of "Mr." and "Miss" in the handwriting, giving titles to the African American couple that the white world at the time did not always give. The couple also added other information to mark their marriage, including the location of Rebecca Harris's family home. Emmanuel and Rebecca Christian would die before their son Marcus's thirteenth birthday, so it is all the more touching that he saved this memory of them.

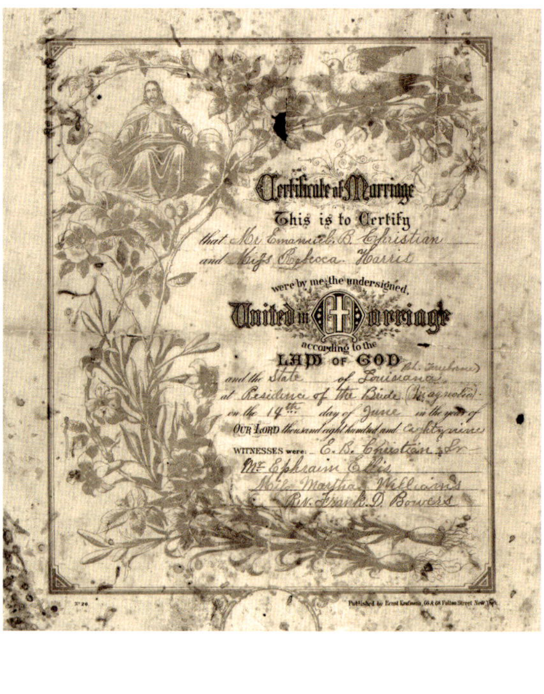
Certificate of Marriage
This is to Certify
that Mr Emanuel B. Christian
and Miss Rebecca Harris
were by me the undersigned,
United in Marriage
according to the
LAW OF GOD
and the State of Louisiana
at Residence of the Bride (Magnolia)
on the 14th day of June in the year of
OUR LORD thousand eight hundred and eighty nine
WITNESSES were: E. B. Christian Sr
Mr Ephraim Ellis
Miss Martha Williams
Rev. Frank D. Bowers
Published by Ernst Kaufmann, 66 & 68 Fulton Street New York.

Scrapbooks

In the nineteenth century, the scrapbook also grew in popularity. Families without the means or inclination to purchase specific types of memory books took the common album or often enough a blank book and made what the New England Historic Genealogical Society later called "scrapbook genealogies." Someone in the William Hyde family, for example, purchased vellum-bound notebooks, dated them 1710, 1713, and 1715, and recorded births, marriages, and deaths that occurred between 1690 and 1756.[20] Another handwritten record of birth, marriages, and deaths, that of the Flint, Buttrick, and Brown families, was given the prominence of a title and named in a way entirely recognizable to today's family historians and album makers: "In Memory of the Family of the Flints by John Flint (1722–1792)."[21]

Since the 1830s, scrapbook makers and publishers have reshaped blank books with the addition of memorabilia. Sometimes they can be purchased, or even commissioned and elaborately bound. At other times they remain a homemade venture created within a published volume with pasted materials over the printed pages.

Scrapbooks specifically made around family history are often called heritage albums. Such albums are associated with various religious communities. Scrapbook making in its current incarnation—and heritage albums especially—are often attributed to the work of an LDS couple, Anthony J. and Marielen Christensen, who gained attention at the World Conference on Genealogy in Salt Lake City in 1980. Marielen Christensen began designing pages for her family's photo collection in the 1970s, experimenting, much as Mark Twain and others had done in the early twentieth century, with various bindings and templates to contain information on ancestors, images of artifacts, and copies of family records. One key element of Christensen's product was that the binders could accommodate the addition of new pages.[22]

She and her husband found such interest in her solution that they opened a store, which sold archival paper and other products for scrapbooking. They called their store Keeping Memories Alive, and they called their heritage albums by a name used by early twentieth-century scrappers, "memory books."[23]

In all such books, family historians could affix memories in photographs, correspondence, and other memorabilia. In some periods, scrapbooks have enjoyed extreme popularity, and in others none at all. For example, scrapbooks were revived in the 1990s to become one of the most popular of all hobbies by the early twenty-first century.[24]

In New Orleans, Catherine (b. 1959) showed me scrapbooks she had created for her children and grandchildren. Her paternal grandmother taught her to make such books. About them, she remembered:

> Both my grandmothers were interested in the family and providing that history. . . . One grandmother said if I wanted to learn anything about the family, it was in her mother's Bible. Both of the grandmothers passed down a lot of pictures, and it's really interesting because . . . on both sides, I'm the family member that ended up with their collections. And on my father's side, my grandmother died early. The day she died, the day before, I was at her home. . . . I was young. Twelve. And she basically said, "Take these things. You'll never get these, if you don't take them now." And, I had to walk [home] with it. Because she was too sick. . . . She said, "Take these."

That day, she carried home a hatbox full of small scrapbooks created from family letters, receipts, certificates, and business letters.

Albums

Like scrapbooks, albums are hybrids of manuscripts and ephemera, or, as Ronald J. Zboray and Mary Saracino Zboray called them, "boundary-blurring forms."[25] More so than scrapbooks, however, albums are by-products of the invention of photography.

The popularity of compiling photographs in one book began almost as soon as paper photographs were invented, and has never really waned.[26] As early as 1861, photography journals urged their readers to collect their multiplying carte-de-visite images into albums produced especially for keeping memories of family and friends. The carte-de-visite album became an established institution by the 1870s, and albums for cabinet photographs (images mounted in cardstock) remained popular until World War I. Almost every middle-class woman compiled such a volume.[27] An 1872 proclamation by *Godey's Lady's Book* proclaimed the ascendancy of this form for family images, noting that "[p]hotograph albums have become not only a luxury for the rich but a necessity for the people. The American family would be poor indeed who could not afford a photograph album."[28] One of these was an album devised in 1864 by Dr. A. H. Platt, called *The Photograph Family Record of Husband, Wife, and Children: Adapted to Recording in a Plain, Brief, and Intelligent Manner, the Name, Birth-Place, Date of Nativity, Descent, Names of Parents, Number of Brothers and Sisters, Education, Occupation, Politics, Religion, Marriage, Stature, Weight, Habit, Complexion, Color of Eyes and Hair, Health, Time and Place of Death, Disease, Age, and Place of Interment of Each Member of Any Family, with Album Leaves for the Insertion of Photographs of the Same.*[29]

Platt included pages on which to inscribe "authentic" signatures and to attach not one but two copies of marriage certificates. Additional marriages were to have their own albums so that the family stayed intact even after the death of one spouse and the remarriage of the remaining partner. The album also supplied enough space for information about eleven children. Platt suggested that, upon maturity, each child be given

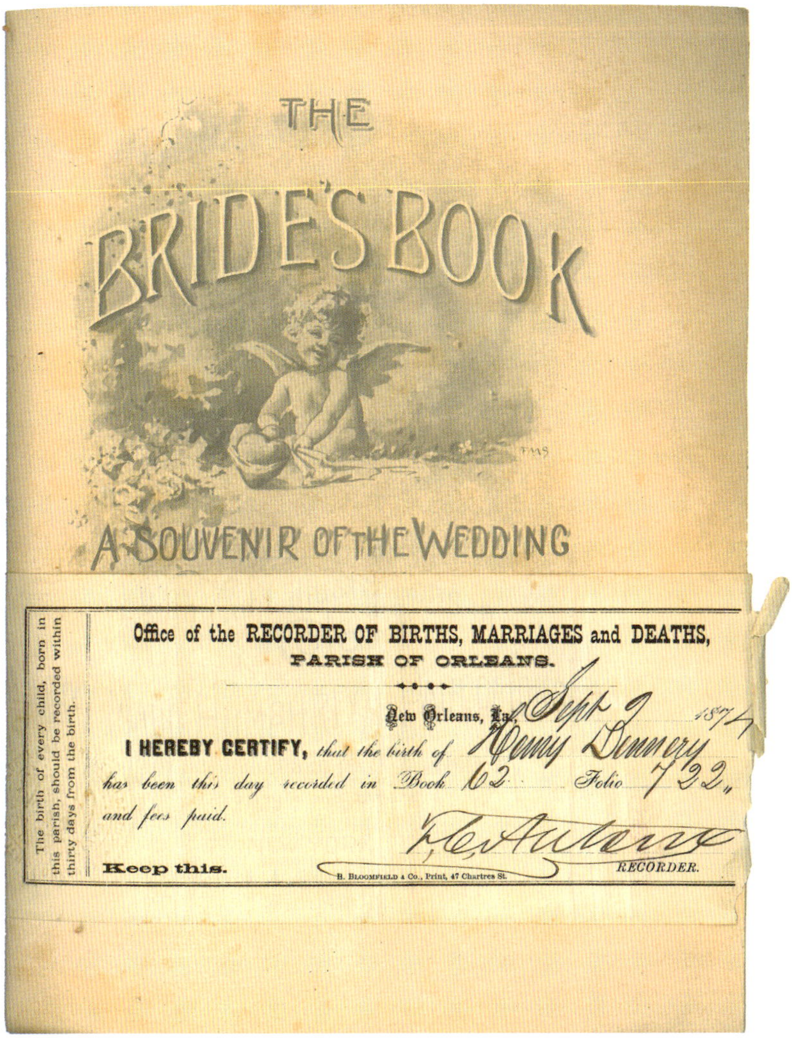

FIGURE 5.15
Title page of *The Bride Book*, Augusta Waldhorn Dennery Scrapbook. Newcomb Archives and Vorhoff Library Special Collections, Newcomb College Institute, Tulane University. ➳ This blank book was published in 1900 by Frederick A. Stokes and included frames for entries alongside pastel drawings by Maud Humphrey. Augusta Waldhorn Dennery felt no compunction about pasting her marriage certificate onto the first page.

his or her own album.[30] Another album maker was the printer William H. Shepard, whose *Family Memorial* (1876) could, when completed, arrange genealogical, biographical, and statistical records of ancestors and descendants within even more categories than those of Platt, and it included a request to supply a "view of homestead."[31] The goals for similar albums continue in contemporary family history albums and also in scrapbooks, with an emphasis on handwritten contributions from family members and depictions of living spaces.

Genetic Genealogy

Now thousands of family trees, accounts from books, and scanned registers are online, hyperlinking individuals across great divides of time and space, facilitating nearly instantaneous transmission to other branches, other families, other formats.[32] Family lineages now can also extend much, much farther back in time, linking individuals through genetic studies to ancient ancestors in prehistory, whose names are unknown, as well as to closer relatives.

On a global scale, testimonials for DNA testing are glowing and somehow reassuring. As one subscriber wrote: "I not only found out that my ancestors were Hungarian Jews, but I found two distant cousins. First relatives I've ever known other than my children."[33]

John B. Windham (b. 1938) of Metairie, Louisiana, who has studied genealogy since the 1960s, began a Y-chromosome DNA project in 2006. His surname group now has access to the various genetic markings for nearly one hundred ancestors born between the 1100s and the early twentieth century.[34] Windham chose Family Tree DNA, one of the first companies to offer a database of genetic test results. Its publicity asserts the necessity for large numbers of test results, critical for linking disparate branches in family trees.[35] The Windham color-coded charts show paternal ancestor names, countries, haplogroups (a set of DNA variations inherited together, the set forming patterns that allow us to see kinship), and short tandem repeats (STRs) on Y-chromosomes. The latter, once called "junk DNA" and now known by the more respectable name "noncoding DNA," are repeats, somewhat like hiccups of the genes in a specific, or closely ordered, manner. So in Y-DNA tests, men who have the same ordered repeats are related. Windham's and other charts show markers for various individuals. Such DNA linkages appear amazing to our early twenty-first-century sensibility. Here, spelled out in body chemistry, are letters indicating that *you, you, and you, across time and across the world, are my family.*

Another New Orleans genealogist, Cheryl Loup Curole (b. 1954), called the whole experience of DNA testing "profound." She had not been a believer in testing and only chose to try it reluctantly. But she found two relatives who would certainly otherwise never have been discovered, one whose connection to her extended back nine generations and another who is more closely related. She has also now visited Ireland to meet relatives.

Windham and Curole are two of only three individuals I could locate who had tried DNA testing in New Orleans, and the excitement about DNA research in the city seems muted. Among the fifty-two people I spoke with during 2006–2009, only three discussed plans for testing. By 2014, I expected those numbers to be larger. Yet, when I asked at meetings of genealogists how many had completed such testing, I was met first with silence. I do not know if this is a reflection of New Orleans genealogists as a group or just of the people to whom I spoke. In 2006–2009, family historians in the city (as elsewhere, my reading indicated) expressed lingering fears based on earlier uses of racialized genetic studies, which had targeted marginal and poor groups and resulted in forced sterilizations. Genealogists were not so sure they wanted to embrace genetics in their practices of finding ancestors.[36] Most experts have argued successfully, however, that science offers the chance "to refute bigoted or essentialist positions."[37] Henry Louis Gates Jr., for example, almost always includes research based on genetic testing in his popular television series and books on genealogy. He also presents his subjects with an album or scrapbook.[38]

Recent interest in genetic genealogy first arose in the 1990s, when scientists began to study major genetic groups, haplogroups, based on national or regional areas.[39] The National Geographic Society's Genographic Project, initiated in 2005, extended this early work internationally, although a number of indigenous people were wary for the very reasons genealogists were. The National Geographic Society and other funders then began to emphasize that only volunteers would be studied, that the study participants would remain anonymous, and that the tests and results would be "nonmedical and nonprofit." They emphasized as well the need for many types of participants in order to study "where humans originated and how we came to populate the Earth." Cheek swabs have been sent to them from 705,343 individuals, and these individuals have learned how their genomes fit within dozens of regions of the world, thereby adding to our knowledge of human migration patterns over centuries.[40] The project is participatory, then, such that with little effort one can contribute to a worldwide group.

As one journalist noted, the network of our history is wrapped more tightly now; with knowledge of our connections to one another, we can learn much more about ourselves and even about how we might get along more peacefully. Physical evidence may corroborate or offer new family stories with such testing.[41] One has to be ready for stories that go against what one has always thought.

There are many types of tests. One might prefer tests showing relationships with cousins, families of origin, ethnic groups, or surname kinships. One can combine tests, overlaying findings so that one can establish multiple perspectives. For example, in 2012, Ancestry.com launched a project to provide DNA testing and then link results from other testing companies across time and space.[42] One can test for mitochondrial DNA (mtDNA, the DNA passed down on one's maternal line in mitochondria that live just outside cells), Y-chromosomal make-up (chromosomes passed only to males), autosomal chromosomes (the other twenty-two matched pairs of chromosomes), and, most recently, X-chromosomes (two chromosomes inherited by women and one by men from their mothers and their paternal lines).[43]

In 2015, there are some thirty commercial firms that offer genealogical DNA testing. All these companies help people find out about their ancestors, explaining how these ancestors lived and coped in the world centuries before records were written down.[44] Some call this practice

FIGURE 5.16
Family photographs used to consider art pieces on family history, 1940–1997, Jan Gilbert. Photographic collage. Courtesy of the artist.

FIGURE 5.17
Biography of a Ball Player, Jan Gilbert, 1997. Silkscreened print. Twenty-three by thirty-eight inches. Courtesy of the artist.
This work was commissioned by the New Orleans Contemporary Arts Center as its 1997 Century Club Print. It incorporates memorabilia of artist Gilbert's father, Charles Mader Gilbert (1919–1983). He was a major league baseball player from 1940 to 1947 playing with the Brooklyn Dodgers, Chicago Cubs, and Philadelphia Phillies.

"deep genealogy," signifying the placement of self within a human network of relatives over centuries. "Of course we know we are linked to all these generations who lived in primitive circumstances, who had to walk to find water, who had to hunt and gather. We have heard of them before. But this makes them real, makes us know that every one of them has a little part in us."[45] Brian Sykes, through his company Oxford Ancestors, offers research that will link a person to one of thirty-six ancestral mothers worldwide. Persons with European ancestry, for example, are linked to Ursula, Xenia, Helena, Velda, Tara, Katrine, or Jasmine, an approach that involves again the power of names, just as genealogists told about. Oxford Ancestors clients receive this information as well as a certificate of membership in a World Clan, not unlike those of membership in patriotic societies.[46]

How many people have tried DNA testing to further their research in genealogy? In 2007, genealogist and scientist Blaine Bettinger estimated that between three hundred thousand and seven hundred thousand people had done so. By 2015, he found that the number had risen to more than two million.[47]

There is every indication that other innovations also will allow science, genealogy, and medicine to be combined in such a way that profound results will be achieved. Already, home films can be added to genealogical databases, and apps on phones. Inventors also promise that the voices of ancestors, one day, will be able to tell us about places they visited, and even offer advice on living.[48]

FIGURE 5.18

Biography of a House Chandelier, Jan Gilbert, 2008. Photo of mixed/photo media light work with sound installation. Original, 18 x 12.5 feet in diameter, On Piety Prospect.1 Satellite Exhibition, New Orleans. Photo by Luna Bella, Girls Club of New York.

This piece incorporates photographs of four generations who shared the residence at 6875 Vicksburg Street, Lakeview, New Orleans. There are photographs by Jan Gilbert, her father Charles Mader Gilbert, and her nephew C. Michael Higgins, with sound recordings by Charles Gilbert and sound design by Jan's nephew William Gilbert. This chandelier was first exhibited as part of the large-scale, collaborative 2007 Lakeview Sunset Bus Tour project, which Jan Gilbert directed.

Art about Family History

In 2011, when I visited the Family History Library in Salt Lake City, I saw genealogical art and artifacts displayed on each of the building's five floors. There are realistic and abstract paintings, drawings, and mixed-media pieces; there are traditional register pages, samplers, and family trees. Some present recent generations, while some show the diaspora of peoples over continents.

One of these is the work of Valerie Atkisson, whose three-dimensional sculpture represents her ancestry. "Hanging Family History" is crafted of copper, wire, rice paper, and ink and includes thousands of small folded triangles, each bearing names or other information about ancestors. The piece starts with the artist at its apex and moves downward to represent persons born two thousand years ago. Like many family historians, Atkisson completed her research at one of the more than 4,600 LDS Family History Centers.[49]

In New Orleans, too, I was shown a number of art pieces depicting family history. Artist Jan Gilbert, for example, worked with old family photographs that influenced her themes of memory, loss, and transition in mixed-media pieces. Family historians also presented other visual and artifactual responses that concern collecting in general. One woman collected dolls named for ancestors, while another collected cups inscribed with the words "Remember Me."

Struggling with the Incompleteness of Family Knowledge

All these formats of family history characterize the unrelenting passion that drives family historians to preserve the past and to extend the present beyond one's lifetime, extending the lives of others as one does so.

FIGURE 5.19
Crazy quilt, ca. 1880. Silk and cotton. Unknown creators, passed down in the family of Susie Owen Quigley (1862–1944).
Quilts and samplers are often the most valued of family heirlooms, but they are difficult to maintain over generations.

Lemuel Shattuck (1793–1859) was a founder of American-style genealogy as practiced in New England, and he would have understood clearly these efforts. Shattuck saw that both public and private forms would be needed for a full genealogy. Perhaps because he came from a family stricken by communicable diseases, Shattuck was interested in what were called the "life tables" of an insurance company, or what we call today mortality tables. A teacher, bookseller, and publisher, Shattuck was also in fear of losing his wife's money. He saw genealogy as linking him to elites but also as a passage back in time to ancestors whose names had been forgotten.[50] While writing a history of his hometown of Concord, Massachusetts, he was struck by the difficulty of finding records. In 1841, he created the first bound blank book, in which families might record information on births, marriages, and deaths. This was an "enhanced register" called *The Complete System of Family Registration*. It was designed to offer the "many advantages of a good Family Register" that could "furnish the evidence of relationship, settle the rights of connexions, [and] prevent disputes about property, expensive litigation, anxiety of mind, and contention and alienation in families, which too often take place."[51]

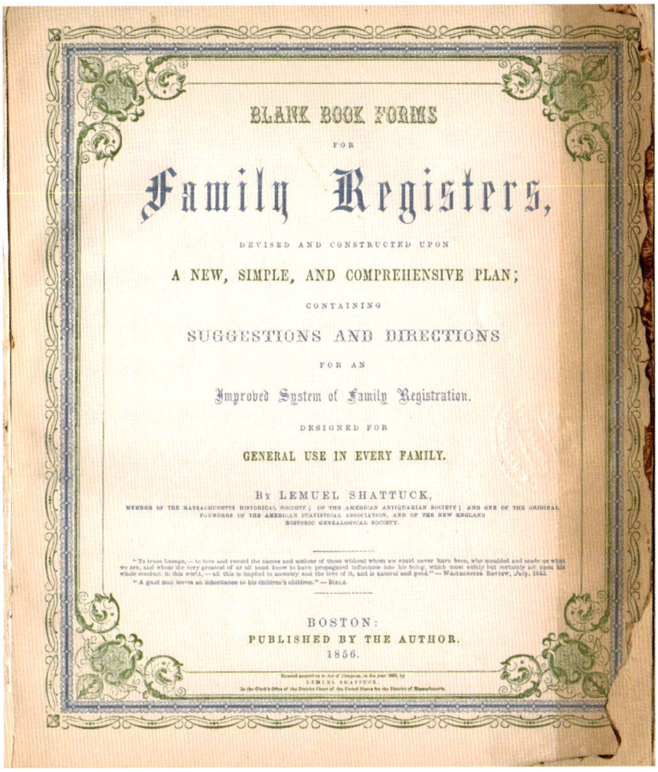

BLANK BOOK FORMS

FOR

Family Registers,

DEVISED AND CONSTRUCTED UPON

A NEW, SIMPLE, AND COMPREHENSIVE PLAN;

CONTAINING

SUGGESTIONS AND DIRECTIONS

FOR AN

Improved System of Family Registration.

DESIGNED FOR

GENERAL USE IN EVERY FAMILY.

BY LEMUEL SHATTUCK,

MEMBER OF THE MASSACHUSETTS HISTORICAL SOCIETY; OF THE AMERICAN ANTIQUARIAN SOCIETY; AND ONE OF THE ORIGINAL FOUNDERS OF THE AMERICAN STATISTICAL ASSOCIATION, AND OF THE NEW ENGLAND HISTORIC GENEALOGICAL SOCIETY.

"To trace lineage, — to love and record the names and actions of those without whom we could never have been, who moulded and made us what we are, and whom the very greatest of us all must know to have propagated influences into his being, which most subtly but certainly act upon his whole conduct in this world, — all this is implied in ancestry and the love of it, and is natural and good." — WESTMINSTER REVIEW, *July*, 1853.

"A good man leaves an inheritance to his children's children." — BIBLE.

BOSTON:
PUBLISHED BY THE AUTHOR.
1856.

Entered according to Act of Congress, in the year 1856, by LEMUEL SHATTUCK, In the Clerk's Office of the District Court of the United States for the District of Massachusetts.

FIGURE 5.20
Title page for Lemuel Shattuck's *Blank Book Forms for Family Registers, Devised and Constructed upon a New, Simple, and Comprehensive Plan: Containing Suggestions and Directions for an Improved System of Family Registration* (Boston, 1856). Hun Family Collection (Mss A 6392). R. Stanton Avery Special Collections Department, New England Historic Genealogical Society.
The Hun family of Albany, New York, used this bound volume, which Lemuel Shattuck, one of the New England Historic Genealogical Society's founders, had devised for family history.

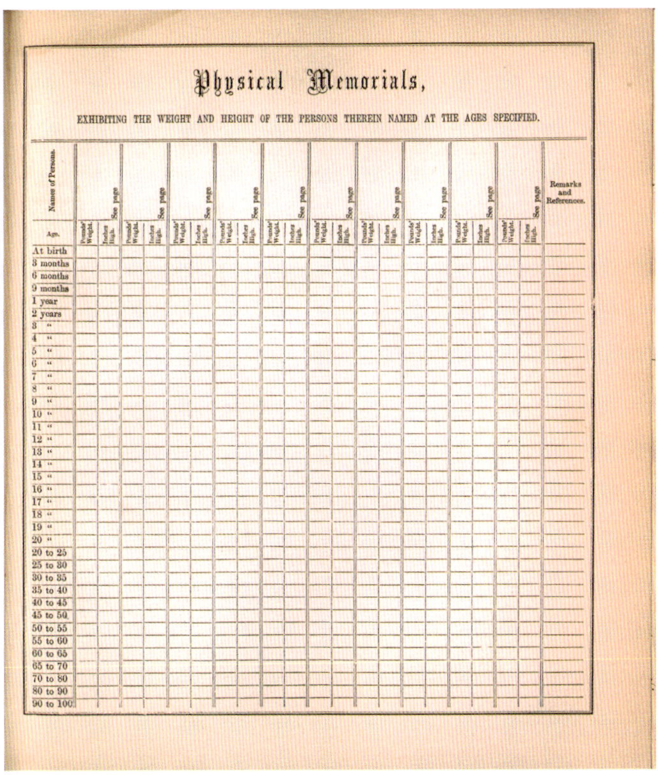

Physical Memorials,

EXHIBITING THE WEIGHT AND HEIGHT OF THE PERSONS THEREIN NAMED AT THE AGES SPECIFIED.

Names of Persons. / Age.	Pounds' Weight.	Inches High.	See page	Pounds' Weight.	Inches High.	See page	Pounds' Weight.	Inches High.	See page	Pounds' Weight.	Inches High.	See page	Pounds' Weight.	Inches High.	See page	Pounds' Weight.	Inches High.	See page	Pounds' Weight.	Inches High.	See page	Pounds' Weight.	Inches High.	See page	Pounds' Weight.	Inches High.	See page	Pounds' Weight.	Inches High.	See page	Remarks and References.
At birth																															
3 months																															
6 months																															
9 months																															
1 year																															
2 years																															
3 "																															
4 "																															
5 "																															
6 "																															
7 "																															
8 "																															
9 "																															
10 "																															
11 "																															
12 "																															
13 "																															
14 "																															
15 "																															
16 "																															
17 "																															
18 "																															
19 "																															
20 "																															
20 to 25																															
25 to 30																															
30 to 35																															
35 to 40																															
40 to 45																															
45 to 50																															
50 to 55																															
55 to 60																															
60 to 65																															
65 to 70																															
70 to 80																															
80 to 90																															
90 to 100																															

FIGURE 5. 21
"Physical Memorials, exhibiting the weight and height of the persons therein named at the ages specified." Section heading in Lemuel Shattuck, *Blank Book Forms for Family Registers* (Boston, 1856). Hun Family Collection (Mss A 6392). R. Stanton Avery Special Collections Department, New England Historic Genealogical Society.
The Hun family did not choose to add this information. Shattuck's interest in public health oriented him to these "physical memorials."

He hoped that this type of book would help prevent families from losing touch with their past. The mid- to late nineteenth-century profusion of Bibles meant, in Shattuck's mind and experience, that there was no *one* repository for records. "Bibles are now so common that there is seldom found one which by way of distinction is called *the* family Bible, and which is peculiarly suited, or can contain proper forms for a family record."[52]

Shattuck was simultaneously working on public recordkeeping. In the late 1830s and early 1840s, he authored the first vital statistics law in the United States, the Massachusetts law that, by 1842, had become a model for other states.[53] He also proposed other measures providing for the "preservation and publication of city documents, creation of a municipal library, and preparation of an annual city register." Ultimately, he became known as the father of public health.[54]

Shattuck's work as a consultant would influence future genealogists in the most significant ways. His revision of the structure of Boston's census form in 1845 led to every person being listed. In turn, federal government officials looked to him for help in designing the national census of 1850. Shattuck's innovation was that each person should be counted; a person became the census unit, not a family, and each person was recorded as to age, birth place, marital status, and occupation.[55] The national census of 1850 also included space for the names of some slaves, although still under the names of slave owners and without instructions indicating that individuals rather than families were the key units to be counted. Still, "slave schedules" brought some democratization to the census process, as Shattuck advocated.

Shattuck believed in the importance of census records, but there is no one person to whom we can give credit for the 1908 publication of the first transcription of the census returns for 1790, with each state in a separate publication.[56] Imagine that one would no longer have to travel to distant archives to see the paper censuses. Could Shattuck have imagined the present? There was no inkling of the possibilities of computer-generated information for genealogy until the 1970s, when Utah genealogist Ronald Vern Jackson began to provide a computerized index for open census records. Again, LDS influence on sealing the family extended out to others. Jackson's work was part of a commercial venture called Accelerated Indexing Systems. In 1984, the microfiche version of these indexes was released. They are now available online through the Family History Library, as are all other censuses up to 1940.[57]

Richness in Evidence

This chapter is a quick overview of a few of the physical objects of family history and genealogical representations of human lives. From the time of the first Bible entries, the first ledgers taken from accounting projects and made into family registers, to the plenitude of the Internet today, genealogists have seen public records as their most important evidence. They have set about providing access to these records by way of many small projects, concentrating on the populations of their immediate areas. They have contributed to the drive for access, making the world today so bountiful in terms of family information.[58]

But family historians have not forgotten the emotional tug of private forms; they have not forgotten them even in New Orleans, where they say there are not as many examples as elsewhere. Lemuel Shattuck would have completely understood this drive and the attachment to personal records, along with other advancements in genetics and electronic information. He would no doubt be amazed, as every genealogist with whom I spoke also was, that the Internet has made access to public records so easy.

He would no doubt also be amazed that family historians can turn to certified genealogists who bring a world of expertise and a formidable skill set to finding evidence; he would no doubt be having his own genetic genealogy tested. In some ways, this formal and scientific world is very different from the work of most of the family historians with whom I spoke. In other ways, especially in terms of Louisianans' fierce pride in their records, the two sides clearly share a dedication to work in common. The two groups together certainly enable the continuing democratization of American genealogy.

Today, both depend upon on oral accounts, private materials, and "documentary sources," with the last far outweighing the first two.[59] Yet, like the pipe that Belsom's family retained and its usefulness in helping Belsom find a birth certificate, genealogy also depends on a *private* starting point.

CHAPTER SIX

The "Most Wonderful Collections": New Orleans Recordkeeping

Almost every day, from the time she was forty-five until she reached seventy-four, Laura Louise Porteous (1875–1952) went to work in one of the two magnificent New Orleans buildings flanking Saint Louis Cathedral on Jackson Square. Here, in the center of the French Quarter, first in the Cabildo and then in the Presbytère, she translated Spanish colonial judicial records. Every three months, from 1923 to 1948, she published thirty to fifty pages of her work in the *Louisiana Historical Quarterly*. She also assisted many others, including genealogists, working with the court records. In her correspondence, some of it about her own family history, she had a way of signing her name that indicates the skills she knew she possessed. She called herself "(Mlle.) Laura L. Porteous, Assistante Archiviste, Paleographe pour l'Espagnol" or "(Señorita) Laura L. Porteous, Asistente del Archivero."[1] She called the New Orleans records with which she worked during those long years, "the most wonderful collection of original documents in the United States."[2]

Genealogy requires passion to continue, family historians repeatedly said, and Laura Porteous worked with records that proved a never-ending source of such passion. Both her unusual job and her deep appreciation reflect other New Orleanians' approaches to genealogy. The city's family historians believe in a grand legacy of records. This chapter is about the specifics of those records, those that Porteous knew so well and others that are unique to the city. As the previous chapter presented national and private forms that engaged family historians, here we turn to local and public forms.

Genealogists call the records that Porteous translated by many different names: "black boxes," in reference to the color of the wooden boxes built to house the manuscripts; "Cabildo records," because they were created in the Cabildo; or simply "colonial records." Whatever their name, they include both notarial and judicial minutes, mingled because notaries assigned to the court maintained private practices, and because the court—where civil and criminal matters were adjudicated—was also a place of notarial practice.

Notarial Records

But because most notaries served individuals, businesses, and families, their records were not part of the judicial records Porteous knew so intimately. An 1867 law, enacted largely in response to the politics of Reconstruction, specified that upon the death or resignation of a notary, all his records should be sent to a central repository. When this law was made, the judicial records beloved by Porteous were missing, and so they did not come to the new Notarial Archives. Today, the Notarial Archives Research Center houses records from 1735 to 1970.[3]

FIGURE 6.1
Laura Louise Porteous, ca. 1894. Studio Print, by Gustave Moses. Courtesy of the Archives of the Ursulines of Brown County.
Porteous (1875–1952) attended New Orleans's Ursuline Academy and then the School of the Brown County Ursulines, Ohio. She also studied at the University of Salamanca in Spain before returning home to New Orleans, where she worked for almost thirty years translating Spanish judicial documents. She kept up a steady correspondence about her own family's genealogy and assisted others in gathering information as well.

The notarial work from the past remains important because, as genealogist Sonja McCarthy (b. 1937) said of all the people she has researched, "if they had a shoestring, they went to a notary and had it written down." The notaries were the draftsmen, guarantors, and archivists of legal acts. Recall that the notaries were charged with oversight of all transactions of commerce and that this commerce included wills, marriage contracts, partnership arrangements, and many other formalized agreements in the private sector. Before the Civil War, notaries also oversaw the purchase and emancipation of slaves. The notaries' records, bound in ledgers, were open to the public.[4]

A retired professor of education, McCarthy is a small, thin woman with a powerful voice. She can be dismissive and she can be welcoming, but most of all she can be passionate. For her, family history practice involves just the right mix of the personal with national and international politics and economics. She researches Creoles of color, whites, and African Americans. She started with an aunt's birth certificate and the surprise of discovering something obvious: this aunt had been born in an earlier century and had seen both the beginning and the ending of the Jim Crow laws. This aunt's mother (McCarthy's grandmother) had been born when "slaves still walked the streets of the city." Today, McCarthy "knows" people on both sides of her family tree and beyond. Like those of many other genealogists, her lists contain some thousand names. Her growing database puts both living and dying in a different perspective. She told me that "all these people accompany" her in life, that she "would not be here without them and the lives they led," and that each "forms a little tiny piece in who we are."

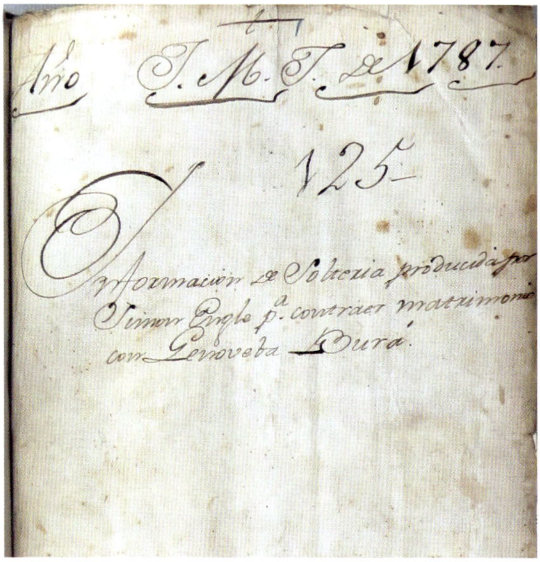

FIGURE 6.2
Title page of the notarial acts of Estevan De Quinones, 1787. Courtesy of Dale N. Atkins, clerk of the Civil District Court and ex-officio recorder, parish of Orleans, Louisiana.

De Quinones was also a notary for the Church and thus recorded marriage applications. These applications included the testimony of residents, or official documents that could prove that one had never married, or that one was a widow or widower (*información de soltería*). There are also suits concerned with breach of promise, divorce, and separation. De Quinones wrote of happy times but also sad ones, and of matters that seem dated today, at least in the language of today: purity of bloodlines, anguish of betrayal, and family honor and dishonor.

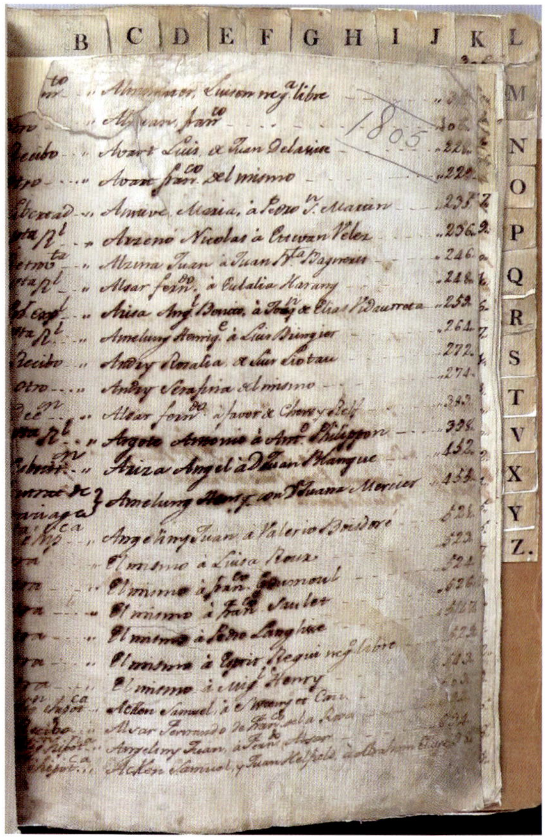

FIGURE 6.3
Index page for notarial acts of Estevan De Quinones, 1787. Courtesy of Dale N. Atkins, clerk of the Civil District Court and ex-officio recorder, parish of Orleans, Louisiana.

Each notary was required to keep such a listing, and the numbers correspond to the bound acts, binding being also a requirement.

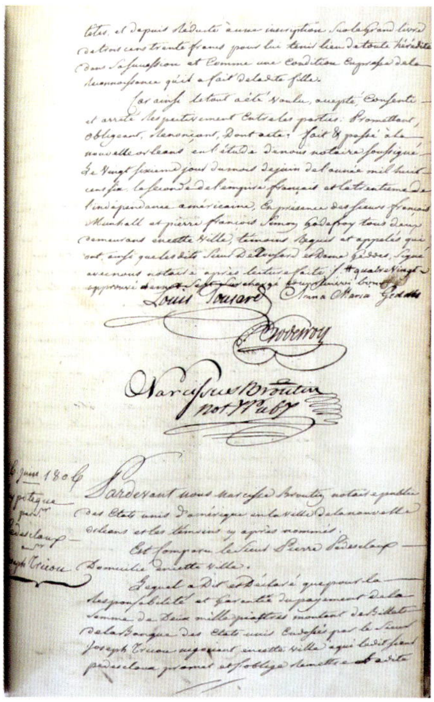

FIGURE 6.4
Signatures, marriage contract of Louis de Toussard and Anna Maria Geddes, June 26, 1806. Acts of Narcisse Broutin. Courtesy of Dale N. Atkins, clerk of the Civil District Court and ex-officio recorder, parish of Orleans, Louisiana.

This marriage contract is four pages and like other such agreements specifies the property that was brought into the marriage by the wife and retained, as well as the property that the couple will hold henceforth in common.

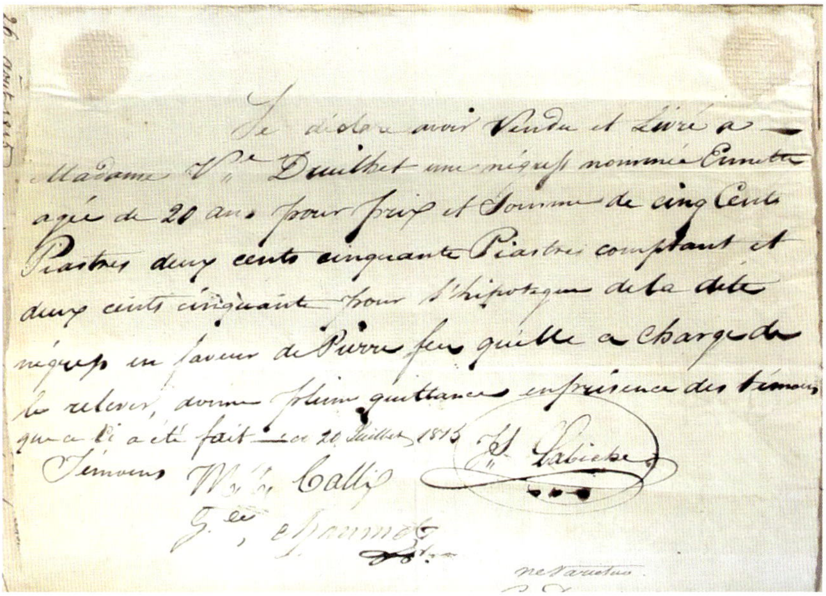

Je déclare avoir Vendu et Livré a Madame V.ve Duilhet une négresse nommée Emma âgée de 20 ans pour prix et Somme de cinq Cents Piastres deux cents cinquante Piastres comptant et deux cents cinquante pour l'hipotèque de la dite négresse en faveur de Pierre [illegible] qu'elle a charge de le relever, donne pleine quittance en présence des témoins que ce Ci a été fait le 20 Juillet 1815 J. Labiche
Témoins W. Callis
G. Chaumet

FIGURE 6.5
Tipped-in information regarding a slave sale, August 25, 1815. Acts of Marc Lafitte. Courtesy of Dale N. Atkins, clerk of the Civil District Court and ex-officio recorder, parish of Orleans, Louisiana.
This piece of information was pasted into the bound volume to show additional evidence about prior ownership of a slave named Emma.

On her father's side, McCarthy has gone back nine generations to Ireland in the 1700s. A favorite story is that of Victor-Eugene Macarty, who gave a different spelling to the family name, following the pattern of French pronunciation. The son of a white planter and his Creole of color mistress, Victor-Eugene Macarty studied music in Paris in the 1840s. McCarthy found records of a case he had filed against a white official who had asked him to move out of the section reserved for whites only in the New Orleans Opera House.

McCarthy has other favorite stories that concern the simplicity of her aunt's life and its contrasts to that of Victor-Eugene. New Orleans offers McCarthy what she calls "a wealth in retirement." Again, she places much of this wealth in the richness of notarial records. Others do also. As another genealogist said, "We have here a true archives, not a collection of papers kept only for history but a collection of records kept in their original order."[5] Or as the Notarial Archives staff added to the glossary of the Society of American Archivists: "In New Orleans, nearly every property transaction that has occurred since the founding of the city was recorded by, or found its way to, a notary's office."[6]

The notarial records are like the fraktur of the Germans in Pennsylvania; both types of documents are beloved because the earliest ones preserve the first languages of the first colonial settlers. Spanish notarial records particularly are testaments to strong and beautifully textured paper and legible penmanship, especially in the flourish of signatures.

In content, notarial records are templates of accord. Genealogists like the formality of the records, and the imagined ancestors going to an office with their hopes on cementing negotiations that often promised to better their lives. Civil law arrived in the city with the French in 1718.

The early French especially desired to maintain official procedures that they had known in France and other parts of French North America. As legal historian Hans Baade writes: "The colony in Quebec in 1667 had made a judgment on the inadvisability of sending many lawyers to New France." Lawyers could be prickly and untrustworthy, "likely to exploit the ignorant, stir up unnecessary litigation, and question the legality of colonial administrative acts." Notaries represented less of "a threat to the . . . primitive colonial government." In New Orleans as in Quebec, notaries followed the rules they had learned with promises of honor. "Especially . . . where neither the public nor even most government officials could be expected to be familiar with legal and administrative formalities, notaries were quite naturally viewed as the agents of stability rather than discord."[7]

In New Orleans, the notaries' work also eased changes of ruling governments. Pedro Pedesclaux, again, is a good example. In 1784, Pedesclaux inherited the records of his predecessor from the 1750s onward and kept them safely until 1816. His successors kept them until 1859. Thus, his notarial acts form part of an unbroken chain from France's Louisiana through Spain's Luisiana (and momentarily back to France) to American territory, then to statehood, and then to the eve of the Civil War. His signatures on various acts reflects this adaptability: he signed as Pierre, Pedro, and Peter in accordance with the varying administrations and sometimes in accordance with the individuals with whom he was working. Pedesclaux and the other Spanish notaries also set in place important traditions that facilitated preservation of records. They were more apt than the French to follow rules about binding records, for example. They also provided genealogists today with more reading matter, more details, than did the French. The Spanish notaries did not skimp on paper but wrote on large sheets (some 15.5 by 10.5 inches in size) not only because paper was more readily available to them in the well-organized Spanish empire but also because they were paid by the page.[8]

Judicial Records

Besides his own practice as a notary, Pedesclaux was also clerk and notary for the Spanish government, recorder of mortgages, and clerk of the Cabildo. In these roles, he was caretaker of all the records of the Spanish and the French governments, or the working records of the people of the colony. This archives included the proceedings of the French Conseil Supérieur (1714–1769) and various courts of the Spanish (1769–1803), especially those of the *alcades ordinarios* who heard cases and functioned as a higher court of the Cabildo.[9]

It is the survival of these judicial records that presents an extraordinary, complicated, and mysterious achievement that genealogists like to tell about, because, for long stretches at various times, the records were known only as either missing or too precious to be handled by anyone less esteemed than a paleographer or translator such as Laura Porteous or various leaders of the Louisiana Historical Society.

The story of these records' journey to becoming a genealogical path begins with the last French colonial governor of Louisiana, Pierre Clément de Laussat (1756–1835). In 1803, when he was packing up and leaving all to the Americans, he took the time to consider what records would be needed by the residents and therefore should be left in New Orleans. Land and commercial records, marriage contracts and successions, and judicial records, he decided, should remain. He ordered these records, especially the judicial records in the étude of Pedesclaux, to be guarded with special attention, to be "sealed."[10]

Pedesclaux had his own problems in the transition to becoming American. He did not know what his status, his place as a notary and as the holder of other offices, would be. He had a large family, and his devotion to them was well known. It was also widely known that he had saved the records from the fire of 1788 that had devastated nearly the whole city, the whole of what today is the French Quarter. Would this role be respected by the Americans, who did not practice civil law? He needed money; he wanted the prestige he had had under Spanish rule. In the transition, then, his troubles seem all the more poignant, the stuff of one family history and its trajectory in becoming American in New Orleans.[11]

After some discussion, civil law remained in Louisiana, and Pedesclaux prevailed in making himself known enough to American authorities that he remained custodian of the judicial records, and a notary for private families as well. After his death, all his work was passed to one son, and then another, and then was placed with another notary. But were these records, this body of work from the colonial courts, more than just records needed in the working lives of residents? Were they also the heritage of the colony? Legislators began to ask these questions, and in 1826 they ordered indexing and improved storage in the form of cedar boxes for the judicial records.[12] We know that some indexing was begun (because of some numbered pages) and that the cedar boxes may have been made then too (because, from 1893 onward, the records have been described as "black boxes" and because there is one very poor photo of cedar boxes, even though this dates from the 1960s). Another order came in 1860, when the legislature resolved that "all the old Notarial and Colonial Records, touching the early history of Louisiana, now in the hands of H. Pedesclaux and Octave de Armas, notaries public of the city . . . be delivered to the State Librarian, whose duty it shall be to deposit the same in the room in the Capitol set apart for the historical society of the state."[13] This was the Louisiana Historical Society (LHS). But no one knows if the records were ever so delivered.[14]

In 1893, the LHS rediscovered these "documents of the time of the

FIGURE 6.6
Unidentified clipping about the translations of the French and Spanish judicial records. Laura Porteous Collection, Mss 1200, Box 6. Courtesy of Special Collections, Hill Memorial Library, Louisiana State University.
Heloise Hulse Cruzat (1862–1931, right) and Laura Louise Porteous (1875–1952, left) worked in New Orleans during the first half of the twentieth century transcribing, translating, and indexing the Louisiana Historical Society's vast collection of French and Spanish colonial judicial records.

Top picture shows collection of ancient files and historical documents at the Cabildo. Bottom picture, left to right, Miss Laura Porteous, Spanish translator, and Mrs. Heloise Hulse Cruzat, French translator of Louisiana Historical Society Archives. In front of the ladies are some original records of Colonial times.

FIGURE 6.7
Petition of Louis and Catherine Connard asking Bienville to honor the freedom given to them by their late owner, March 6, 1739. Judicial records of the French Superior Council. Courtesy of the Louisiana State Museum and the Louisiana Historical Society.
This was part of a succession. Yet it also presents descendants with evidence of the difficult process that African Americans experienced in maintaining their freedom. Successions often included multiple parts such as wills, estate inventories, and acts of sale.

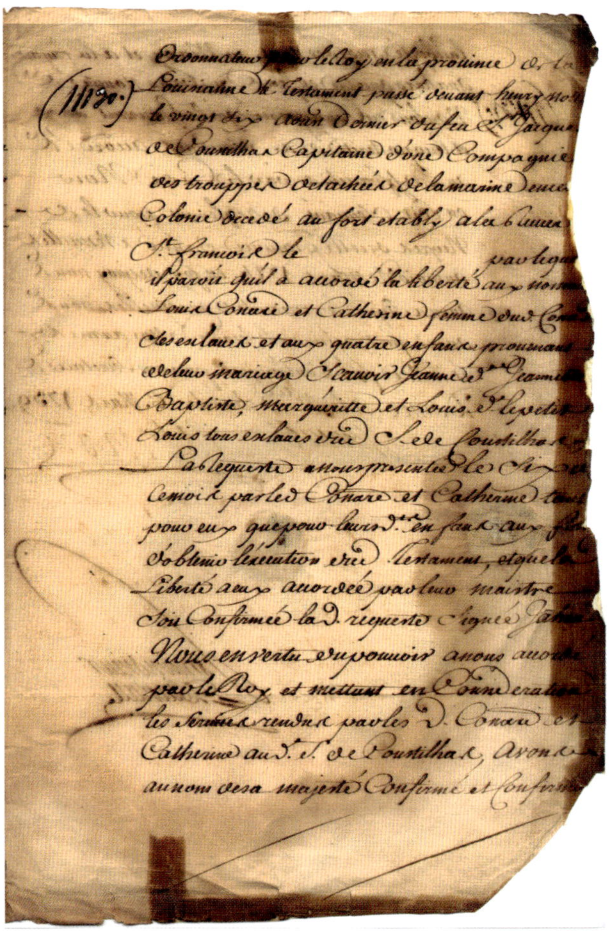

French and Spanish dominations" housed in a "number of wooden boxes" at Tulane University.[15] In 1908, the city council granted both the Louisiana State Museum and the LHS permanent homes in the Cabildo, the Presbytère, and surrounding buildings, and the records came to live there. They have been there for over a century now but no one knows where they were between 1860, when Pedesclaux's heirs were responsible for them, and 1893. No one knows, in essence, who saved them from the ravages of the Civil War.[16]

In the first decade of the twentieth century, these court records found their first use as information, rather than solely as evidence, when Tulane University German professor Hanno Deiler began research for his book *The Settlement of the German Coast of Louisiana and the Creoles of German Descent* (1909), essentially about genealogical and local history.[17] He must have had quite a job. Packed in eighty boxes, fragile and dirty, the records had not been regularly bound like the notarial records had been, or placed in bundles, a common archival method. The LHS saw clearly that it would take many years to make these documents accessible to anyone but a privileged few. Yet they also knew that the records were critical to colonial history, being the state's oldest secular records. As Grace King proclaimed, to ignore them would be "a sin of deplorable neglect."[18] Another LHS leader, lawyer Henry Plauché Dart (1858–1934), began to promote efforts to find solutions for their care, especially their translation. Dart visited the records every day and himself was called the "state archivist" on many occasions to honor his concern and advocacy for them. He never ceased to marvel at them. The records, he believed, would reveal something that all genealogists understand: the chance to know earlier lives. As he wrote: "There before me lay fifty thousand documents or more that told of the daily life of our ancestors; of their births and deaths, of their marriages and their children; their contracts and disputes, their purchases and sales, their wills and their estates."[19]

For him and for others, access meant both translation and organization by family name.[20] In 1917, Heloise Hulse Cruzat became the French translator, and Laura Porteous joined her as the Spanish translator in the early 1920s. The calendars and English synopsis of their work (and that of others), along with selected records translated in entirety, appeared in the *Louisiana Historical Quarterly* until 1948.[21]

Yet more work was still needed; the records themselves, not merely selected translations, had to be considered. In the late 1930s, the Works Progress Administration was called in for service. Genealogists still use what they call the "black notebooks" created by the WPA workers, which contain English-language synopses of each record, a necessity since not every case appeared in the LHS translations and calendars. The WPA also assisted in the first microfilming of the records, moving them from an old jail called the Calabozo, which was infested with termites, to what was called the "safety vault" on the first floor of the Presbytère.[22]

FIGURE 6.8
WPA translation of the petition of Louis and Catherine Connard, March 6, 1739, Black Books. Courtesy of the Louisiana State Museum and the Louisiana Historical Society.
The WPA translations usually included, as this one does, a citation to the *Louisiana Historical Quarterly* calendars of the judicial records created by Heloise Cruzat, Laura Porteous, and others who translated them, at least in synopsis form. The black notebooks were literally that, notebooks commonly sold in any office supply store; their name has been known to generations of researchers, as has the name "black boxes," which held the judicial records.

FIGURE 6.9
Works Progress Administration archives project room and picture cataloging section, Louisiana State Museum, ca. 1940. Courtesy of the Louisiana State Museum.
The WPA workers created large scrapbooks, some two feet by three feet, and bound them. They also took compiled pages of genealogical information and bound them into books.

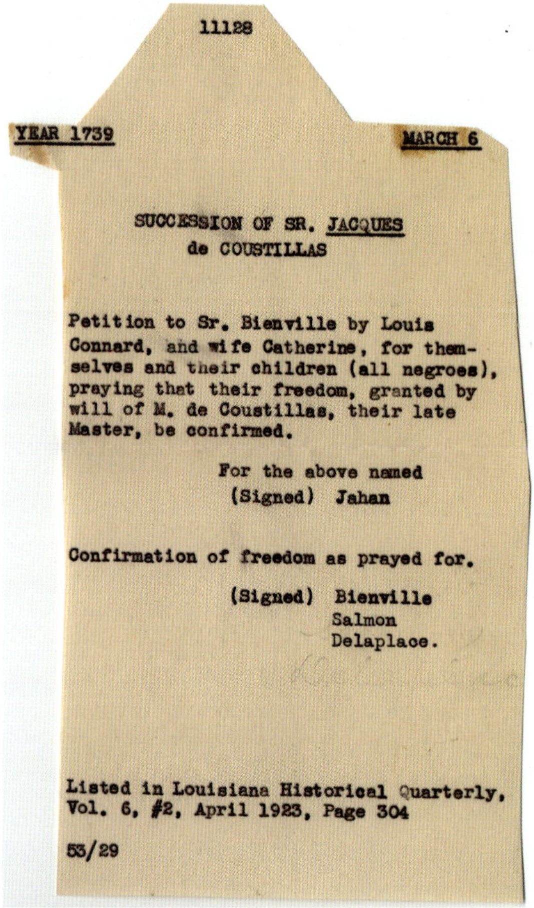
11128

YEAR 1739 MARCH 6

SUCCESSION OF SR. JACQUES
de COUSTILLAS

Petition to Sr. Bienville by Louis Connard, and wife Catherine, for themselves and their children (all negroes), praying that their freedom, granted by will of M. de Coustillas, their late Master, be confirmed.

For the above named
(Signed) Jahan

Confirmation of freedom as prayed for.

(Signed) Bienville
Salmon
Delaplace.

Listed in Louisiana Historical Quarterly, Vol. 6, #2, April 1923, Page 304

53/29

FIGURE 6.10
Presbytère building, ca. 1940. Courtesy of the Louisiana State Museum.
The location of the State Museum in the French Quarter in the Cabildo and Presbytère was always important to its status as the repository of the early city records, art, and artifacts. Some of the city's first records were created there. The WPA's work throughout the Quarter as well—in archival work and in the renovations of buildings—made public history visible across the landscape.

FIGURE 6.11
WPA worker at the Louisiana State Museum, initial microfilming, 1940. Courtesy of the Louisiana State Museum.
Microfilming was an experiment at this point; genealogists both praised it in terms of access to documents and lamented it in terms of quality of the film.

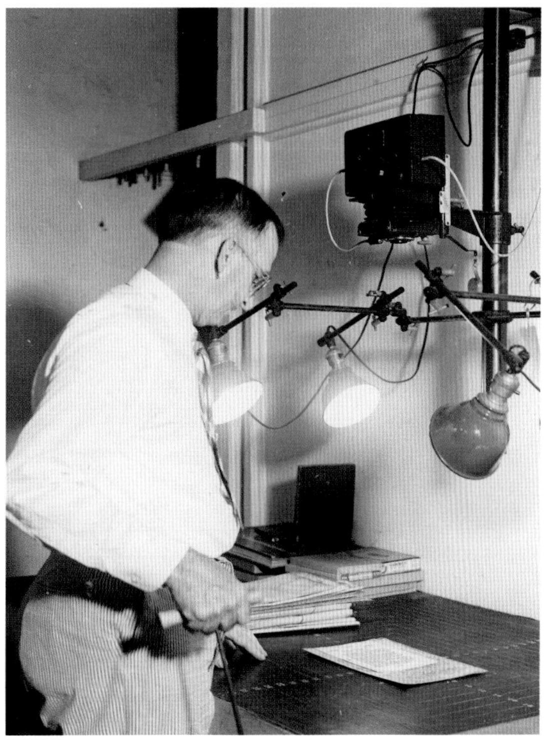

But this "safety vault" was dank and eventually cluttered with other items. In the 1960s, genealogists were among those citizens who mounted a public outcry for better care of these judicial and notarial records.[23] Genealogist Winston De Ville brought historians' attention to the mismanagement that seemed to circle about "the most talked about and least understood, the most quoted and least often consulted [records] of any in the nation."[24] As a result, family historians began work on the records as volunteers, creating, for example, card catalogs by names mentioned in the records, and other indexes, which appeared in the magazine of the Genealogical Research Society of New Orleans, *Genesis*.[25]

Advocacy helped, and the records were moved again, this time to a new humidity-controlled vault on the second floor of the Presbytère. In the 1970s and early 1980s, the records were microfilmed once more, this time by LDS missionaries working in New Orleans.[26] A digital project with the ultimate goal of publishing the records in an online database began in 2009 and continues to the present (2015).

Would Laura Porteous be astounded at how long this all took? Probably not. As genealogists always say, work on the past never ends.

Porteous's path to leaving a record herself, though, tells another story. Her own family history is located in New Orleans; she grew up in a French-speaking home and lived in the same house until her death in 1952.[27] But the movement of her papers, like those of the judicial records, suggests something about both the fragility and the resiliency of paper. The paper slips she used in compiling the index to the translations, and her letters to archivists in Spain and France about her own family history, are today all outside her home city, amassed during an ambitious program initiated in the 1940s by the Louisiana State University Library to save the state's records and manuscripts. LSU leaders perceived these materials as overlooked by the State Museum and other repositories. A bookseller, Albert Lieutaud of New Orleans's Royal Street, sold Porteous's materials to LSU. To this day, Porteous's family does not know how this came to be, and indeed neither the staff at the State Museum nor the family was aware of her notes to the records at LSU until 2010.[28]

This general movement of papers, their separation from one another, their division between private, professional, and public—all are part of family history. Genealogists often lament how much is lost in family papers, but even when saved, they also sometimes ask: *Why didn't such and such ancestors save their papers* ***here, close to me***? The answer is that sometimes one chooses an institution (or person) far away from where one has worked oneself. As one family historian confessed, "I know I had too much stuff so after [Hurricane] Katrina I wanted to find a safe place somewhere, safer than at home. I gave the photographs to the library here, sent the letters away to the State Archives in Mississippi. Too private now for those here. In forty years, they will be of interest for something more than gossip or idle curiosity."[29]

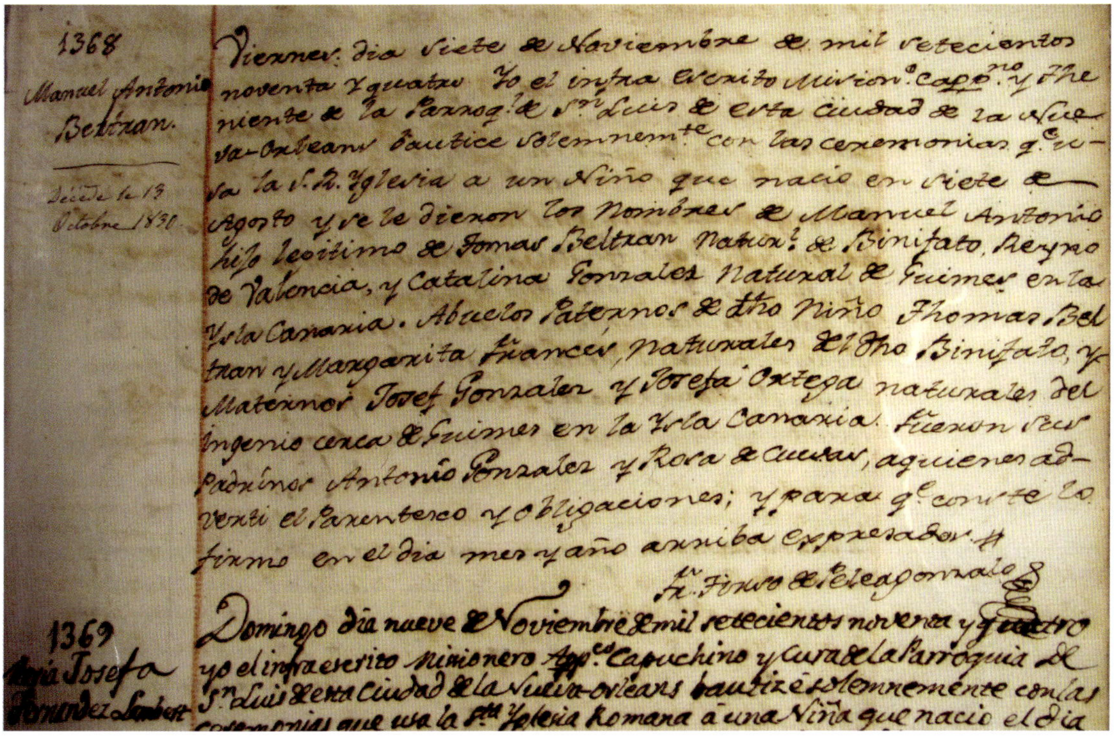

1368 Manuel Antonio Beltran. Decedio le 13 Octobre 1830

Viernes dia siete de Noviembre de mil setecientos noventa y quatro Yo el infra escrito Mision.o capuchino y Theniente de la Parroq.l de S.n Luis de esta ciudad de la Nueva-Orleans bautice solemnem.te con las ceremonias q.e usa la S. R. Yglesia a un Niño que nacio en siete de Agosto y se le dieron los Nombres de Manuel Antonio hijo legitimo de Tomas Beltran Natur.l de Binifato, Reyno de Valencia, y Catalina Gonzales Natural de Guimes en la Ysla Canaria. Abuelos Paternos de dho Niño Thomas Beltran y Margarita Frances, naturales del dho Binifato, y Maternos Josef Gonzales y Josefa Ortega naturales del Ingenio cerca de Guimes en la Ysla Canaria. Fueron sus Padrinos Antonio Gonzales y Rosa de Cuevas, a quienes adverti el Parentesco y obligaciones; y para q.e conste lo firmo en el dia mes y año arriba expresado.

Fr. Firmo de Peleagonzalo

1369 Maria Josefa Fernandez Lambert

Domingo dia nueve de Noviembre de mil setecientos noventa y quatro yo el infraescrito Misionero App.co Capuchino y cura de la Parroquia de S.n Luis de esta Ciudad de la Nueva-Orleans bautizé solemnemente con las ceremonias que usa la S.ta Yglesia Romana a una Niña que nacio el dia

FIGURE 6.12
Baptism of Manuel Antonio Beltran, November 7, 1794. Saint Louis Cathedral, New Orleans, Baptisms, vol. 2, 1786–1796, p. 335, no. 1368. Courtesy of the Office of Archives and Records, Archdiocese of New Orleans.

Here one can see that the father was a native of Spain (Valencia) and the mother, of the Canary Islands. Canary Islanders, or Isleños, were important to the history of New Orleans, coming in the late eighteenth century to guard the Spanish city from the English. The handwritten note on the left of the page shows that the priest followed the child to manhood and death.

Sacramental Records

Privacy issues also govern genealogists' perspective on other colonial records that continue to the present and that are most often described as the foundation of New Orleans's genealogical culture: the sacramental records. The Church was and remains, according to genealogists, the principal "registry of record." But the Archdiocese Archives, as their website states, is "NOT open to those engaged in genealogical studies or family research." Instead, "All requests for individual sacramental and cemetery records are handled by email or written mail."[30]

Family historians almost always focused first on the "richness" of the Church records, then turned their thoughts to the policies of the Archives, and then to accessibility made possible by current digitization projects. The "richness" is hard to ignore since the Church's records are the second oldest in the city, following the judicial records by six years. The registers for Saint Louis Cathedral began in 1720, and those for Saint Charles Borromeo on the German Coast (upriver from the city) began in 1739.[31] As one genealogist said, "It would be hard to imagine a more spectacular listing of humanity anywhere than [what] the priests here left." Or as another said, "These records show an amazing gathering of evidence: all classes, all colors filled out on the line, daily sometimes, and they functioned really as vital statistics."[32]

Knowing the Church records, one knows the city more deeply. Jack

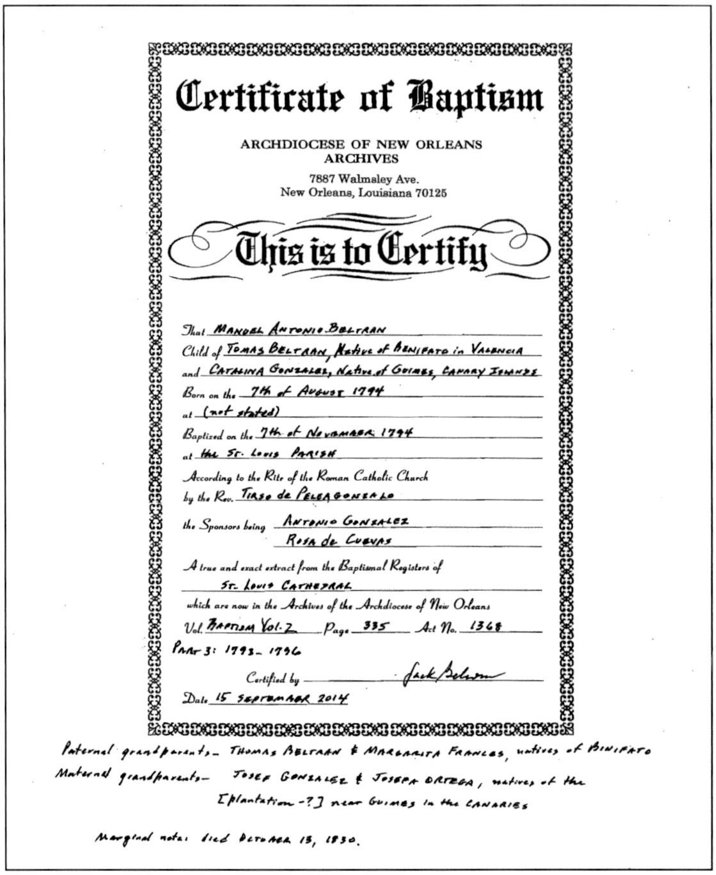

Certificate of Baptism

ARCHDIOCESE OF NEW ORLEANS
ARCHIVES
7887 Walmsley Ave.
New Orleans, Louisiana 70125

This is to Certify

That MANUEL ANTONIO BELTRAN
Child of TOMAS BELTRAN, Native of BENIFATO in VALENCIA
and CATALINA GONZALEZ, Native of GUIMES, CANARY ISLANDS
Born on the 7th of AUGUST 1794
at (not stated)
Baptized on the 7th of NOVEMBER 1794
at the ST. LOUIS PARISH
According to the Rite of the Roman Catholic Church
by the Rev. TIRSO de PELEAGONZALO
the Sponsors being ANTONIO GONZALEZ
ROSA de CUEVAS
A true and exact extract from the Baptismal Registers of
ST. LOUIS CATHEDRAL
which are now in the Archives of the Archdiocese of New Orleans
Vol. BAPTISM Vol. 2 Page 335 Act No. 1368
PART 3: 1793–1796
Certified by Jack Belsom
Date 15 SEPTEMBER 2014

Paternal grandparents – THOMAS BELTRAN & MARGARITA FRANCES, natives of BENIFATO
Maternal grandparents – JOSEF GONZALEZ & JOSEFA ORTEGA, natives of the [plantation-?] near GUIMES in the CANARIES

Marginal note: died OCTOBER 13, 1830.

FIGURE 6.13
Certificate showing the baptism of Manuel Antonio Beltran, November 7, 1794. Prepared by Jack Belsom, 2014, extract of entry, Saint Louis Cathedral, New Orleans, Baptisms, vol. 2, 1786–1796, p. 335, no. 1368. Courtesy of the Office of Archives and Records, Archdiocese of New Orleans. A "certificate" or "extract" is the name given to the document attesting to a sacramental record. A certificate, not the record or a copy of the record, is issued to genealogists. Only scholars can use the actual records. The certificate format has varied over the years, and examples from the early 1800s are available in family papers. Certificates from the early twentieth century from nearby cities such as Mobile, Alabama, seem not to be as elaborate (in imitation of the ceremonies they represent) as the Saint Louis Cathedral ones.

Belsom is a longtime volunteer in the Archdiocese Archives. As he noted, to understand genealogy, one must learn the city itself, or "any place your ancestors lived. And by this I don't mean just knowing who settled there but really who was there keeping the records." He commented:

> From the late part of the nineteenth century the Catholic Church here established what they called national churches to deal with the immigrants. So up in the Irish Channel, you used to have three churches within a two-block radius. You still have Saint Alphonsus–which was the Irish church. Right across the street, Saint Mary's Assumption–which was the German church. On Jackson Avenue a block away, it was destroyed after the 1920-something hurricane, was the French church, Notre Dame. So you had three big Catholic churches within a three-block area serving the immigrant population, and those were the, quote, national churches. Downtown, the national German church was Holy Trinity and the French church, which was on the other side of Rampart Street, was Annunciation Church.

This again is the landscape of the city genealogists love to learn about.

In the late 1970s and early 1980s, the archdiocese began to gather all the parish records into the central archives. They also began another project that endeared them to genealogists. This was the release of abstracts in book form of the sacramental records in different parishes, which "came out for many years, and, in essence, began to make the records more available than they had ever been." *The Sacramental Records of the Roman Catholic Church of the Archdiocese of New Orleans*, now in nineteen volumes, covers the period 1718–1831 and "provides entries for births, marriages, confirmations and burials for those persons with legible surnames." Although lacking notations of race, which are highly prized by genealogists, the *Sacramental Records* volumes eventually covered churches in the present civil parishes of Jefferson, Orleans, Plaquemines, Saint Bernard, Saint Charles, Saint John the Baptist, and Saint Tammany. Some of the early acts took place throughout New France in places such as Old Biloxi, Rapides, Mobile, Natchez, Natchitoches, Illinois Territory, and Quebec.[33]

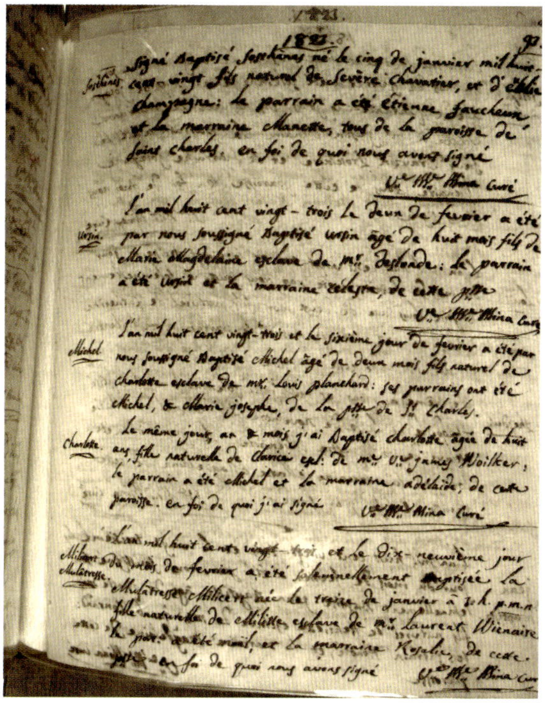

FIGURE 6.14
Page from baptismal records for people of color, 1823. Saint John the Baptist, Edgard, Baptisms, PC, vol. 7, 1818–1825. Courtesy of the Office of Archives and Records, Archdiocese of New Orleans.
Note that the listing of names on the right-hand side of the page only includes first names, as was the custom for people of color. Note also, at the bottom of the page, Milicent Mulâtresse, another designation evocative of what was included and excluded in records, even though here the book was for all people of color.

It was rare in general for Catholic dioceses and archdioceses to have published such volumes. The diocese of Baton Rouge set the precedent when, in 1978, it began compiling an ambitious series listing names from the sacramental registers, publishing them in twenty-two volumes.[34] An even earlier precedent was set in 1974 by the Reverend Donald J. Hébert in his thirty-five volume set entitled *Southwest Louisiana Records*, which compiled church and civil records.[35]

Selected dioceses, parishes, and genealogical societies in Canada, New Mexico, and Mobile, Alabama, are among the few other establishments that have offered similar, but smaller, publications. Some diocesan archives in other places have sacramental records available in microfilm but not in book form.[36] Yet the books are not the records themselves. The books contain merely a listing, which is frustrating to genealogists.

The Church has its reasons for privacy. Even though the records *may function* as vital statistics, in courts, they are not exactly so. They are "sacred records" and, according to the Church, therefore deserving of confidentiality. They were not always even considered *in part* as vital statistics. As genealogist Winston De Ville recalled, "The former chancellor [1962–1992] of the Archdiocese of New Orleans, Msgr. Earl Woods, loved to tell genealogists that church records were NOT public records and researchers could look at them only with his permission. That permission was not granted to genealogists."[37]

In requesting a certificate for a sacramental record, a genealogical researcher must know the name of a particular person or request copies of particular microfilm images. There are many reasons the copy is not satisfactory to genealogists. "It is not real, it is not the record" is the first reason. Context is not available in the copy either; there is no chance to see the handwriting, no chance to consider how the record is dated or what other entries surround one's ancestor's entry. Copying also means that errors can be made. The archdiocese is straightforward in acknowledging that in writing the certificates mistakes can be made, but for family historians, finding a slip of the hand is discouraging. As all family historians are told in general about all records, each time a record is copied, there is always a chance for error, "but one cannot help but lament when a typographical error meant that 1813 was written for what should have been 1913," as one genealogist noted.[38] Another genealogist claimed that archivists there "who can read eighteenth-century French and Spanish adequately are far and few between." She would have rather "tried her own eyes and resources" in deciphering the handwriting of the priests.[39]

Academic and public scholars, too, have been barred from these records. Writing in her 1991 book on free people of color under the Spanish in New Orleans, historian Kimberly Hanger described her experiences:

> Since the 1970s the Archdiocese Archives of New Orleans has not permitted researchers access to colonial sacramental records, with the exception of one or two individuals who have "the right connections." I have petitioned several times to gain access and submitted referral letters that attest to my capabilities and sensitivities as a professional researcher. All to no avail. The archdiocese's official position is that the sacramental records are personal documents belonging to the Catholic Church and are under litigation at the time.[40]

On the other hand, six genealogists in the city urged caution in such condemnations. To them, there was reason for privacy. Belsom noted especially that there was a reason for

> a "wall" between [the archdiocese] and the "state," i.e., civil authorities, [maintaining Catholic records as] private rather than public. I rather suspect, also, that its reluctance to open them to researchers in many cases stemmed from wanting to avoid litigation on sensitive topics. . . . For example, I distinctly recall—although now I can't identify the priest or the baptismal book—where, in the baptism of a child with a *père inconnu*, the priest wrote something like "the father of the child is reputed to be," the kind of thing that could have led to a lawsuit. I think legitimacy, even more than racial mixture, was the chief concern.

Another person reminded herself that she should consider what the Church had done "right," not what they had done "wrong. The records are inclusive of everyone who lived in the city, who were born here or converted to the Church," she noted. Even if she does not have access to the registries, "they are there," and that is to be respected, especially so considering earlier racial segregation. At least "they included everyone, from whatever background."[41]

A project to digitize some of the sacramental records has ended some

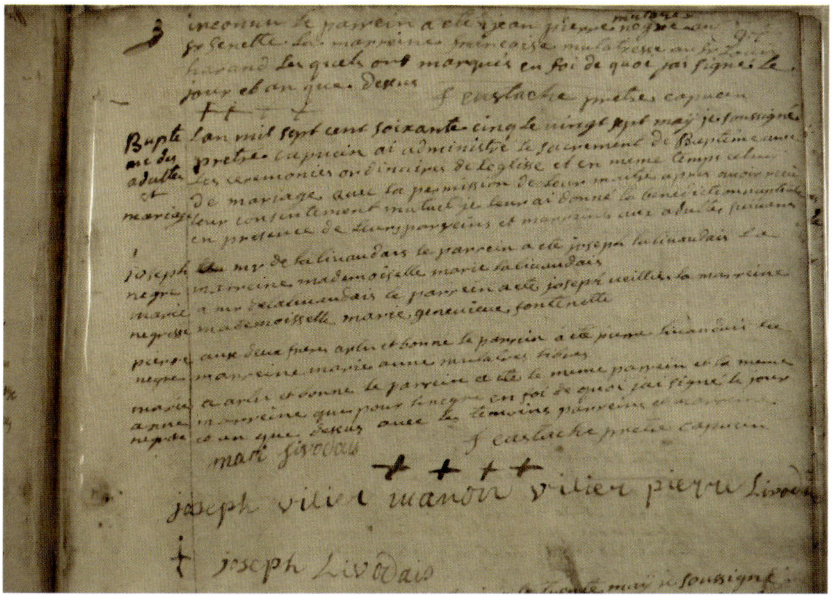

FIGURE 6.15
Baptême des adultes et mariage of Joseph Livaudais and Marie and others. Saint Louis Cathedral, New Orleans, Baptisms and Marriages, vol. 5, 1763–1767, p. 94. Courtesy of the Office of Archives and Records, Archdiocese of New Orleans.

In this record, all four parties signed the register with a mark of "x." While literacy was high among women in colonial Louisiana, something that family historians attribute to the work of the Ursulines, it was not uniformly so. The handwriting of the priest was not always legible either.

of the complaints. During the years 2012 to 2015, the "Slave and Free People of Color Baptismal Records in the Archives" from 1777 to 1812 were put online. The choice of these records, rather than others, seems like compensation from the Church. The digital records about the ancestors of African Americans show "openness," genealogists said. The change came, one said, "not only from [varying] views toward the lives of African Americans . . . but also because the archbishop himself understood the needs of those seeking the records. . . . The current archbishop of New Orleans is a native of Louisiana. . . . Understanding . . . the community that came from growing up here prompted the archbishop to make the records available."[42]

Again, New Orleans family historians feel luckier than those in other places.

Obituaries and the Story Their Indexing Tells about Genealogists, Librarians, and Archivists

Unlike the Archdiocese Archives, the New Orleans Public Library stands, as most libraries do, welcoming and open to all. Among those documents most widely used there in the past by genealogists was a huge and always growing catalog card file containing names and dates of obituaries.

Obituaries, while not strictly an archival record type, are a form of information fundamental to family history research. The circumstances surrounding the creation of the *Louisiana Biography and Obituary Index*, called by most the *New Orleans Obit Index*, highlight the importance of death notices and the constancy of family historians to their craft. The *Obit Index* is today an online list of articles about persons who died between 1804 and 1972. Its publication on the Internet follows almost one hundred years of compilation. It appeared online in the same year that it was, in part, made obsolete by a tool that family historians before the Internet age could not even have imagined: GenealogyBank.com, which contains well over 200 million obituaries and death records including scans of the original newspapers, and an index of 1.3 billion newspaper articles. As one blogger noted for the 2006 debut of this resource, this is similar to a "genealogy library containing 100,000 books" in which "you can search all the books simultaneously, finding any word or phrase in any book within seconds."[43]

FIGURE 6.16
Indexing the city's newspapers, ca. 1941. Photograph. Courtesy of the Louisiana Division and City Archives, New Orleans Public Library.
WPA workers were among the first to index the city's newspapers, both for obituaries and for news articles. They thought of obituaries as local history. Their work continued under the City Archives, then the City Library, then volunteer genealogists, then via a joint effort of the library and the Historic New Orleans Collection, until the early 2000s. First created in a card catalog, the index was produced in a digital version in 2006.

At the same time, New Orleans family historians don't forget how precious and valuable the New Orleans Public Library's millions of cards once were, and how the online *Obit Index* is valuable because it is free, open, and most importantly their own city's achievement. It contains a few sources that GenealogyBank missed, as well. "Right up there with our music [and] our food, our *Obituary Index* is one of the treasures of America," said one genealogist.[44] New Orleans is the only large city in the United States to have such an index.[45]

In addition, the *Obit Index* reflects a local fascination with New Orleans publications and, more centrally, on the work of the City Archives, itself a rarity in that it has operated since the eighteenth century. Very few repositories elsewhere have had the same sort of continuing central role that the New Orleans's City Archives has had. Indeed, municipal archives in the United States were few and far between before the mid- to late twentieth century. One 1970s writer penned an article titled "The Shame of the Cities: Public Records of the Metropolis."[46] No such shame for New Orleans, where, nevertheless, in the 1930s the WPA saw much work to do on the archives' department newspapers.

This indexing work was divided into a general news index and an obituary index, and it continued until 1942, when WPA work ended.[47] Others would continue it, later, of course, working periodically into the twenty-first century, largely because of the city's passion for genealogy. These evolutions tell a story of assistance from family historians and philosophies about genealogy and archives, and that story begins in 1946, when the city government decided to move the City Archives from the magnificent but crowded Gallier Hall to the Public Library. There were the card indexes themselves to move, and then the whole of the archives, with records dating to the 1700s. From 1946 to 1952, the library worked to accomplish this physical transition.

FIGURE 6.17
Newspapers stacked in a City Archives storage area, ca. 1940. Photograph. Courtesy of the Louisiana Division and City Archives, New Orleans Public Library.

The first newspaper in New Orleans was *Le Moniteur de la Louisiane*, which began in 1794. As early as the 1850s, the City Archives made it part of their mission to collect all newspapers printed in New Orleans.

The change was not exactly a smooth one. It required uniting different philosophies of providing access to materials. The archives had been run in the manner of a European archive, where archivists thought not of subject access but of the creators of documents and the order in which the records were created. Researchers were not permitted to use materials until completion of a lengthy interview process overseen by as many as four archivists. Researchers could wait for days for their requested materials to be placed on the desk assigned to them in the archives.[48]

In the move to the New Orleans Public Library, the librarians wanted to change these practices. They visited and corresponded with other archives, notably the Mississippi State Archives (one of the oldest in the nation and, of course, a neighbor); LSU's Special Collections Department; and the Illinois State Archives. Advice from the last institution is especially significant, since Illinois was a leader in early and rare efforts to assist genealogists.[49]

The *Obit Index* fit well enough with what the librarians had learned from these other institutions. In addition, newspaper collections, always a specialty of the City Archives, made sense to the librarians. Newspapers had, after all, titles and could be easily cataloged. The WPA work on the cards involved some subject access (names of people), an approach involving library principles; more importantly, creating access to information on people from the past would mean gaining the support of a large segment of library users, genealogists. The library's collection of New Orleans newspapers dated to 1794 and so was considered important to archivists as well. Thus, work on the index would continue for over half a century. The librarians and archivists could only work intermittently on the index, and so they involved many volunteer genealogists, and, in the past decade, staff paid by the Historic New Orleans Collection. As the index's website says today: "What began life in the first half of the 20th century as an ambitious effort to make biographical information more readily accessible has now been transformed, through the technology of the 21st century, into a research tool that the index's originators could not have imagined possible."

The Public Library and the City Archives within it are located today in a very different kind of milieu than the neoclassical Gallier Hall, the Carnegie-built library on Lee Circle, or the Historic New Orleans Collection with its wood-paneled, high-ceilinged research center located in a Beaux Arts–style building on Chartres Street. The 1958 New Orleans Public Library has a steel *bris soleil* or sunshade, a design of a series of open blocks that allow light to filter through. Pollution from cars and buses and other sources has now dirtied these clean lines and walls of glass. Inside, on the third floor and right across from the City Archives, is an interior courtyard where smokers and homeless people find a place to rest. Yet genealogists see the library as central to their work; a cohort of them, the same some half-dozen persons, come almost every day, and it is a stop for all visiting genealogists. The professionalism of the staff there befits the records they house, not only the beginning of the *Obit Index* project but the earliest Cabildo records, yet another pillar of colonial recordkeeping. The building also befits the records, protecting them in a way that might not be apparent on first glance. The building, its basement filled with records, was designed by Nathaniel Curtis and Arthur Q. Davis. Curtis told librarians that the building would not flood, and it remained dry following Hurricane Katrina, while just next door water reached the second floor of Tulane University's Medical Center.[50]

Margaret Ruckert (1914–2011), head of the City Archives from 1942 to 1968, oversaw the transfer of the archives to the library. Her successor was Collin Hamer (served 1969–2004), and it was Hamer who initiated other programs for genealogists in the library and continued the work of making archival practices fit with library ones through genealogists. He collaborated with members of the LDS not only in microfilming but also in finding many records in warehouses, city offices, and courthouses. He literally rescued nineteenth-century civil court records and vital records when a call came that they would be dumped on the streets.[51] As Hamer noted, characteristically modest as public librarians are, or perhaps just

FIGURE 6.18
WPA worker in survey of New Orleans records during the Survey of Federal Archives Louisiana, ca. 1937. Photograph. Courtesy of Historic New Orleans Collection (1981.310.36).
The WPA Guide to New Orleans is generally hailed as a model for other states due to the leadership of Lyle Saxon, but the research for the guide was also facilitated by the abundance and knowledge of records of the state.

tired by the many duties his work involved without adequate funding: “The civil court records were headed to an unsupervised, un-airconditioned warehouse near the river front where they were destined to be destroyed by roaches, rats and mildew. Officers of the Genealogical Research Society of New Orleans tipped me off about it and we negotiated a permanent loan of the material.”[52] As several of the LDS microfilmers and twelve family historians noted, the library staff there has often taken the extra steps needed to ensure the safety of records.[53] To the community of genealogists, the public library is at the center of their lives, and the librarians there are nothing short of heroes.

Forging Identities

These public and Church records, these obituaries and access to them, represent something little known outside the communities of genealogists, historians, archivists and librarians, priests, civil servants, attorneys and notaries, architects, and a few others who have had reason to trace the past. Perhaps that is a large enough community, large enough anyway to make continual demands for the materials. In these demands, genealogists especially forge their personal identities, but also ones of the city, by making stories. The stories are sometimes about the records themselves, joining disparate strands of the past into simple questions: what was written down, what was preserved, what is here now for me to test out my theories, what can let me understand how my ancestors lived? Like Sonja McCarthy believed, the records give a richness to lives being lived, and “lives once lived.”

CHAPTER SEVEN

One Account: Many Branches in Family Trees

The enormity of family history rests upon a foundation of huge numbers of seekers, huge numbers of records, instances of hierarchy within democracy, a positivist background, and yet a populist tradition welcoming and tolerant across many boundaries. No one represented these varying perspectives better to me than Augusta Elmwood (b. 1947) who, like most of the other genealogists in this book, is a lifelong New Orleanian. She descends from eighteenth- and early nineteenth-century immigrants from France, Saint-Domingue, and Genoa, and from nineteenth-century immigrants from Germany, Portugal, and Poland. From all of them except the French Cossé family, Elmwood remembered humble attachments: "nothing big, nothing showy," she told me.

FIGURE 7.1
Cotton and silk dress for crowning ceremony, 1913. Photograph by Yuka Petz. Courtesy of Augusta Elmwood.

More so than the others, Elmwood has a distinctive New Orleans accent that suggests the deeper tones and inflections of French and other languages. She was always good at German in school and now speaks flawless French. She has traveled often and owns a small house in Spain. About her ancestors, Elmwood began with myths, large ones and local ones:

> We are, most Americans and New Orleanians here specifically, a people convinced of a promised land and knowledgeable now enough to know this promised land will never be reached, that its pursuit itself will be tiring. But think why they left and what they had to do to get here. The message is *you try in life*.

For her, the private stories of adversity, love, and even the slightest moments proclaiming some joy—these details of life are the interesting parts of history, and yet they are so often left out of academic history. "They are eclipsed, always, every day, for schoolchildren. Schoolbooks," she said, "do not show how little one brings on a ship across the sea; or how poor one's family once was in another country; or even how little is documented about every life." She then turned to the scarcity of records concerning

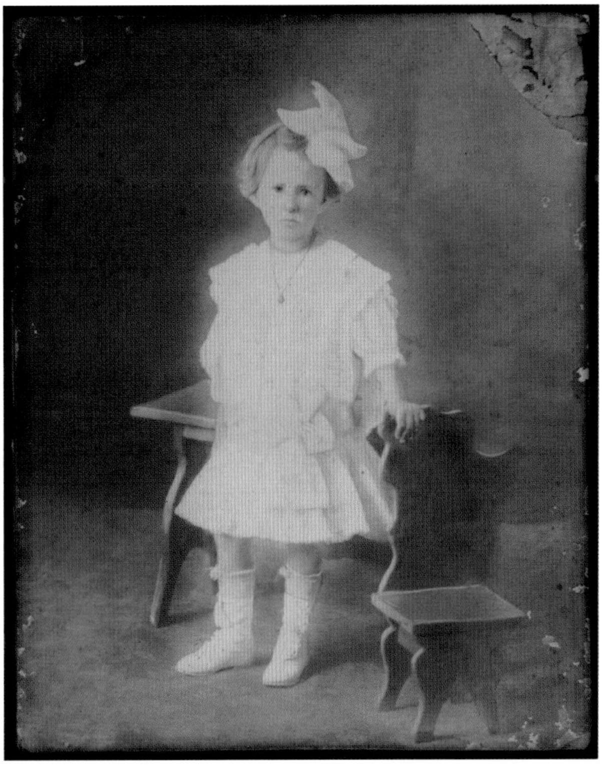

FIGURE 7.2
Agnes Mary Bethancourt, dressed for crowning ceremony, 1913. Studio print. Courtesy of Augusta Elmwood. Not only did the family retain this dress but they also tell a story about it, of both a practical and social nature. Walking home from the Star of the Sea Church, where she had placed a wreath of flowers on a statue of the Virgin Mary, a little girl fell into a deep gutter of water, a familiar feature at that time on New Orleans streets. Her mother wanted to punish her for arriving home with her dress coated in mud. A neighbor begged for leniency toward the child; she took the dress, washed it, sprinkled it in corn meal, and rolled it up. With repeated efforts the dress came clean, to be worn again by children in successive generations.

one of my ancestors . . . named Dominique Cossé. Now I know something about him because his father-in-law, Bacas, devoted about four pages of his will to this son-in-law. He especially wants everyone to know what he had done wrong to his daughter. The will is written in 1817, and apparently the son-in-law had gone through all the family money. "*Il a mangé tout*"–"He's eaten everything up"–I think the father-in-law said. Cossé is not to be found in the census or anywhere else after 1810. But he is alive since [he is] in the will. I couldn't find him in any records. But one day, when I was looking for something else–I was in the Mint [the Historical Center of the State Museum] scrolling through microfilm and I just happened to see his name fly by, the name Cossé and a reference to the notary Broutin. 1791. So I went there to an inventory of the estate of one Don Frederico Carlos Villain. From this estate, "Dominque Cossé dit Chevalier" purchased one "libro titulado Sobre el Blazon." He bought a heraldry book! He also bought a lot of other materials–expensive clothing and other books. So, like I said, I cannot find him in Louisiana after 1810, but I believe that the book then stayed with the family, long enough to suggest such lofty ancestors as Roman senators within a noble French family, within a humble one here in Louisiana. Perhaps Dominique showed his daughter and other family members the book so that they would know the heraldry he wished them to see, so that they could understand him.

I liked this story for many reasons: the serendipity of research (*I was looking for something else*), the simultaneous readiness (the recognition of the notary's name and that of her ancestor), and the explicit reference

FIGURE 7.3
Research notes, "From the Notarial Records of Francisco Broutin." Courtesy of Augusta Elmwood.
This shows the trail of Augusta's work as she discovered that her ancestor had purchased a heraldry book.

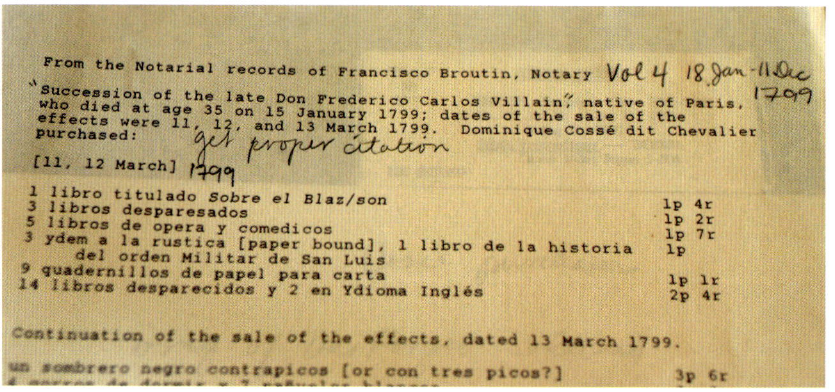

From the Notarial records of Francisco Broutin, Notary Vol 4 18 Jan-11 Dec 1799

"Succession of the late Don Frederico Carlos Villain," native of Paris, who died at age 35 on 15 January 1799; dates of the sale of the effects were 11, 12, and 13 March 1799. Dominique Cossé dit Chevalier purchased: get proper citation

[11, 12 March] 1799

1 libro titulado Sobre el Blaz/son	1p 4r
3 libros desparesados	1p 2r
5 libros de opera y comedicos	1p 7r
3 ydem a la rustica [paper bound], 1 libro de la historia del orden Militar de San Luis	1p
9 quadernillos de papel para carta	1p 1r
14 libros desparecidos y 2 en Ydioma Inglés	2p 4r

Continuation of the sale of the effects, dated 13 March 1799.

un sombrero negro contrapicos [or con tres picos?] 3p 6r

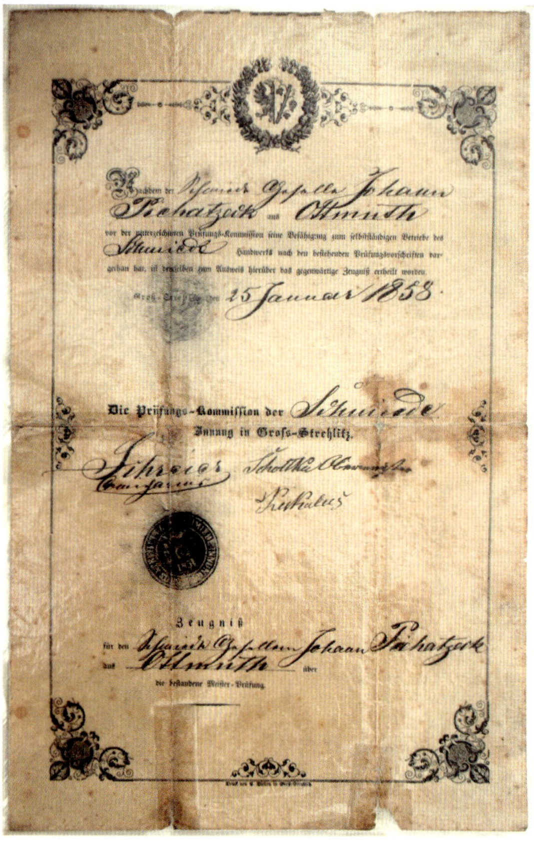

FIGURE 7.4
Detail from Polish document, ca. 1870. Photograph by Yuka Petz. Courtesy of Augusta Elmwood.

to the aspirations of so many families for nobility (*He bought a heraldry book!*). As Elmwood noted about this find: "I may be a bit paranoid but, because of the way he appeared and disappeared from New Orleans and because of the time period—the French Revolution—I suspect he may have been a fake, a deceiver, looking to marry his way into a well-off New Orleans family. Did he use the heraldry book to create for himself a set of very honorable and noble ancestors? In any case, according to his daughter's obit in *Le Meschacébé*, the family believed he was a member of a noble family."

Family history in general is framed within many families by such stories, told and retold, tested and retested. Family history is also embedded often with this reputation of the desire for nobility, or more often with the desire for some connection to the well known, but this impulse also is transformed as it has been here. Elmwood knew enough to doubt, to suggest humility.

In Elmwood's accounts, I also heard about the intersections of public and private records. Her mother was a "great album maker." Besides gathering memorabilia for her grandchildren, "she had her rituals, and every August third, she would take out this picture and she would say this is Johann Piechaczek and he was born in Ottmult, Prussia, it was at the time," Elmwood recalled, adding her own connection. "He was my great-great-grandfather."

From his life, she had "some kind of document, the sale of a part of a stand in a market to a man named Matthias Rygol." She also found his service record and his master smith certificate. He was a gunsmith and

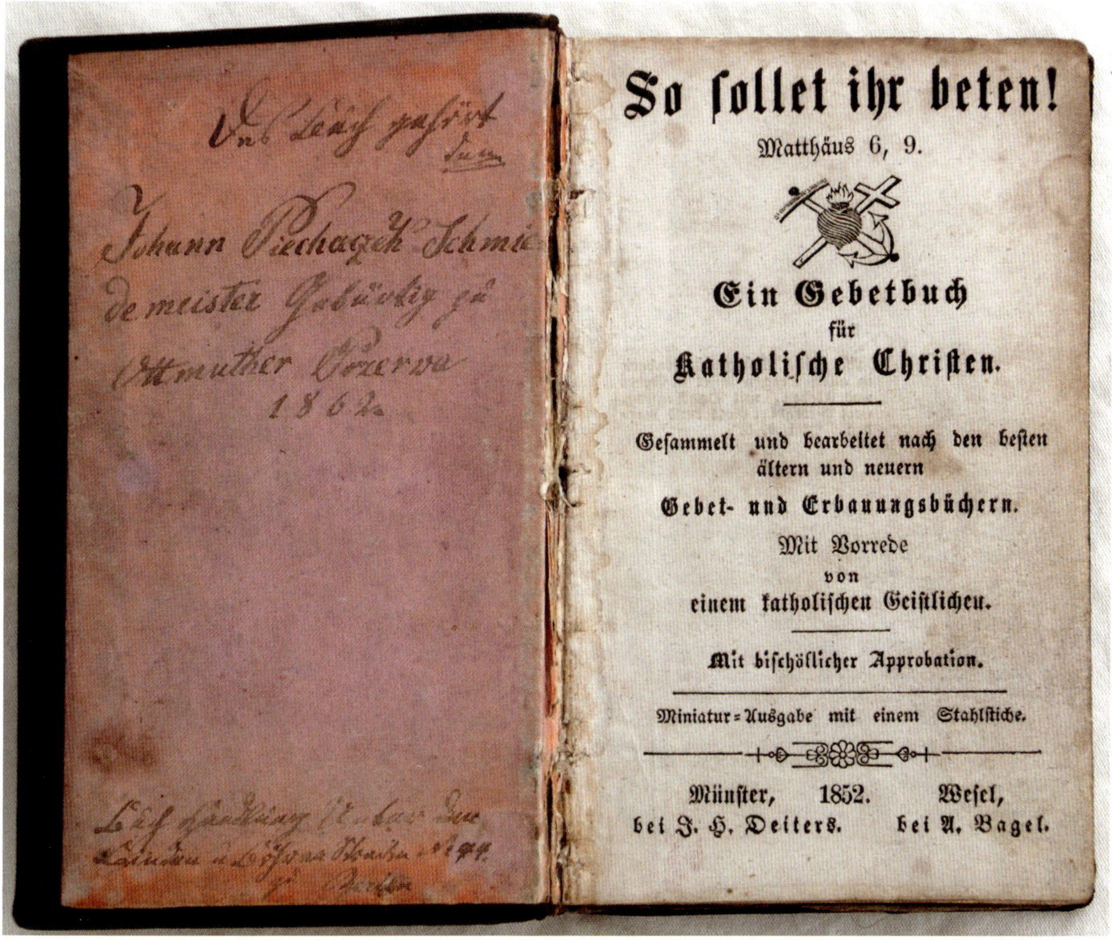

FIGURE 7.5
Inscription within a prayer book brought from Prussia in the 1870s to New Orleans by Johann Piechaczek. Courtesy of Augusta Elmwood.

a locksmith, and these documents were evidence that "he had passed some exams, some apprenticeship"—proof that the family retained. She has some business cards, too, of his.

That was on her mother's mother's maternal side. From her paternal side, Elmwood showed me three letters concerned with the Bethancourt/Bettencourt family. The three letters were addressed to Elmwood's ancestor, João or José de Bettencourt de Ataide, in the city of Boston from his parents in the Azores.

Such documents represent the past in the same way that a record in an archives, in a repository of official records, would. They show a transaction that has become historical. Elmwood told me that she was working again on her Polish ancestor because she is curious about "how he got here, what leaving meant, the struggle of knowing he had to leave one place and go to another."

She considered the quantity and the quality of her accumulations, kept in boxes, as she pulled out papers, fabric, photographs, and other memorabilia (a smoking hat and, of course, albums) to show me what

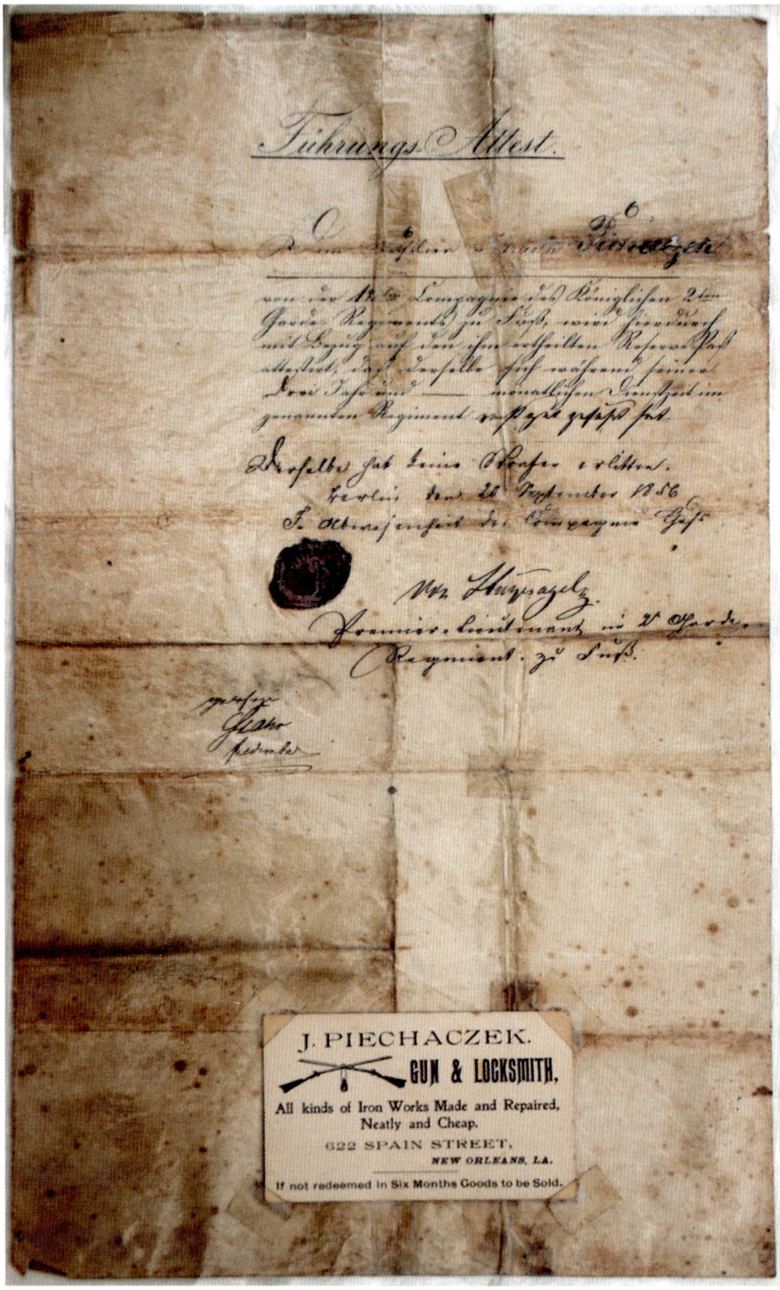

FIGURE 7.6
"Führungs Attest," brought by immigrant ancestor Johann Piechaczek to New Orleans in the 1870s. Courtesy of Augusta Elmwood.
Apprenticeship papers such as these had a practical value to an immigrant and, later, evidentiary value to family historians. The business card in English shows us that Piechaczek found work for which he had been trained.

FIGURE 7.7
Letter from parents in the Azores to their son, a new Boston resident, 1844. Courtesy of Augusta Elmwood.

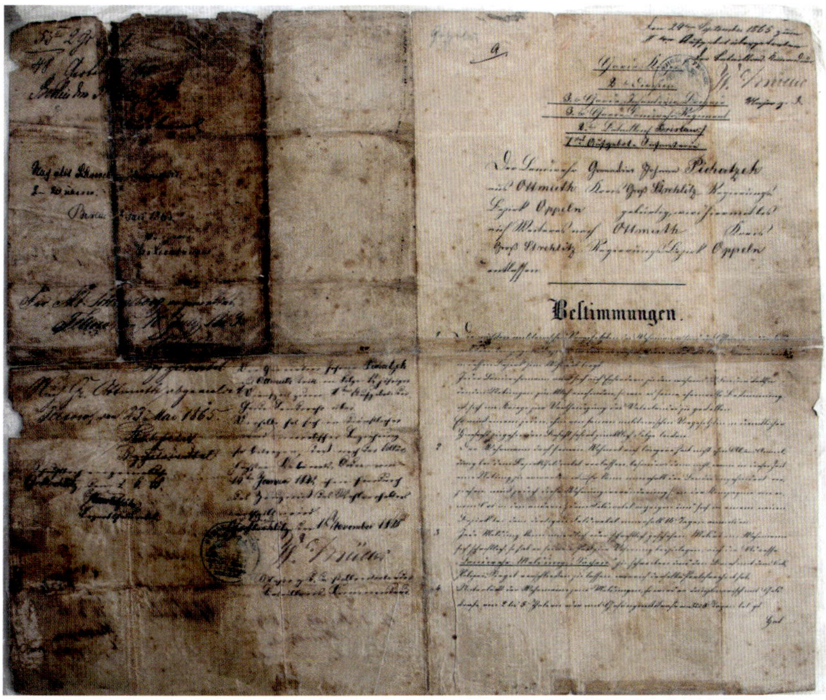

FIGURE 7.8
Smoking hat from the Polish side of the family, ca. 1890. Photograph by Yuka Petz. Courtesy of Augusta Elmwood. Fabrics are some of the most perishable of family heirlooms, hence especially valued.

FIGURE 7.9
Military papers from the Prussian army, ca. 1869. Courtesy of Augusta Elmwood.

she had long saved: "Some people have nothing, but of course some people have piles and piles of letters and portraits and stuff. I am grateful for what I have and that my mother saved them and that she also passed on these memories to me."

Elmwood spoke of other ancestors who had had no chance to save such memorabilia, as they had fled the slave rebellions that would create Haiti, and even of her ancestor Cossé, fleeing France in the late eighteenth century: "If he was a nobleman, it makes sense that he would flee the revolution there." For her, contemplating the objects was "another part of the privilege of genealogy."

She considered then again to me, Dominique Cossé. He had had

FIGURE 7.10
Saint Roch's Cemetery, New Orleans. Photograph by Yuka Petz.

enough money to buy the heraldry book and to be recorded in an estate record, now still available in a notarial record. His daughter, Josephine Cossé (later, Berthelot), had reason to believe, disbelieve, or ignore her father's nobility. He was known, after all, as a scoundrel, and was specifically mentioned as one in her grandfather's will. She might have thought that his very bad behavior was part of his "noble" character. The New World was being formed in opposition to such men who stood only on their inherited rights. On the other hand, in the milieu of nineteenth-century trials concerned with "mixed blood," Cossé's descendants would have been glad for noble status, as one more proof that they were different. They might have wanted this distinction "considering that Cossé's brother-in-law, Barthelemy Bacas, cohabitated with and had nine children by a free woman of color, Adelaide 'Pouponne' Beaulieu." Elmwood has assembled these stories that could have shaped her ancestors.

During the time that Cossé made his life in New Orleans, there were also many other immigrants pouring into the city. Cossé's grandchildren and great-grandchildren could have been pleased with their hierarchy in the history of Louisiana. They were descendants of the older white settlers, noble or not.

Gathering

Elmwood lives on Saint Roch Avenue in one of the many houses built in the late nineteenth and early twentieth centuries. She grew up in the same neighborhood, once called New Marigny to distinguish it from the older Faubourg Marigny. Before the Civil War, these *faubourgs* (as the older neighborhoods outside the French Quarter are called) were home to one of the nation's largest populations of free people of color and, within New Orleans, one of the largest groups of German immigrants.[1] It is currently the neighborhood of choice for young and artistic people, who live alongside lifelong residents like Elmwood.

Elmwood's house is on a "key lot," meaning it faces one street and then has a long garden that runs from the back of the house parallel to the whole of the block, behind other lots. Hers is a modest shotgun house (room after room) with a side hall such that the doors of the rooms open to one's right on the path from the front door to the kitchen. Her house is unpainted, elegant, and un-air-conditioned for the most part, cooled for most of the year only by tall Victorian-era ceilings. It sits on a divided avenue whose neutral ground (median) offers shade from old oaks. Down the street, there is a well-cared-for park. It is a beautiful although crime-ridden place. Most of her nearby neighbors are African American. Elmwood is white.

FIGURE 7.11
Saint Roch's Cemetery grave, New Orleans. Photograph by Yuka Petz.

The entire neighborhood, and especially Saint Roch's cemetery, two blocks down from Elmwood's home, are the types of places one would find nowhere else in the world and the types of places family historians seek out with passion. The late nineteenth-century chapel predates the cemetery and was built under the supervision of Father Peter Leonard Thevis of Holy Trinity Catholic Church in a nearby neighborhood. During the yellow fever epidemic of 1868, Father Thevis evoked the good works of a fourteenth-century French priest (later Saint Roch) who had cured hundreds during an outbreak of the plague in various Italian cities. In New Orleans, Father Thevis's prayer worked; rumor has it that no one from his church died of yellow fever in that particular season. He built a chapel dedicated to the saint. It was completed in 1876 and resembles a small Gothic church. The overwhelming feeling of both the chapel and the cemetery is one of whiteness in sunshine.

As in other New Orleans cemeteries, there are aboveground "houses of the dead." Also as elsewhere in the city, there are four sides of walls that contain smaller vaults, pocket doors (called "ovens") for the remains of the less affluent. In one corner of the chapel, people have hung plastic and ceramic replicas of body limbs, polio braces, and crutches—signs of healing or wishes for healing.[2]

They are literal "accumulations." Sigmund Freud, in pursuit of the traces on the "mystic writing pad," would have been pleased to visit.[3] So would others who have worked on the layers of literal archival materials, on the complications of remembering, as Elmwood has.[4] South African archivist Verne Harris emphasized that, in uncovering the different places where a society accumulates records, we come to "the heart of archival endeavour—disclosure of context."[5] This neighborhood and indeed the work of Elmwood and so many genealogists revealed just those contexts of the past as they are brought to use in the present.

Like others interested in family history, Elmwood spoke about both European and local settings, and a sense of herself as growing through the pursuit of family lines:

> I've been doing this since the mid-1980s and I have now a complete college education pursuing my ancestors. I can speak now French and German. I can read some in Portuguese. I can read the old German script . . . and I've learned about weather patterns, I've learned about politics. I've learned about sociology and history, of course. At some point it stops being a collection of names, places, and dates. It becomes why and where and what was going on. It broadens your worldview. It takes off the blinders and you realize there is something besides your immediate life.

As if studying genealogy, history, and archival science at once, Elmwood said, records are "a true snapshot of both the bleakness and the triumph of life. The record is actually what happened, the nuts and bolts. It can't be twisted about or manipulated."

For her, genealogy demanded the gathering of records, the search for patterns, the construction of questions about the patterns, and the disruption of patterns. Who was a witness at a marriage, who was the godmother at a baptism, how many children survived to adulthood, who were the neighbors and what were their occupations, and what church registered their births, marriages, and deaths? And why, suddenly, does one ancestor pick up belongings and move? For family historians, these discoveries yield "an iterative process," an ongoing search that builds question upon question.[6]

Eric Ketelaar provides a starting point for this incremental building of questions as both a consequence and an example of *archivalization*: "the conscious or unconscious choice (determined by social and cultural factors) to consider something worth archiving."[7] Family historians decide to collect materials, and they use materials that have been collected.

Here, there is a continuum of reciprocity where oral accounts and personal and official practices come together to define what counts as a representation of the past. Family historians also create new materials and make new records, a process by which the past and present become part of one another.[8] Archivalization and later stages in genealogical inquiries are considered parts of *collective memory*, the socially organized or mediated representation of the past created via socially produced artifacts, and held in common by a group.[9]

In her talk with me, Elmwood made vivid these concepts of collective memory. She spoke of circling back to records, of retracing her steps as she found the children born of a second wife rather than a first. She spoke of learning to work with forms, of finding a way to rapidly make a document readable and of searching for hints that point to authenticity. About some French records that were in tattered condition when microfilmed, she noted: "I learned to look first for the extract of the record and then to scroll down the signatures on the right side of the page. When I found a signature of the family, or a neighbor, then I could go and take time with going through the whole record." She also noted that the reliability of a name, say, of her ancestor Dominique Cossé, is only as good as what he said. Similarly, the reliability of the sacramental records depends on the priest who wrote the record. "Since the French registers [of slaves and people of color] have gone online, I have railed at many a seventeenth-century priest who filled these precious record books with illegible names and dates," she added.

There is another, more emotional approach, however, collectively held by many family historians; they often refer to ancestors "leading" them to sources, to specific insights. When Elmwood found "the right name" in a registry, it was a "sign" not only about how she has learned to work but also, at least at times, of "the ancestors talking."[10]

Other genealogists in New Orleans, finding some record by happenstance or finding a way to see the past differently, similarly spoke of "hearing the voices of the dead." Elmwood qualified how these ancestors speak, nonetheless. It is a cumulative process involving a trip to the church registry office centuries ago, with decisions made to keep copies and with instructions on filing them so they can later be retrieved. It is the enlargement of collective memory and its materiality: the papers saved from war and fire, the departing family and what they brought to prove they could leave and to prove who they were, their New Orleans lives. Then there was her own process of return, to the records in France or on microfilm via Salt Lake City and the LDS satellite library in suburban Metairie.

Collective memory formation also can be compared to the formation of records, an analogy that extends the interpretation that scholars, especially in archival studies, can find in studying family history practices. Family historians and indeed all private recordkeepers both

FIGURE 7.12
Clipping with hair of child. Courtesy of Augusta Elmwood.

seek and create "persistent representations," and they have "prototypes" in specific inscribed records and the more distantly associative "not-quite records" of family albums and oral accounts.[11] Like record formation, memory formation also displays "recursive processes" embodying "multivalent temporality," that is, the "simultaneous presence of multiple chronologies and contexts in a single document or body of documents." Creation, capture, classification, and other steps go back to the event that is being represented, in Brien Brothman's schemata, as "a helical model" that is always complexly located in various mediating points.[12] Genealogists similarly circle back to records and stories and, as they do so, come to different conclusions even as the materials and stories themselves remain the same. Michael Young's statement in *The Metronomic Society* prevails: "The cyclical depends on the linear as much as the linear depends on the cyclical."[13]

The protective cover for Elmwood's mother's clipped obituaries was the Bible, although she did not observe any organizing structure. Elmwood was careful to tell me that her mother did not match the obituaries to any chosen biblical passages, so they have been removed, inventoried, and refiled in boxes. She is, in other words, telling why she has not kept them in the order her mother kept them, why she is not observing the original order" of archival terminology. On the other hand, she has added to the knowledge of the past as any trained archivist would do, noting the earlier arrangement on her inventory, "no particular order." Likewise, her mother preserved clippings of hair inside clippings of print. Today, as Elmwood noted, these pieces of saved material can be used in other ways, even perhaps for the study of DNA, adding future paths to knowing the past.

FIGURE 7.13
Autograph book, ca. 1917. Courtesy of Augusta Elmwood. Photograph by Yuka Petz.

Connections

Like other family historians, Elmwood extends connections from the past into the present. Family historians also form a bond with one another, and they have it in mind that their materials matter to those who follow them. This connecting function of family history concerns the transmission of knowledge through various forms and genres. Family historians make a continuum of records, taking the first record and reshaping its meaning when they find another record. All materials passed along to others "derive their significance from the different 'invisibles' they construct and from the ways in which they mediate these to spectators or users."[14] For generations, archivists thought of family history albums and other family history forms as derivative, unoriginal, and not suitable for donations to archives, but lately we have changed this thinking.

Album makers, painters, and others who approach family history from outside its records argue that their work is important because it facilitates connections among people; their work enriches our understanding of how people lived and wanted us to remember them. This belief is complemented by a certainty that records are created in a communal sense *for* the people. Many family historians recalled the 1973 Freedom of Information Act, increasing openness, transparency, and accountability in government.[15] They also discussed issues of access before the Internet: minimal open hours at archives and libraries, laws preventing access to birth certificates, the cost of travel to distant repositories, and so on.

They had some sense that they have changed, even created, the online environment. They have created access to records; they have created an environment where people contribute records. In possession of records, family historians also are growing their personal archives and posting them online for others to see. They bring then a change in the concept of "consignation" of records.[16] Many individuals and groups now share authority over the past; authority is no longer restricted to the historians but shared with other researchers, the LDS Church and other Utah Internet providers, the grand historical societies, academic collections, various levels of government, and religious bodies. Elmwood takes part in this authority over the past on her website, where she has added information, responses from others, new sources, and so on.[17]

Returning to the documents about her ancestor Cossé, "the rascal one," Elmwood showed me again his daughter's obituary. Her full name was given, its spelling somewhat different from others Elmwood has seen: Josephine *de* Cossé Berthelot (1802–1875). The obituary itself is one mediation of the past, especially since it carries forward the idea that Cossé was a "Chevalier." The obituary states that Josephine had in her possession a letter dated "le 6 mai 1874" whose goal it was to correct an error, to tell the American family about their connections in France, "rectifier une erreur . . . par un journal sur l'histoire de sa famille, le duc [a relative, according to the paper] ecrivait." He described how the Cossé family had always been a noble family, with papers from 1611 to prove it.

Elmwood noted then her recurring skepticism of this nobility and, of course, of her ancestor. But, as time goes by, she also could see the overall matter differently. She has rethought it often enough to question, and to know that there will be no single conclusion: the clipping "makes his claim to nobility—by appending 'dit Chevalier' to his name—more believable, at least in some fashion." Maybe Josephine had more correspondence than the one letter and so "was in touch with her father's family back in France; maybe Dominique returned to France when Napoleon was exiled, and maybe he maintained contact with his daughter Josephine over the years, and perhaps relatives continued to maintain the ties even after Dominique had died." Genealogy offers these sorts of cerebral reconciliations. They are sympathetic responses, which cost very little.

The obituary appeared in the newspaper *Le Meschacébé*, published from 1853 to the mid-1940s in the area of Louisiana known as the German Coast. This area was home to early eighteenth-century farmers from Germany; the French colonists had recruited them to help the starving colony. Their work and their memory as both French and German are other instances of collective memory. Elmwood looked to the German Coast in her search for Dominque Cossé. By the time of his daughter Josephine's death there, she had some one hundred grandchildren and great-grandchildren. Josephine's husband's family, the Berthelots, had arrived on the Côte des Allemands after the British takeover of the Poste des Alibamons (in present-day Alabama) in 1763. The Berthelots now appear on countless genealogical websites. These sites join cousins—many, many cousins; this joining, Elmwood says, is part of the joy of living in Louisiana. She knows a number of fellow genealogists—white and black—who turn out to be distant relatives. They all extend "generational memory," that process that links specific historical events with current identities.[18]

Websites act as other mediators of transmission. One part of Elmwood's website is called "Saint-Domingue Page: Exploring the Genealogy and History of the French Colony of Saint-Domingue (1664–1804)." Elmwood recalled that growing up, nothing was ever mentioned about this side of her family. She also recalled how, until the 1990s, New Orleanians called Saint-Domingue "San Domingo" or "Santo Domingo." This was true of the early New Orleans genealogical writers (Charles Patton Dimitry, Grace King, Stanley Arthur, George Campbell Huchet de Kernion) and also of members of the Louisiana Historical Society. As Elmwood stated:

> They didn't teach this part of our history where so many of us came from in school. It was always given a Spanish name and it was never really mentioned, never did anyone say you know this revolution in this place called Saint-Domingue changed the history of New Orleans, of Louisiana, and of the world really. It was a slave rebellion in which the white man was defeated and I guess that is why it was never discussed.

It is a curious absence for the descendants of Saint-Domingue refugees. The very use of the Spanish name for the island could be explained by noting that New Orleans was a Spanish colony when the first of those fleeing the island arrived. Yet other French words were common among the population, and the people who came were French. Many more of these Saint-Domingueans had made interim stops in Jamaica, Cuba, and even France before arriving in the new American New Orleans, and so perhaps no one name was ever given for their origins. Many were multicultural people, or of mixed origin, when they arrived.

In 1998, Elmwood established a special interest group on Saint-Domingue within the Jefferson Genealogical Society (JGS, Jefferson being the parish where many of the suburbs of New Orleans are located). The group has its own website (with a link at Elmwood's website), and its purpose is "to meet the special needs of those researchers who have a specific or general interest in the political, economic, and social history and genealogy of the French West Indies colony of Saint-Domingue."

About the open access to the website, Elmwood remarked: "It started out as being just for JGS members, but I did not feel it was right to deny access to information to those who were not members. Genealogical information should be free and available to everyone." While many webmasters and other administrators have taken similar approaches, first borrowing from an older model (and one more often economically sustainable) and then going to an open model, Elmwood's comment about genealogy being "free" and "available" is significant in other ways. Writing in 1978 about the democratization of genealogy in the immediate aftermath of *Roots*, Tamara Hareven looked to the simultaneous needs for exploration of different ethnic groups and for less exclusiveness and separatism in genealogy.[19] Elmwood showed me something about how these hopes have evolved. While the next two chapters tell of some of the divisions within and between genealogical communities, Elmwood represented the more typical response of sharing.

Recalling how she had learned that one of her ancestors had been born in Jamaica and another in Cuba, Elmwood noted on the group's website that the group is devoted to "any of the other French West Indies colonies" as well as "the island-colonies in the Caribbean and North Atlantic, belonging to Great Britain, Spain, and other European nations, as they relate to the French refugees that sought shelter on their shores, settled there, and/or married into their families."

An annoyance to Elmwood is that these people are often called "Haitians." "They were French when they left and French when they arrived. They were even kicked out of other places because they were French. The country's name was not Haiti until 1804. They were leaving to save their lives so it seems odd to call them Haitian. And besides, I think of the Haitians of the 1970s, the 1980s—the boat people—when someone says they are from Haiti." She attributes the fault to historians as well. "Perhaps they think it is more politically correct to say Haiti, or perhaps they think it does something else to say Haiti."

The special interest group on Saint-Domingue completed a project that "involved researching the National Union Catalog of Manuscript Collections [a Library of Congress catalog of manuscripts] for references to collections of colonial West Indies–related materials that exist in repositories in the United States," and completed another project "indexing the surnames" found within a 1954 dissertation entitled "French Refugees in the Southern United States in the Years 1791–1810." Members also assisted in "arranging for the microfilming of the early Catholic registers of Kingston, Jamaica." Finally, for many years the group has exchanged publications with such groups as the Généalogie et Histoire de la Caraïbe of Le Pecq, France. All their materials are available at the Jefferson Parish Library, in a suburb of New Orleans.

Elmwood's recorded family trees are broader than those of her ancestors, not only because she necessarily has more ancestors than they did but also because of the technological improvements in recordkeeping and even in the mere formalities of providing context, a necessary part of the "new genealogy." She uses statistics to understand and present her background. They are available on a web page where she has listed the names of her family branches. Here, she also tabulated the frequency of names in her own family trees: Berthelot, 3 percent; Brelet, 3 percent; Bacas, 3 percent; Jungeblut, 3 percent; Tregre, 2 percent. That is her order of family. Genetic genealogy will likely permit her descendants to confirm or change these percentages. Online family trees currently give instantaneous connection to other branches, other families, other trees—demonstrating kinship's movement across space and time.[20] Science, via DNA testing, is now giving us and will continue to give us more such connections online, no doubt.

These will all enhance collective memory, just as Elmwood's research and activities demonstrate *social memory*, as defined over the years from Maurice Halbwach's *Les Cadres de la Mémoire* (1925) and *La Mémoire Collective* (1950) to contemporary interdisciplinary memory studies. The work of Daniel R. Woolf is especially helpful; he characterized personal, community, and social memory in early modern England as necessary to collective memory. The first, personal memory, was often transmitted orally; the second, community memory, was performed (that is, transmitted in other ways as the aggregate of experiences); and the third, social memory, was "mediated" in some "narrative form."[21] As in the example of Elmwood's statistics and her website, technology today enables transmission in a combination of forms. Memory becomes both "a product and a process."[22]

Because of technology, Elmwood can view the register from a Polish village in the 1830s. In one moment, she can consult the census of 1870 in New Orleans, joining a boy born in Silesia to his self as a grown man working in New Orleans. This type of sharing involves an authentic and reliable collective and social memory, the extension of records within and beyond the archives.[23]

Elmwood can determine when her ancestor left Poland, and she can do so without talking to any official guardian of records. Here, another complexity of the Internet age becomes apparent, since there are "inherent or potential rights of others in records" and thus "challenges" to "the notion of recordkeeping as existing within the domain of one single entity. Recordkeeping of this kind becomes a dynamic relationship to be managed across time."[24] Family historians and memory keepers are centrally located as part of this dynamic relationship. One such public and private online archives, that of Rick E. Barry, shows letters, photographs, records, and texts in a project he describes as a "personal and ongoing exercise in personal electronic records."[25] In brief, he recontextualizes his family's genealogy online to give access to anyone who chooses to look.

Seeing and hearing about the steps involved in the creation of collective memory from these groups and these people, *their accumulations of materials*, therefore has the power to enlarge the understanding of the future of records and genealogy. More and more often there will be personal archives, online and in homes. Family historians, album makers, and others are part of new "recordkeeping regimes," carrying records "forward" and enabling "their use for multiple purposes by delivering them to people living in different times and spaces."[26]

Elmwood likened genealogy to collecting in general: "One gets one ancestor, one wants more." What is collecting, what purpose does it serve? Scholar Susan Stewart observed something that would be entirely recognizable to Elmwood:

> While the point of the souvenir may be remembering, or at least the invention of memory, the point of the collection is forgetting—starting again in such a way that a finite number of elements create, by virtue of their combination, an infinite reverie.[27]

Therein too rests the appeal of family history: identities are not fixed, they are moving, as more and more records reveal new interpretations. It is this movement that makes genealogy particularly appealing to Americans, to their dream of a society that is not static.

CHAPTER EIGHT

Complexities of Gender in Family History

Ina Fandrich (b. 1957) holds a doctoral degree in religious studies. She is also a genealogist, but it is her scholarly work that led me to want to interview her. That's because it is this scholarly work that allowed her time to carefully study page after page in the baptismal and marriage records of Saint Louis Cathedral—the registers themselves, not their certificates provided on request.[1]

Her approach shows the determination, precision, and critical thinking required in all work on records, but especially on records of free people of color and slaves, registered often in official documents by only their first name, and then often given inconsistent spellings for what names there are. Her approach shows, too, why genealogists rejoiced when some of the archdiocese's baptismal records of slaves and free people of color (1777–1812, for selected parishes) were made available online over the period 2013 to 2015.

I asked Fandrich to talk about genealogy also for another reason. Her best-known work is on Marie Laveau and female leadership in the nineteenth century, so I wanted to know if she had had other thoughts on how women figured in family history work.[2] I asked her if she thought women more than men seem inclined to practice family history.

She gave a qualified answer, stating that nowhere in the world has she heard so many people tell of their ancestry as in New Orleans. "This has to do with loss," she said. "For the New Orleanians have lost many battles, only winning in the War of 1812. The loss has included . . . the eradication of equality in *Plessy v. Ferguson*, and much more. All the same," she concluded, "women have had more loss, the loss *for* others, for their men, and the double burden of being segregated by gender. They become the story bearers," she said, "the storytellers, if they are lucky. They can parcel the family lore out when needed. It is part of their caretaking."

Other genealogists turned to the issue of power for women in genealogy. "Women didn't get the name you know. The family history was the compensation prize," one family historian told me.[3]

One can use current statistics to frame both these functions of caregiving and the strategic power in knowing the past. Since the early twentieth century, women have predominated within family history groups in the United States. Today, women generally make up from 65 to 71 percent

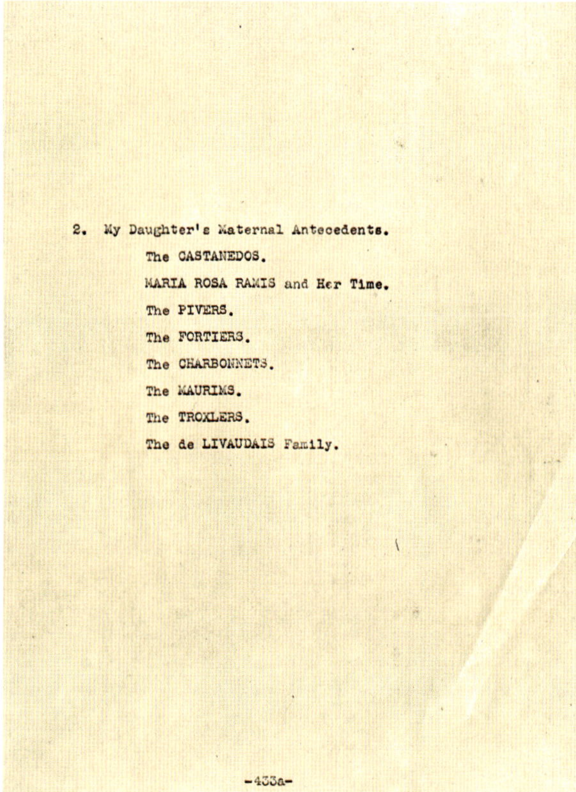

2. My Daughter's Maternal Antecedents.
The CASTANEDOS.
MARIA ROSA RAMIS and Her Time.
The PIVERS.
The FORTIERS.
The CHARBONNETS.
The MAURIMS.
The TROXLERS.
The de LIVAUDAIS Family.

-433a-

FIGURE 8.1
Title page to chapter within commonplace book: *My Daughter's Maternal Ancestors*, ca. 1940. Castaneda Genealogy Commonplace Book, David Graham Copeland Collection, Genealogical Paper Series, 504 (33), Louisiana Research Collection, Tulane University.
In genetic genealogy, the term "daughtered out" means that one cannot locate any female descendants on which to test mitochondrial DNA. On the other hand, for many long years, it meant that a family had no surviving sons to carry the family name, and thus the line was "out." This simple heading above, *My Daughter's Maternal Ancestors*, is a testament to the unusual nature of searching primarily for female ancestors.

FIGURE 8.2
Marriage contract between Jean Jacques Montfort of New Orleans, free man of color, and Marie Eulalie Blais of New Orleans, free woman of color, 1829. Personal Documents Collection 525, Louisiana Research Collection, Tulane University.
This contract lists Marie Eulalie Blais's extensive dowry, including a thirteen-year-old slave. Marriage contracts were common under civil law and often provided a woman with explicit rights to her property. Family historians note that all classes of people used such contracts. Today, the contracts almost always give plentiful information such as the names of other family members and the places of birth of the new husband and wife.

of members of such organizations.[4] Among certified genealogists in the United States, women also outnumber men. In Utah, for example, there are fifteen professional genealogists who are women and seven who are men. In Pennsylvania, there are seven women to three men. In Louisiana and Alabama, there are four women and no men.[5] In a few studies that compare goals for genealogical pursuits, academics report that men have a more public role and women a more private one in finding and using the records of the past. Most men begin family history in order to pursue a dream of publication or to fill spare time, whereas women tend to begin with an idea of connecting generations.[6] Scholars also found that women are more likely than men to assume roles concerned with sharing photographs and other records among family and friends.[7] Seemingly women have always been cast as private recordkeepers within families. An example from the European past is found in the biography of Dhuoda, a ninth-century Frankish noblewoman who lived in the prosperous area around Nîmes. Since her teenage son William had been sent from her to be groomed for leadership, she wrote a manual for him on good conduct, one part of which prescribed the necessity of knowing his paternal ancestors. "You will find written down at the end of the chapters of this book who they were and what their names were." Although Dhuoda's handbook and literacy were unusual, her emphasis on memory keeping was not. Memory was seen as a process of social commemoration to be overseen by women, embedded in "care for the dead, prayer for the salvation of the souls of kin, and child rearing."[8]

Renaissance society continued and expanded these roles for women memory keepers even as most were denied the chance to learn to read and write.[9] Women created and sought alternative forms of evidence and dissemination of family history. They took what was at hand to shape memories in the form of quilts and other textiles, oral accounts, and names given to their children.

Throughout later centuries as well, women's memory work was seen as foundational, alternative, and more informal than that of men.[10] In other words, women's part in remembering was seen as instinctual rather than learned. Even as women were finding their place in historical and genealogical work among men, leaders stressed this "natural" role for the females among them. For example, by 1825, when the president of the Historical Society of Pennsylvania attempted to make various changes that would represent a new, more inclusive American approach to understanding the past, these ancient roles of women as memory keepers were taken into consideration.[11] As William Rawle boldly reasoned in his argument for giving them entry into a hitherto all-male organization, women had "superior memories" and acted as "living records of oral traditions."[12] Similarly, when, in 1897, a few men who were described as "audacious" dared to bring up "the subject of opening the membership to women" within the New England Historic Genealogical Society, one member offered his opinion "that women were naturally interested in the records of family history—more so, probably, than men."[13]

The professionalization of history in the late nineteenth century exacerbated the marginalization of female and also male genealogists. The existence of prejudice toward genealogy was discussed earlier, but it is worth reiterating that women did attain professional status and could find employment usually in liminal positions in history and cultural fields.[14] They were also then more likely to become the "handmaids" of historians as genealogists.[15]

Male genealogists, as well, came to produce what might be called "a genre of recollection" that was given less prestige than academic history. But women's roles, built upon centuries of family memories, became the most pronounced stereotype of a genealogist.[16] To understand how often this stereotype blossomed and deviated from what was expected, however, one must look closely at individual families and see how they tell their accounts over time.

One Acadian Louisiana Story

In their shared family history, genealogist Carolyn Ivy Shimek (b. 1934) and her distant cousin, primitive artist Mary Anne de Boisblanc (b. 1925), present something of the complexity of considering that one sex more than another is the more practiced or natural family history keeper. Shimek and de Boisblanc have a common ancestor named Marie Rosalie Préjean (later Pécot, 1741–1813), and, rare among families, this female ancestor (as opposed to a male one) is the focus of their most cherished accounts. This is likely because Marie Rosalie had such a vivid, sad, and yet fruitful and long life. Her story begins in the mid-1700s when she was yet a teenager and, along with many others, was expelled from Acadia (the three present-day maritime provinces of Canada) by the British. With her brothers and a sister, she was sent to Massachusetts, then made her way to Saint-Domingue, then to Jamaica, and then to Louisiana. In the course of her life in these different places, she was married twice and widowed twice. Her second husband and one son were beheaded during the Haitian Revolution. In the exile from Acadia, two older sisters and their husbands were separated from Marie Rosalie and other family members. Some forty-five years later, the sisters, as very old women, were reunited in Louisiana.[17]

Shimek has traced all the family's various steps in becoming American. Using her cousin's findings and those located by other researchers, de Boisblanc has painted and drawn her imagination of journeys, settlements, celebrations, and other contexts of their ancestors' lives. Besides the most obvious sorrows of the expulsion from Acadia and the beheadings in Haiti, there are other tales of sickness, missed opportunities for the education of children, harsh labor, and dangerous ship voyages.

FIGURE 8.3
Autumn Reunion of the Four Préjean Sisters in Bayou Teche, Mary Anne de Boisblanc, 2004. Acrylic. Courtesy of the artist.
De Boisblanc painted the reunion of sisters who had been parted for some fifty years in *le grand dérangement*, the exile of the French from Acadia in the mid-1700s. In the early 1800s, Marie Rosalie Préjean Pécot and her family, including her younger sister, had arrived in Louisiana and only by happenstance heard that their two older sisters were living in the countryside not far away. The family story tells of a barge ride through the bayou in the evening and a celebratory bonfire. De Boisblanc included the participation of Native Americans in her art, since they had given assistance to the new arrivals in learning how to live in a new environment.

There was also a community of kinship enduring through time. She tried to show this survival in primitive works.

Before the late nineteenth century, the memories of Marie Rosalie's life were not inscribed within the family and only scantily inscribed by church and government authorities. Narratives, it is said, "simplify." The presence of a beginning, middle, and end—or an "original state of equilibrium, a disruption, and a resolution"—make the past both tenable and interesting.[18] But in genealogy this simplification can take decades, awaiting the time until the story is "needed" (thus attending to identity) and the time when records can be gathered (thus attending to evidence). For the broader Pecot family (whose name was Americanized in dropping the accent over the *e*), a story from the years 1750 to 1815 has been told in increments over more than two centuries, and told in different ways by men and women.

Shimek first encountered the family story in 1960. She found an 1890 clipping that her mother had saved that told about two granddaughters of Marie Rosalie (Hermina Bouillet Martel and Mathilde Perret) and how they had been told by their mother (a daughter of Marie Rosalie) of the family's experiences in coming to Louisiana. They spoke in French, and Hermina's grandson, Gabriel Martell, translated their words into English and wrote them down. Yet it is his father (and Hermina's son), J. Sully Martel, who was considered the "heroic custodian" of the story. In the late nineteenth century, he was the featured center of attention. He "went to great lengths to track down the story of the four exiled sisters." One of Marie Rosalie's sons, Charles Pecot, was also praised, since he was "one of the French pioneers who settled on the [Bayou] Teche."[19]

In other words, in that era, the focus was on these two grown men

FIGURE 8.4
Daily Life in Acadiana, Mary Anne de Boisblanc, 2008. Acrylic on paper. Courtesy of the artist.
De Boisblanc spoke of the networks of families she wanted her art to show. Here, she recalls her grandfather's work as doctor, and his office as also a drugstore where everyone in the little town visited from time to time.

FIGURE 8.5
Driving to Natchitoches, Mary Anne de Boisblanc, 2004. Acrylic on canvas. Courtesy of the artist.
De Boisblanc commemorated the paving of roads by Governor Huey Long's administration and her mother's ability then to attend teacher training school in Natchitoches.

rather than the female storytellers or their youthful male translator. Nevertheless, de Boisblanc was riveted by the account of the sisters' reunion, and as a genealogist she was interested in the two granddaughters who told the story.

Shimek also told of another storyteller, a distant male cousin who had published "a little book" in 2002. The cousin, Thomas Frère Kramer, reinforced J. Scully Martel's efforts in making known the story of Marie Rosalie.[20]

Disregarding questions of voice and assignation of authority, the reunion of the four sisters remains the focus of the Pecot family story. The sisters lived into old age, and had many occasions to tell of their lives and the life of their mother. They also had many children, and ultimately grandchildren and great-grandchildren, such that Shimek would say about Marie Rosalie, "Her descendants are everywhere. So they are interested in her."

De Boisblanc has painted an image of how the reunion of the sisters might have looked. She included Native American onlookers, since they are said to have helped the new arrivals. In other works, she painted the lives of their descendants, representing widows and their children on the way to Mass, the post office, and various celebrations of family life. That is, she has painted both secular and religious themes embedded in the lives of Acadian Louisiana, themes she knew in childhood but also stories that Shimek has learned through records.

De Boisblanc and Shimek link their family history to this collective memory about Acadia and Acadian Louisiana, and also to another reunion of those parted in *le grand dérangement*. This is the fictional story of Henry Wadsworth Longfellow's "Evangeline." De Boisblanc is especially moved by a statue of Evangeline in Saint Martinville, Louisiana. In one of her exhibition catalogs, she writes:

> Ever since childhood, Evangeline has had a mystical hold on me as an Acadian woman. . . . It was Evangeline's spirit that guided me to the Acadian Memorial. . . . It was here, I realized, that Marie Rosalie's story belonged. Then my Pecot cousin [here she is referring to Shimek] told me Marie Rosalie was actually buried on February 11, 1813, at St. Martin de Tours [a nearby cemetery].[21]

Symbolically, de Boisblanc then "added" Evangeline to her own family. In some of her exhibition catalogs, a photograph of the statue and a drawing of Longfellow are positioned near her own Acadian family images.[22]

Countless schoolchildren have studied Longfellow's 1847 poem, and it is worth exploring in terms of the transmission of gendered memories and the formation of public memory in general. The poem follows a young Acadian woman in her search for her lost love, Gabriel. The two have been parted from each other, much as the sisters were, during the expulsion of the French from Acadia. Longfellow based his story on a secondhand account told by a Massachusetts Episcopal priest. To learn the landscape of Louisiana, the poet relied upon his sister's telling of a journey to New Orleans. He himself also had viewed a panorama called *Three-Mile Painting*, a moving screen literally being turned so that viewers in Boston could "experience" somewhat a journey down the Mississippi River.[23] Longfellow also visited libraries and read Thomas Chandler Haliburton's *Historical and Statistical Account of Nova Scotia* (1829) and

FIGURE 8.6
Digging for Gold, Mary Anne de Boisblanc, 2007. Mixed media. Courtesy of the artist. De Boisblanc here wanted to remember the games given to children, one of which was the idea of digging for gold. The adults, meanwhile, are having a picnic. She also wanted to portray the style of houses both in Louisiana and in French Canada. Newly arrived in Louisiana, the Acadians imitated the tall slope of their earlier roofs, built for the snow they had been accustomed to in the colder climate of the north.

Guillaume Thomas François Raynal's account of the expulsion published in 1770.[24] It is notable that Longfellow did not rely upon genealogical records, although at least one scholar speculates on his use of records held by the Massachusetts Historical Society.[25]

The Saint Martinville statue of Evangeline was created by sculptor Marcelle Rebecchini during the making of the 1929 film *Evangeline*. Actress Dolores del Río, who played the role of Evangeline, paid for the monument and had it fashioned in her likeness. The statue became an immediate tourist attraction. Some fifteen thousand people, including a group of Canadian Acadians, attended its unveiling.[26]

Both the poem and the statue changed lives not only as traces of the past but also in specific personal ways. The name Evangeline, for example, began to be chosen for girl children, and contests crowning selected teenagers as Evangeline and Gabriel became yearly celebrations. Before the poem attained popularity, the name Evangeline was not an Acadian one. Rather, Longfellow chose it to represent both the angelic nature and the messenger role of an ideal and patient woman—a woman who carried and lived memory.[27]

Evangeline—the exiled woman, the statue, the song, and the poem and its popularity—functions in part as a gendered history within a larger international history. Marie Rosalie functions in much this same way on a smaller scale. Marie Rosalie's story also has been told and "owned" by many different parts of the family and others in Acadiana.

A Croatian Louisiana Story

Another family tells me about a Croatian ship captain named Miho Baccich (1859–1935). A great-grandson of Baccich, Jonathan Jordan (b. 1953), first spoke to me about his family. When he learned that I was interested in family history, he didn't want me to stop my research until I had heard their "family story." He spoke of the 1990 publication of a book by his cousin, Gus Rathe (1921–2007). Rathe told the story of a handwritten family manuscript, translated by his grandmother, describing her husband Miho's survival of a shipwreck in the late nineteenth century.[28] Three women in the family also began their interviews with mention of this book—the published record of a male storyteller, in this case Rathe.

All the family members who spoke to me then told of a teenage Baccich who had left his home on the Dalmatian coast in 1875 as a worker aboard his uncle's ship, the *Stefano*. They went first to England to pick up coal, then started a long journey to Hong Kong.

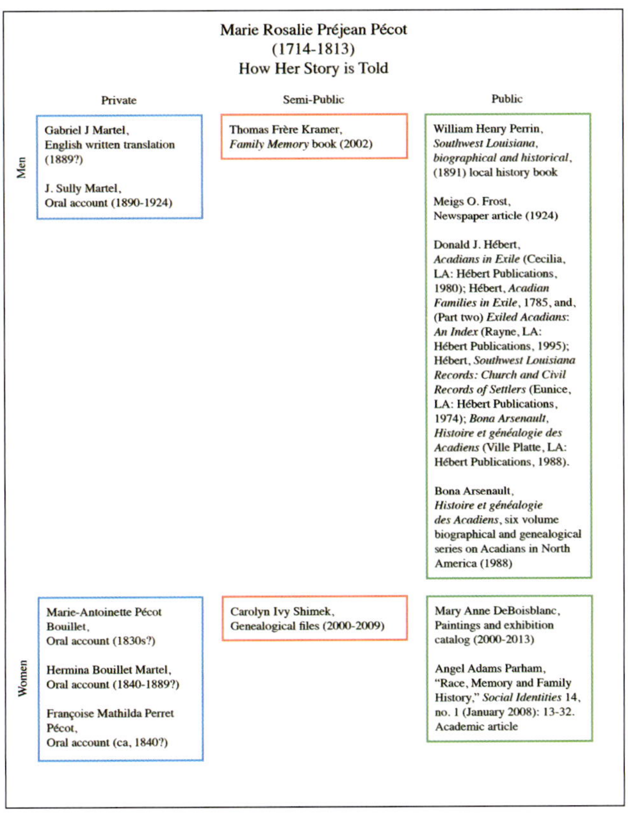

FIGURE 8.7
Marie Rosalie Préjean Pécot (1741–1813): How Her Story Is Told.
New Orleans family historians generally believe that the stereotype of a genealogist as a woman holds true in their families. This chart shows something of that belief but suggests too how men and women of the early twenty-first century increasingly narrate family stories to wider audiences.

FIGURE 8.8
Cadet Miho Baccich, 1875. Studio print. Courtesy of Lesslie Crowell, Gustave Rathe Jr., and others.

Miho Baccich opened his account of the wreck of the *Stefano* by remembering first his mother's worry about his departure. He was only sixteen, and this image makes that youth seem all the more real. He then recalled all the seagoing experience in the family; his grandfather and great uncles had owned ships. A first cousin was captain of the *Stefano*.

FIGURE 8.9
Cutter Jessie to the Rescue. B. Ivancovich, 1877. Oil on canvas. Courtesy of Lesslie Crowell, Gustave Rathe Jr., and others.

This votive painting hangs amid many others that give thanks for survival at sea in Dubrovnik's Our Lady of Mercy Church. Miho Baccich's parents commissioned it. The family in more recent times placed a newspaper ad in Australia and located the great-grandson of the captain of this pearling ship, the *Jessie*, which had brought the boys back to their Dalmatian homes.

The *Stefano* ran aground off the western coast of Australia, and only Baccich and another teenager survived. After near-starvation, cannibalism, and treks through the hot desert, they were saved by indigenous Australians, who eventually led them to a town settled by Europeans. There, the captain of a pearling ship secured their passage back to Dubrovnik. At home, Baccich and the other survivor dictated all they could remember to a Jesuit scholar, who recorded the experiences of the shipwreck: the long journey of survival, the flora and fauna of the land, the rescue by a particular group of Aboriginal people, and the assistance of colonial Australians. Two copies of the manuscript were made. One was given to Baccich and one remained with his parents, eventually passing to his sister, "since she never emigrated." Baccich did; he came to New Orleans.

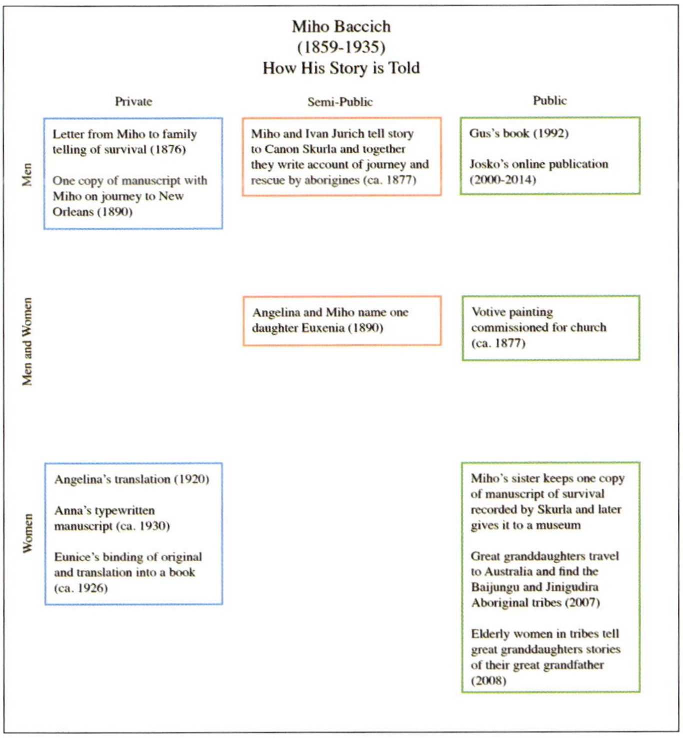

FIGURE 8.10
Miho Baccich (1859–1935): How His Story Is Told. Miho Baccich's story of rescue has been told and retold from the 1870s to the present. This chart shows only a fraction of those tellings. In 1987, for example, divers found the bell from the ship and reported this to the Australian press; in 2001, sociologist Josko Petkovic made a documentary about the shipwreck; and in 2009, Maureen Dowd and Bessie Lyndon, who are Baiyungu people, corrected the spelling of some of the words used in the manuscript.

The society in which Baccich lived influenced how the story was told. His account in the translated manuscript began with his recollection of his mother on the day of his departure, her fear for him. This beginning demonstrates more than just the dynamics of the family; it tells us about the milieu of recordkeeping among seafaring families. Such families then, as now, understood the possibility of death at sea. They also understood the need to keep records of goods and people; they had specific customs for giving thanks for survival. Jonathan's mother, Peggy Jordan (b. 1926), showed a page in Rathe's book with a votive painting, circa 1877, still hanging in Our Lady of Mercy Church in Dubrovnik. Baccich's mother commissioned this painting in gratitude for the survival of the boys—more evidence of memory traditions.[29]

Today, the family thinks not only of Rathe's book but also about the whole of the papers *about* Baccich, the art and artifacts created around his survival, and even rescued parts of the ship. This collection of materials dates from 1876, when Baccich wrote the first letter telling of his survival, to various dates in the first and second decades of the twenty-first century. Some descendants of the Aborigines who had rescued him, for example, have annotated the account. The family and others have spread these various texts literally and figuratively across three continents, and now also in a number of websites. Some of the records still exist in their original form with the family; others are located in archives, museums, a church, and the homes of other families. The "collection" of the memory

FIGURE 8.11
Angelina Cietcovich, ca. 1886. Studio print. Courtesy of Lesslie Crowell, Gustave Rathe Jr., and others.
Angelina Cietcovich Baccich's life in New Orleans is important to the transmission of the story of her husband's rescue. Note the placement of her hand on books. She spoke five languages, since, although born in the city, she came from a Dalmatian family who in their native land had spoken both Croatian and Italian. New Orleans had German- and French-speaking schools, and Angelina, according to her descendants, took her coursework in French at Mater Admirabilis, the school of the Religious of the Sacred Heart of Jesus (later the Academy of the Sacred Heart). She learned German with a private tutor.

FIGURE 8.12
Miho Baccich, 1886. Studio print. Courtesy of Lesslie Crowell, Gustave Rathe Jr., and others.
Not too long after his rescue but after schooling and training, Miho Baccich was named captain of a ship, called fittingly the *Resurrection*, and in 1879 it sailed for America. Yet he did not want to be captain, understandably so, and found a place where he could leave the ship in other people's hands. This would be New Orleans, which had, he recalled "the air of prosperity . . . but also the cultural resources." He stayed. He never went on a ship again, although he always hoped of returning to Australia to thank, even more than he had done earlier, those who had saved him. This desire is one reason his descendants call their own voyages there a "return."

is reshaped in each generation, but it is ordered in relation to the story of Baccich—his shipwreck and survival, and then too his passage to New Orleans, where he settled in the 1880s.[30]

Rathe's book indirectly describes how he found records via the first translation of the manuscript by his grandmother, Angelina Cietcovich Baccich. Family members today recall that Angelina (whose name, like Evangeline, means angel or messenger) was a "scholar," a new role for women of her time. She was educated by Religious of the Sacred Heart nuns in New Orleans, and on her own through her study with some teachers her father met as part of the Croatian community in New Orleans and in his work as a ship supplier.[31] Angelina Baccich's translation of the Italian manuscript dictated by Baccich and the other survivor, and written by the Jesuit priest, made it possible for her English-speaking children and grandchildren to read the account. She wrote in a simple notebook.

Youngest daughter Anna typed the translation from her mother's notebook and made copies for each of the five other daughters and one son. Another daughter, Eunice, bound the typed manuscript. This bookbinder daughter had learned her craft, and later taught it, as part of the art curriculum within the coordinate college for women at Tulane University, Sophie Newcomb College. Much about family history depends upon these types of circumstances of transmission: who is taught to type (or use other technology such as bookbinding equipment), who is allowed to study and learn, and who lives in circumstances that present opportunities and reasons for recordkeeping. The bound volume and the notebook were given to the oldest daughter, and Rathe was the son of this daughter.

Rathe shared the manuscript with people in the part of Australia where the ship was known to have sunk and where the boys were known to have been helped by natives. An Australian film scholar and activist, Josko Petkovic, then provided another translation of the manuscript (online) and annotated it to discuss issues of authorship and translation, noting what Angelina added and what she left out of the original Italian. The manuscript was itself a translation of the original spoken Croatian account into Italian, the language of the recorder-priest and the primary language for many along the Dalmatian coast at that time.[32]

Petkovic and others continue work on the meaning of the story. In 2015, two conferences, one in Perth, Australia, and the other in Dubrovnik, brought together descendants of colonials, as well as members of the Yinikurtira people who had rescued "the boys." The conferences also explored the ship itself, the land the boys described, and their heritage along the Dalmatian coast.

Baccich himself represented his survival in Australia in another way that his descendants continue to articulate via women in the family. A name—that most familiar and living form of a genealogical legacy—was given to one of his daughters to convey the way Miho and Angelina Baccich wanted the story remembered. Their second daughter was born on October 27, 1890, the fifteenth anniversary of his shipwreck. He initially chose the name "Australia," but his multilingual New Orleanian wife had different ideas. She suggested a Greek name—Euxenia—from *eu-xenos*, which translates literally as "high [regard for] the stranger."[33] That name was chosen because "of the lifesaving care bestowed on their husband and father, the stranger, by the people of the distant land."[34] Today, the name has been passed down through three generations of female descendants.

One of the great-granddaughters, Mary Lee Gregory Baccich (b. 1945), spoke about another instance in which names figure, an early twenty-first century example:

> I changed my [last] name to Baccich when I entered the seminary, to invoke the strong spirit of Miho. After doing so, I have gone to Australia twice and am rebuilding in New Orleans, the [part of the] city here [that] he and his partners built, the Gentilly Terrace area. I believe changing my name evoked all his genetic material within me and influenced my life to include his own history. Meeting with the Aborigines fulfilled a dream he had of returning to Australia and meeting with them again.

She reverses in part the genealogical amnesia of women's names, the "patrilineal problem" caused since girls and single women usually carry the names of their father, and married women so often take the surnames of their husbands.[35]

Gendered Family History

There were once very few other ways to enter "back" into family trees the many maiden and married names of female family members. On a mundane level, an album from 1915 tried to do so. In *Bailey's Family Ancestral Album*, one could find maternal lines though "strategically placed cutaways," a kind of pre-Internet linking that permitted jumps across the convention of taking a male surname.[36]

The other approach to negotiating gender within family history has been rooted in material culture. Laurel Thatcher Ulrich makes a strong argument that female identity was not made "fragile" or "derivative" when women took their husband's names or were otherwise left out of official records. Rather, she found that eighteenth- and nineteenth-century American women responded to "the force of patriarchy" by mediating between their families of origin and families of marriage. They established female lineages in objects, making sure that the chests, for example, of the grandmother went to a girl child.[37]

That men in most societies possess and hand down a name that survives the test of time remains one of the big challenges for genealogists. One has only to remember Dickens's *Great Expectations* and little Pip standing at the graves of his parents, reading over and over the name "Philip *Pirrip*, late of this parish, and also Georgiana *wife of the above*." Similarly, Donald Harman Akenson looks at the "kernel genealogical narrative," using as an example the tombstone inscription showing the names, dates of death, and ages at death of two people ("John Teskey" and "Anne, Beloved Wife").[38] Anyone who has walked through a cemetery has seen such examples. To Akenson, the omission of the wife's last name is purposeful, at least in terms of a societal habit, a primitive response to the idea that all that is actually needed for any genealogical trail is for a woman to give birth to a child who lives. As Akenson concludes, the history of so many genealogies beginning with a male and sometimes even leaving out his female partner is significant. Genealogies, in other words, can be seen as being "dictated by cultural desires rather than by biological reality."[39] A recent exhibit on women's needlework showing colonial US family lineage illustrates this proscription, with its vernacular title, "Who's Your Daddy?"[40] In short, the practice of concentrating on the male line, as Dhuoda described in the ninth century, continued and indeed continues.[41]

Those are all reasons that I asked New Orleans's genealogists about their understandings of women as family recordkeepers. Like Ina Fandrich, most responded thoughtfully to my question about gender. I prefaced my remarks to them by stating, "In general, some of the publications on family history I've seen begin with the statement that every family has its own historian, someone who keeps family records. Can you tell me what you think about this statement and also how this plays out in your own family?"

After answering this question, they were then directed back to a general overview with the question, "Do you think this person is more likely to be a woman or a man?" As one told me, "Women are socialized to keep the records of their families, the birth certificates, the school records."[42] Or, as another said, "Women are also usually more tenacious in their research, usually the ones willing to dig down to bedrock with a camel-hair brush." She recalled her mother and other women as "the most persistent family recordkeepers."[43]

She also linked her practices of family history to her role as a mother, to her own mother, and to other women in their family. "I was expecting our third child . . . my mother was not getting any younger, I was sitting in her kitchen, and she was telling me the litany of ancestors. I took out a plain old, eight-and-a-half-by-eleven lined sheet of paper and I drew a crude little family tree. I don't even know how I knew to do that. My mother, after she dredged up all she could remember—she said, let me call your daddy's sisters. And then through them we found a lady who had done some work, real genealogical work, and we visited her and she made us copies." She talked of their work in terms of family history traditions and private sources:

> My mother and my aunts were not going to the library and looking at records. They were pasting in photos and agreeing to take in the old letters and keep them. They wrapped things in tissue paper when they could, they placed things in shoeboxes and drawers emptied of clothes.[44]

Sociologist Pierre Bourdieu describes the responsibility of women in the celebration that occurs when families share photographs and other artifacts. It is women who generally organize gatherings of people and photographs.[45]

Another motive for women to collect the past was because their names *did* change. Recall Ina Fandrich's account of women making up for loss, and the other genealogist who talked of family history as consolation prize. For centuries, one of the only routes to adulthood for women was marriage, and this required taking the name of one's husband. A girl's family name, after all, was a part of childhood, not adulthood: maiden name, *nom de jeune fille*. Yet, in New Orleans, family historians also were quick to tell me that French women usually used their full name, writing their *nom de jeune fille* along with their husband's *nom de famille* on signed documents.

Among the fifty-six family historians I first interviewed, thirty-four felt that a family historian was more likely to be a woman, one felt that a family historian was more likely to be a man, and the rest felt that this status varied. Among those who believed that a woman was more likely to be a family historian than a man, three were men themselves. One of these, Chuck (b. 1937), discussed how he worked with information from other men (his father and a male cousin). I asked then why he thought

FIGURE 8.13
"I wonder what your name will be," postcard inscription, ca. 1917. Courtesy of Augusta Elmwood.
This inscription was found in the small autograph album shown in Figure 7.13. Although not a standard entry for women, it suggests more than the usual consciousness that marriage customs compelled a change of names.

of women as more likely to be the family historians—"Except your father kept all those records, right?" He replied, "He had very few. And my cousin—he had loads of stuff. But he had too much. And so, he told me, 'When I get time, I'll get my wife to copy them, I'll call you to come here [and] pick it up.' So there, again, is the woman."

For the one genealogist who thought that family history more likely to be a hobby of men, her reason revolved around the issue of time. "Men have more time," said Rebecca (b. 1939). She then referred to the reading room of the local branch library of the Latter-day Saints. "We have three men here reading, or four men here reading, and one lady." She was an LDS member herself, and in her generation (born before 1950), it was male children who were encouraged to write family histories. Yet she added, "My husband doesn't like genealogy. He's not a patient person. . . . His aunt lives across the street from us and she knows his family history for him."

Only two family historians were surprised by the question about the gender of the gatekeeper to family history. To most, the question seemed to be one that would be asked (*I have always thought of that*, many said). However, as Thomas (b. 1960) stated,

> It is one of those things, like African American history–until someone asks, people who are not touched by it won't consider it. It may well have been a way for women to have some power and it may have been that they, more than the men, were just interested in families, in the way people were shaped in families.

In a similar vein, Adrienne (b. 1940) mused,

> Never crossed my mind. But then it was important to [know] what diseases the family got. Say your aunt had a child who was blind, well, the woman remembered that when she was pregnant. She might want to write that down more than a man would.

As Thomas continued, "women as history keepers" were sometimes "outside the family." He said,

> Think about who is staffing those courthouses and who is the librarian. All women. And in my case, it was the church historian. One of the mothers of the church did a lot of documentation. And she died at 101 or 102 years of age, and she had a lot of personal information that she gave to me.

On the other hand, as Ingrid (b. 1941) and William (b. 1966) related, the keeper of records is often determined by who remains in a particular house or a particular locale. According to Ingrid,

> [I]n reading how to improve my genealogy process, I was reminded that my dad's first cousins and my mom's first cousins all had the same grandmother. And so, in my dad's case,

FIGURE 8.14
Baccich family, 1911. Studio Print. Courtesy of Lesslie Crowell, Gustave Rathe Jr., and others.
Left to right, Euxenia, father Miho, Eunice, and Ida (standing), Anna (seated), George, mother Angelina Cietcovich, Lydia, and Hilda. Euxenia is the daughter whose name was chosen to give thanks for her father's rescue, a name passed down to other daughters of this daughter and said to mean "high regard for the stranger." Both Euxenia (b. 1890) and Anna (b. 1899) were born on the date of the shipwreck (October 27; the wreck had been in 1875), as if wiping out some of the bad memories of that date.

> since his family's home had been burned, I thought, well, I would check his cousins. And I just found a wealth of information there. And I find that most of the record groups from the immigrants that are maintained usually stay with the last family that that person is living with before they pass away.

As William similarly stated, the family's recordkeeper in his father's family was

> my dad's sister; [because] of all my dad's siblings, she didn't leave the area she grew up in. She stayed there, she married someone local–she pretty much stayed within five miles of where most of them were born. So she was the one. She knew the most family history of her generation of my dad's side.

In other words, if women do not move around the country as much as men, if they stay close to parents, it is they who inherit family papers. Yet, as Thomas said, "It depends on if a family is matriarchal or patriarchal and a lot of that depends on how many daughters, how many sons, how the money is earned if any, if there is a family home passed to the daughters or sons. So many things."

Context, Structure, Content, and Future

These answers and the stories of Marie Rosalie Pécot and Miho Baccich show the complexity in understanding a gendered family history. Yet it could well be that technology will alter the circumstances that gave the mother her role as family memory keeper, and the male (usually her son) his role as public voice. Perhaps private archives will be more likely to be maintained by the young, at least during a time in which they, more than other age groups, are technologically savvy. At the same time, it is wise to remember that men are often missing from family photographs of the mid-twentieth century because they were given the role of photographer. It is a twist on the role of the outsider in any society, as Virginia Woolf once reminded us. Who is the observer and who is the observed? Those are questions that family historians more and more often have to consider as records become more plentiful, and as concepts of families and even people themselves change. The record, in archival terminology, is always an "evolving mediation" of different uses. The context of records changes their status as archival records and thus changes "what they are." Archivist Tom Nesmith wrote of these changes and used the example of women's records, once considered not worthy of placement in archives at all, since women were outside the official historical realm. Their records were not transmitted to archives or were not retained in such a way that they became part of the inscribed past.[46]

Times have changed since Nesmith's observations in 1997, and women's records are now the focus of a number of archives and the work of genealogists. Yet one is still tempted to warn, as did French philosopher Jacques Derrida, that any accumulation of records represents the present of whatever kind of power is being exercised. Or, as Michel Foucault similarly cautioned, an archives is a system of the establishment, and any "truth" it holds must be regarded from that perspective.[47] These remarks underscore the complexity of research in general and that of any insight into a gendered history of genealogy. Those stories outside the official records and public sources (the paintings of Mary Anne de Boisblanc and the notebook of Angelina Baccich being two such examples) teach a more complicated part of any family history. In this complexity, New Orleans family stories are no different from those of other places.

CHAPTER NINE

A Continuum of Family History

On each All Saints' Day for over fifteen years, Barbara Trevigne (b. 1947) has put on a white dress and a white tignon and set up a chair, table, and umbrella before the tomb of the Laveau-Glapion family in New Orleans's Saint Louis Cemetery no. 1. This is the tomb of the fabled Marie Laveau, the most well-known queen of voodoo in New Orleans.

The power and memories of women in New Orleans voodoo eclipse that of men.[1] Trevigne told me of this power. It is mostly women who come to the tomb on November 1, and mostly women "in general" who come to other family burial sites. She also spoke of her own work as an actress, visual artist, and genealogist. From the perspective of all these roles, she wanted to be sure that I understood neither race nor gender "particularly" but Marie Laveau herself. The "wise woman" was not, as people have long held, the daughter of a white man, but rather of a free man of color and his free wife of color.

Trevigne has a captivating spirit. She is generous in sharing this and other knowledge about not only her Laveau-Glapion family lines but also those of others in her family such as journalist Paul Trevigne (1825–1908), who wrote one of the first state histories of African Americans, and Mother Henriette Delille (1813–1862), who founded the African American Roman Catholic congregation known as the Sisters of the Holy Family.

Trevigne once made a series of dolls to represent the past of the African American city: a girl in a white First Communion gown; a girl in a white apron ready to serve her own family, her owners, or her employers; and a woman holding a basket on her way to market. The dolls "are *stories*," she told me, stretching out the word "stories" to an even emphasis on both syllables. The dolls represented what the genealogist in Trevigne sees as missing from the larger, especially the tourist, culture: that African Americans lived lives as other people did.

In the introduction to this book, I began with my own family portraits, for they also suggest to me what is left out of most published and spoken accounts. Was Emily's dress pressed by a slave? Was Calvin's suit made by a tailor in a town who was also a slave?

Near the family portraits, I have hung other paintings of family mem-

FIGURE 9.1
Crowd gathered at tomb of Marie Laveau, Saint Louis Cemetery no. 1, All Saints' Day, 2010. Photograph. Collection of the author.
Saint Louis Cemetery no. 1 is the city's oldest cemetery. Visitors are asked not to deface the tombs in any way. Rather, they are encouraged to give donations to a nearby church, Our Lady of Guadalupe, itself a site of memory for many genealogists since it was specifically built, in 1826, to bury victims of yellow fever epidemics.

FIGURE 9.2
Barbara Trevigne at the tomb of Marie Laveau, Saint Louis Cemetery no. 1, All Saints' Day, 2010. Photograph. Collection of the author.

bers. These are all works of my mother, so I think of her, her losses as well as her privileges. One of the paintings, entitled *Three of My Girls*, was prompted by a photo of my three sisters in nightgowns on a Christmas morning. I am not in the painting. I was often away and so I asked for this painting to remind me of home. I wasn't an easy daughter. I went away because I did not really like Alabama as a home: I was confused by George Wallace, ashamed of segregation, and embarrassed to have a southern accent.

But my family kept pulling me back. American genealogy is like that.

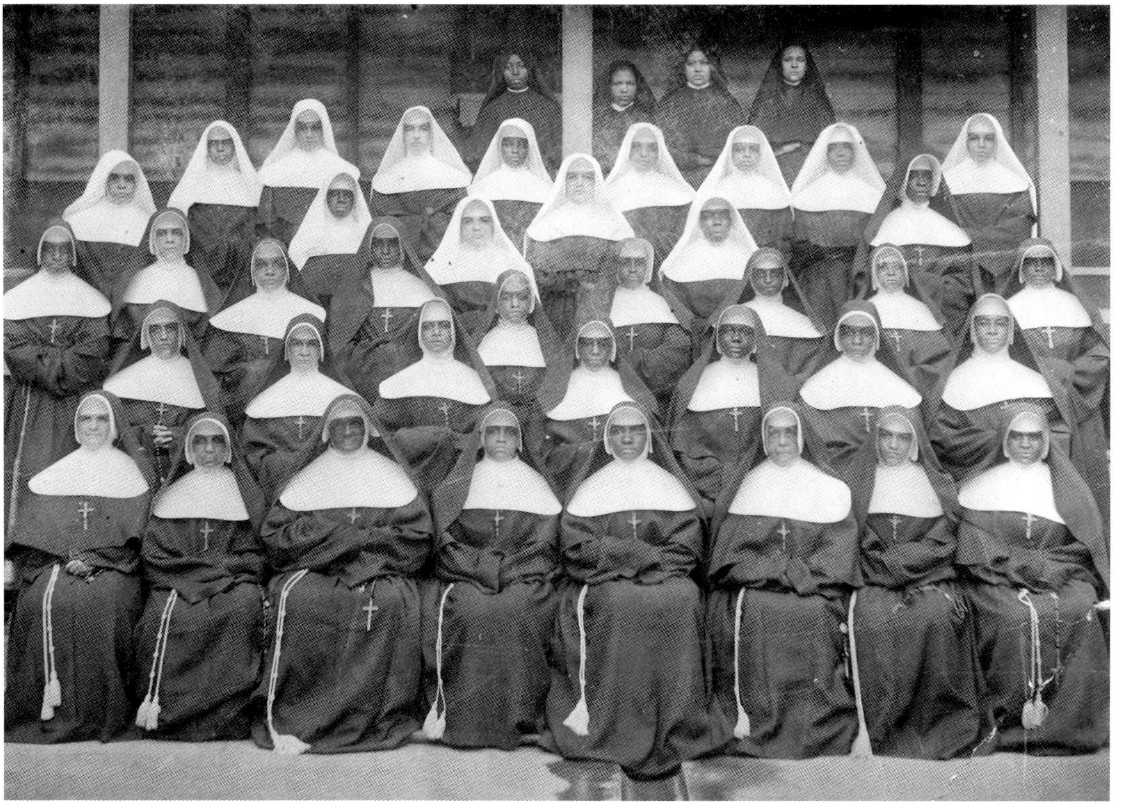

FIGURE 9.3

The Sisters of the Holy Family, ca. 1899. Photographic print. Courtesy of the Library of Congress, American Memory. An image collected by W. E. B. Du Bois and Thomas J. Calloway for the Paris Exposition of 1900, this photograph shows the stalwart nature of the Sisters of the Holy Family. Founded in 1842 by free woman of color Henriette Delille, the African American congregation has a practical and mythical role in the city. The order has created schools, orphanages, and nursing and retirement homes. A number of New Orleans genealogists, and those as far away as California, work on Delille's lineage lines.

It is a pull to attachment, to a glimpse of those who loved those who loved us.

Similarly, in archival studies, there is a model of how records move through stages over time. It is called "the records continuum" and it is visually represented by circles within concentric circles, each representing different phases of creation, capture, organization, and then use, or pluralization, an oddly abstruse term for so practical a field as archival studies.[2]

The recurring work on the memoir of Miho Baccich, as described in the previous chapter, is one example of this continuum. The manuscript was first created to celebrate, document, and possibly also to propitiate. The family today speculates that the boys' parents forced the discussion with the priest, thus forcing the manuscript's creation, because starvation on the Australian coast and subsequent cannibalism of their fellow crewmembers was involved. The votive painting for the church in Dubrovnik is another record of the survival, representing the boys exchanging adieux with the colonial Australians and the Aboriginal people. Recall that successive generations of the family, scholars, and the descendants of the Australian rescuers made possible the preservation as well as the evolution of these and other documentary sources, accounts, and artifacts. Some changes were physical and others intellectual. The family "owned" the story, as did those Aboriginal people whose oral culture retained the story of "the boys." All of them appropriated it, adjusted it, and tried to learn more about it. I do so as well.

FIGURE 9.4
Three of My Girls, Bea Quigley Tucker, 1979. Watercolor. Photograph by Yuka Petz.

In more simple terms, the records of Baccich's survival came to hold different meanings in different eras. The records' continuum model similarly emphasizes "overlapping characteristics of recordkeeping, evidence, transaction, and the identity of the creator." This model is in contrast to the linear movement of records in a life cycle model, wherein records come to the archives only when they are no longer active. In the continuum model, records remain "alive" in other ways. They offer evidence, facilitate transactions, and bolster identity.[3]

The topographical nature of this model suggests related concepts concerned with the use of records in family history. Family historians become record creators themselves as they copy and gather certificates of various sorts, as they make their family charts, trees, and other compilations for relatives. Family historians "move" these materials farther away from their public sources; they make new private records. The Internet especially has made possible such re-creations. Theoretically and in reality, family historians work within or across the continuum as they use records.

Family historians uniformly told me how they never give up their work. Ancestors always have parents. For Lucy (b. 1955), family history work involves

> questioning, yes, but passion is what drives it. . . . It's sweeping and I would say it's melodic because it's peaceful. And it has got kind of [a] flow to it. But it also has this urgency, push behind it, you know, [a] drive—to seek out the answers to the mystery. And I don't throw away. You never know when something later will make sense, will connect.

Others use the word "addiction." No sort of addiction is ever really tolerated, and perhaps this is another reason that reception to family historians has not always been welcoming. As mentioned throughout this book, genealogists have a long history of being relegated to the status of second-class experts.[4]

Yet clearly family historians have formulated and followed for almost a century rules requiring evidence. They have also been the driving force behind increasing access to records for everyone throughout the twentieth century and into the twenty-first. Without the support of family historians, neither the US National Archives nor many of the state archives as we know them today would exist.[5] Thus, over the past century, particularly since the 1970s and the emphasis on social history, there has been some repositioning, some steps away from prejudice against family history.

Across the United States, genealogical methods and genealogists have allowed us as a society more often than not to heal some of the wounds of racial tensions. Think not just of *Roots* but of many other more recent books such as Shirlee Taylor Haizlip's *The Sweeter the Juice: A Family Memoir in Black and White* (1994), Edward Ball's *Slaves in the Family* (1998), Dorothy Spruill Redford's *Somerset Homecoming* (1998), "our" New Orleans story, Bliss Broyard's *One Drop* (2007), and Daniel J. Sharfstein's *The Invisible Line: A Secret History of Race in America* (2011). These writers are telling stories made possible by family history's expansion and access to records, but they also are creating cross-racial dialogue. These conversations would not have occurred without the progression from the genealogical practices brought forth and refined by access to records. The communal networks, rules, and democratization of the ownership of genealogical memory can be seen as proceeding from John Farmer and Lemuel Shattuck in the nineteenth century to Donald Lines Jacobus in the 1920s and 1930s, to twenty-first century ideas that learning family history will influence our conceptions of ourselves and aid in family and national accord.[6] There are, in this lineage of the discourse of a democracy of genealogy, other early examples of biography that deal specifically with race: W. E. B. Du Bois's *The Philadelphia Negro* (1899) and Donald Everett's "Emigrés and Militiamen: Free Persons of Color in New Orleans, 1803–1815" in a 1953 issue of the *Journal of Negro History*. Add to these also an article on African American families said to be the first to appear in a mainstream (i.e., European American) genealogical journal: a 1970 article by Winston De Ville titled "The Free Negro Militia in Louisiana, 1804," in the *National Genealogical Society Quarterly*.

Another episode that could be considered as evidence of much earlier attention paid to race, biography, and the representation of American families occurred when Du Bois gathered photographs from families for the 1900 Paris Exposition Universelle. In this effort, he and others wanted to show African Americans as indistinguishable from European Americans with respect to religion, politics, language, and daily life, but different in their membership in another "vast historic race." As scholar Shawn Michelle Smith argued, the photographs for the exposition made Du Bois's argument more potent; the visual depictions encouraged consideration of the status of African Americans as not so different from that of other Americans. The exhibit did "not lift the Veil that distorts images of African Americans" but rather made visible the evidence that "cultural logics and privileged practices" produced racism.[7] Another groundbreaking work that functioned to provide evidence about race, a work uniformly applauded by genealogists, is Gwendolyn Midlo Hall's "The Louisiana Slave Database and the Louisiana Free Database, 1819–1820."[8] These public efforts brought the possibility that others beyond the genealogical communities would see how family research makes us understand the complexity of the past, the multiple versions of our yet shared society.

Just as Trevigne does today with the creation of dolls and genealogical pursuits, the other genealogists with whom I spoke also considered the community of family historians as teaching about the variety of people on earth. Family history, according to Robert (b. 1938),

> allows you to meet people you would not normally meet. It allows conversations to take place. It allows–you [to] become involved in a . . . community that is worldwide. It educates and, I would hope, breeds tolerance. Because not everybody comes from a socially acceptable family all the way down the line. So you see where you're not purist and, hopefully, it allows you to have a better understanding that we're a global community and not some Nazi, you know, cookie-cutter type thing. I think that's helpful.

Recalling the copy of a notarial record he sent to distant cousins in France, Louis (b. 1946) felt that family history could redeem the past. For him, these relatives "were way over there and yet we had all this in common. It made me consider the world in a more kindly way. I thought of my people, well they had Saint-Domingue, slavery, the horrible things, Sicily, poverty. But they had this sociability. We met through this sociability. It couldn't be all bad."

There are other examples of this type of tolerance and redemption that New Orleans genealogists wanted me to understand as part of their work. For instance, they pointed out the efforts of many who are caught up in the varying definitions of Creole—is it all the people descended from the first French, Spanish, and African colonists, those descended only from white colonists, or those descended only from mixed Africans and Europeans? Is it a smaller group or a larger one? Most agreed that the conversations about families who lived in this mix were helpful in defining the mixture in the melting pot that is New Orleans. They went back to what the families themselves experienced in the nineteenth century and projected forward as they considered race relations in the twenty-first century.

Yet there are still many divisions. Consider those family historians who look back on their ancestors who came from Saint-Domingue. Since the 1990s, there are two groups who have worked most prominently on Saint-Domingue records: the special interest group (SIG) on Saint-Domingue founded by Augusta Elmwood within the Jefferson Genealog-

FIGURE 9.5
General Toussaint, Mary Anne de Boisblanc, 2004. Acrylic. Courtesy of Angel Adams Parham. Photograph by Yuka Petz. De Boisblanc often drew and painted her idea of how Toussaint Louverture might have looked. Some of these portraits she called *First Black General in the World*. Once a European viewer asked her why she would want to place him alongside images of her family, since they had suffered under him. She answered that she thought her family had proved worthy of forgiveness and so could forgive others.

ical Society, and a group called the Louisiana Creole Research Association (LA Creole). Most people who attend SIG meetings are white, while most who attend LA Creole meetings have mixed ancestry.

Sociologist Angel Adams Parham worked with these two groups over a number of years in the early 2000s. Like other scholars, she found that "people of color tend to link their family history to larger national narratives of oppression and progress" more often than do European Americans. She also found that the divisions between the two groups in membership replicated other divisions in New Orleans, notably the separation of different ethnic groups in churches, schools, and social life. Where else then could conversations occur? She noted how two different events exploring Creole identity occurred on the same day in 2005, meaning the groups never consulted with each other at all.[9]

On the other hand, she saw how the "discoveries of family history research can also be used to push public dialogue forward and across racial and ethnic lines."[10] One example of this type of conversation came from the artist Mary Anne de Boisblanc. De Boisblanc is quite the publicist for her work: she sought out both Parham and me with tenacity, like the good family historian she is. I was interested in de Boisblanc's focus on a female ancestor, but Parham was interested in de Boisblanc's interpretation of her ancestors' time in Saint-Domingue.

To understand and come to terms with her ancestors' roles not only as oppressed victims in their exile from Acadia but also as oppressors and then as victims in Saint-Domingue, de Boisblanc had to think about the complexities of imperialism, land ownership, and slavery. Next to her portrait of the leader of the Haitian Revolution, in both her accompanying catalog and on the exhibition label, de Boisblanc has written:

> I wish I could tell General Toussaint [Louverture] that I forgive him for taking the lives of my ancestors in Saint-Domingue during the revolution. I understand that he was a product of his time. In the Pecot name, I would also ask his forgiveness for the Pecot's ownership of slaves. They, too, were products of their time. I pray that all of our souls will rest in peace.[11]

When I asked her about this, she talked of her cousin Carolyn Shimek, the genealogist, and how she had explained the journeys so often forced upon the family and their ultimate ability to leave descendants in Louisiana, where they have lived peacefully now for two hundred years. "So I am the beneficiary of that," she said. "I want to acknowledge that our family had some good luck as well as bad. And I want to . . . somehow [make] Rosalie . . . comforted by my knowing this." As Parham commented, "Mary Anne is attempting to use her family history research as a site of reflection and public social commentary."[12]

Today, such sharing is accomplished through a vernacular knowledge of family records, undertaken by people who display richly textured levels of purposes and meaning making as they compile products of both memory and evidence. Their work is dependent on many increasing social and technological practices that mediate what becomes public or private, and that mediate the democratization of sources.

One remaining question concerns those records not "captured," that are not kept in archives, not organized or often used, or, in the terminology of the genealogists, "overlooked." Return again to Tulane University's Louisiana Research Collection and one of its genealogical collections. The Personal Documents Collection is a grouping of various documents dating from 1671 to 1959. Such accumulations have the appearance of a display amassed to educate on a designated subject. The connecting subject of this collection could only be family history, or archival documents themselves. Again, this is the type of collection created in the early part of the twentieth century to provide subject access to manuscripts and records. To twenty-first century eyes, provenance has been destroyed. Here are New Orleans Catholic Church, notarial, vital statistics, and private records all mixed together.

This new arrangement makes for interesting reading, nonetheless, related to provenance and preservation. Most intriguing is Folder 13, an index of baptismal records created by Père Antoine, that foundational figure among New Orleans record creators and recordkeepers. In this copy he created, we can see again his handwriting on

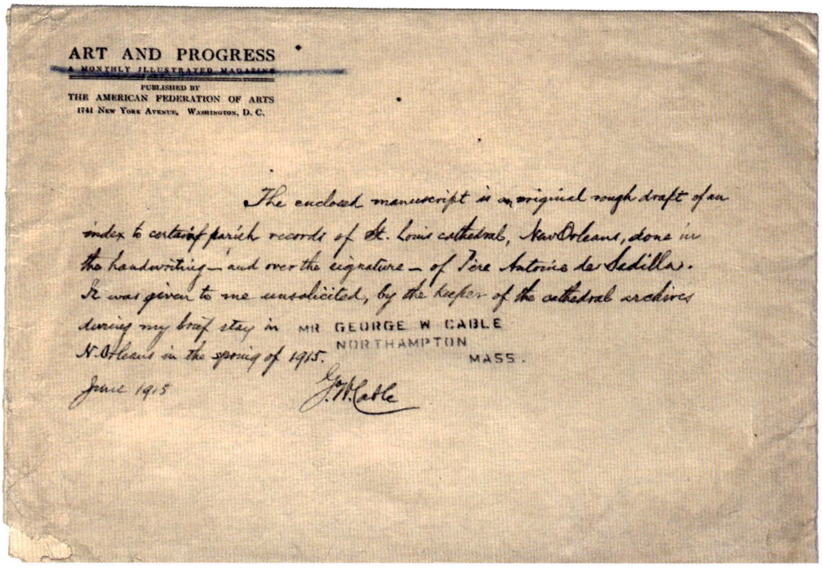

ART AND PROGRESS
A MONTHLY ILLUSTRATED MAGAZINE
PUBLISHED BY
THE AMERICAN FEDERATION OF ARTS
1741 New York Avenue, Washington, D. C.

The enclosed manuscript is an original rough draft of an index to certain parish records of St. Louis cathedral, New Orleans, done in the handwriting – and over the signature – of Père Antoine de Sedilla. It was given to me unsolicited, by the keeper of the cathedral archives during my brief stay in N. Orleans in the spring of 1915.

June 1915

G. W. Cable

MR GEORGE W CABLE
NORTHAMPTON
MASS.

FIGURE 9.6
Manuscript note, George Washington Cable, 1915. Personal Documents Series, Collection 525 (13), Louisiana Research Collection, Tulane University.
This image shows us much about the relationship of George Washington Cable to the hometown that eventually gave him so much trouble. We see evidence of his work for *Art and Progress*, the stamp of his new home in Massachusetts, and his diligent character when he explained here how he came to possess the copy of the parish record.

Queda copiado este Yndice en el libro Tercero de Bautismos de solas Personas blancas, que concluyó en siete de Marzo de 1802.

Fr. Antonio de Sedella

FIGURE 9.7
Title page to the Baptismal Record Copy. Personal Documents Series, Collection 525 (13), Louisiana Research Collection, Tulane University.

heavy, lovely paper that dates to the nineteenth century. There are 2,652 entries in this compilation. "Rough draft," George Washington Cable has written on an envelope housed with the registry pages. It is a document copied from Book 2 of the baptismal record in the cathedral. Cable wrote also that the draft had been given to him on a visit to the city in 1915. He was careful to note that it was an "unsolicited gift."[13]

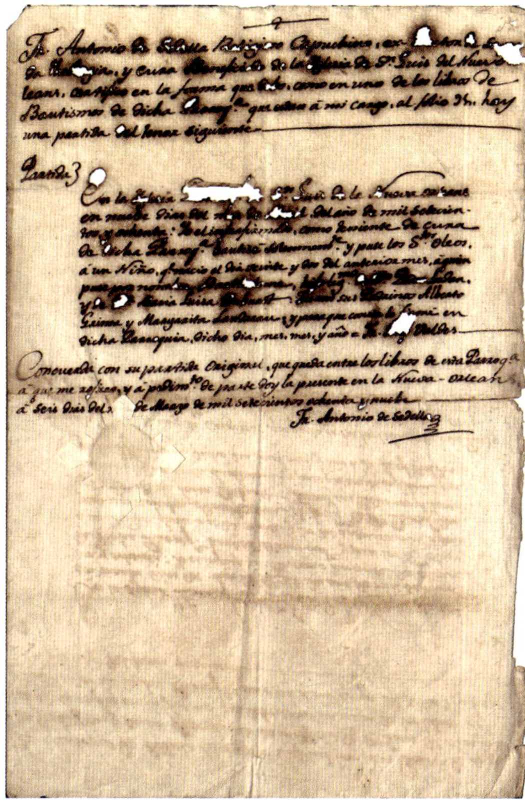

FIGURE 9.8
Back page of the Baptismal Record Copy. Personal Documents Series, Collection 525 (13), Louisiana Research Collection, Tulane University.

Cable, in turn, gave it as a gift. Likely, he did not know what else to do with it. A library would save it. And it has saved it.

It tells its own story: it is a record that has become a manuscript. Overall, an assemblage of personal documents is what archivists call an "artificial collection." They are part of the historical manuscript tradition, being composed of "materials with different provenance assembled and organized to facilitate its management or use. Artificial collections, as distinguished from organic collections, typically do not grow out of a single, specific function, and are often arranged for the convenience of description or retrieval rather than in an order originally established by the creator."[14]

Yet it is only the retention of information on provenance that renders full evidential status. That is the danger of the Internet, that so many documents now lose that provenance. As a family historian told me: "You have to sort of learn to discern between what is reliable and not reliable information [online]. I always tell newcomers, 'Reliable information is stuff where people have gone to foreign countries, or even this country for that matter, but mostly foreign countries and filmed actual records. And then the unreliable stuff is things that have been submitted by people, by individuals.'" She is referring here to the split between records individuals can upload to various websites, including the LDS databases, and those records created by governments and other organizations in their work.[15] She is noting, then, another manifestation of the layers of memory and the need to evaluate the context of records.

One of the scholars most insightful in analyzing the current online genealogical explosion is Canadian Julia Creet. In a working paper she calls "Arborescent Archives; or, The Aesthetic Roots of the Family Tree," she asks if,

> in the course of building their family trees, genealogists and family historians also build the larger forest signing away any rights to personal information they enter into the database. So,

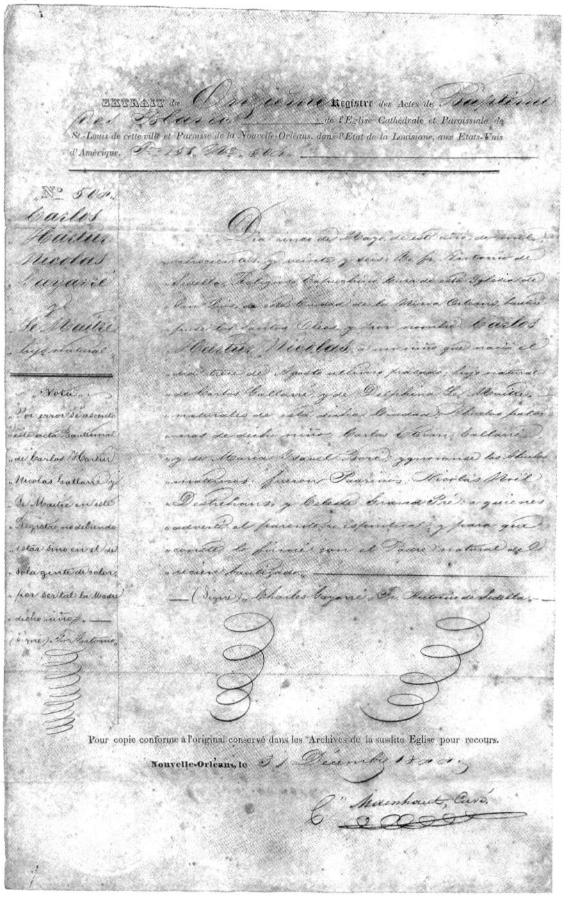

EXTRAIT du ... Registre des Actes de ... de l'Eglise Cathédrale et Paroissiale de St-Louis de cette ville et Paroisse de la Nouvelle-Orléans, dans l'Etat de la Louisiane, aux Etats-Unis d'Amérique.

Pour copie conforme à l'original conservé dans les Archives de la susdite Eglise pour recours.

Nouvelle-Orléans, le

FIGURE 9.9

Baptismal certificate of C. A. N. Gayarré. Charles Gayarré Papers, Mss 156, Box 14, Folder 3, Louisiana and Lower Mississippi Valley Collections, LSU Libraries, Baton Rouge. This certificate was requested in late 1844, and created and signed on December 31, 1844, by Father Constantine Maenhaut, a Belgium-born priest who served both Saint Louis Cathedral and another French-speaking parish, Saint Mary's. Gayarré *fils* was nineteen years old when this certificate was made, and his father, who kept it with other papers, was thirty-nine, about the time he was elected to the State House of Representatives.

> while genealogy was once a private family pursuit of pedigree, it has now turned into a global personal positioning device . . . combined with powerful new technologies that coordinate access to exponentially growing databases, which, in the end, serve commercial interests and the privatization of information as much as [the] drive to know our "roots."[16]

Her comments are part of a larger project, a scholarly genealogy of genealogy, and her own mother's family tree, the wish of her mother never to tell her children about her Jewish heritage in Hungary, her personal connections to the Holocaust. Others have also written of the need to keep private their family's archives, to guard them within their families, to burn them even.[17]

The nineteenth-century Louisiana historian Charles Gayarré left another clue about such decisions to leave behind or to destroy documents. He lived to be a very old man whose last days were spent in a small cottage in New Orleans, "a contracted space," he called it. He sold everything from his beloved home across the lake, including his books. He certainly could have destroyed many papers as he moved through what one writer called his "parade of misfortunes." Yet he left untouched

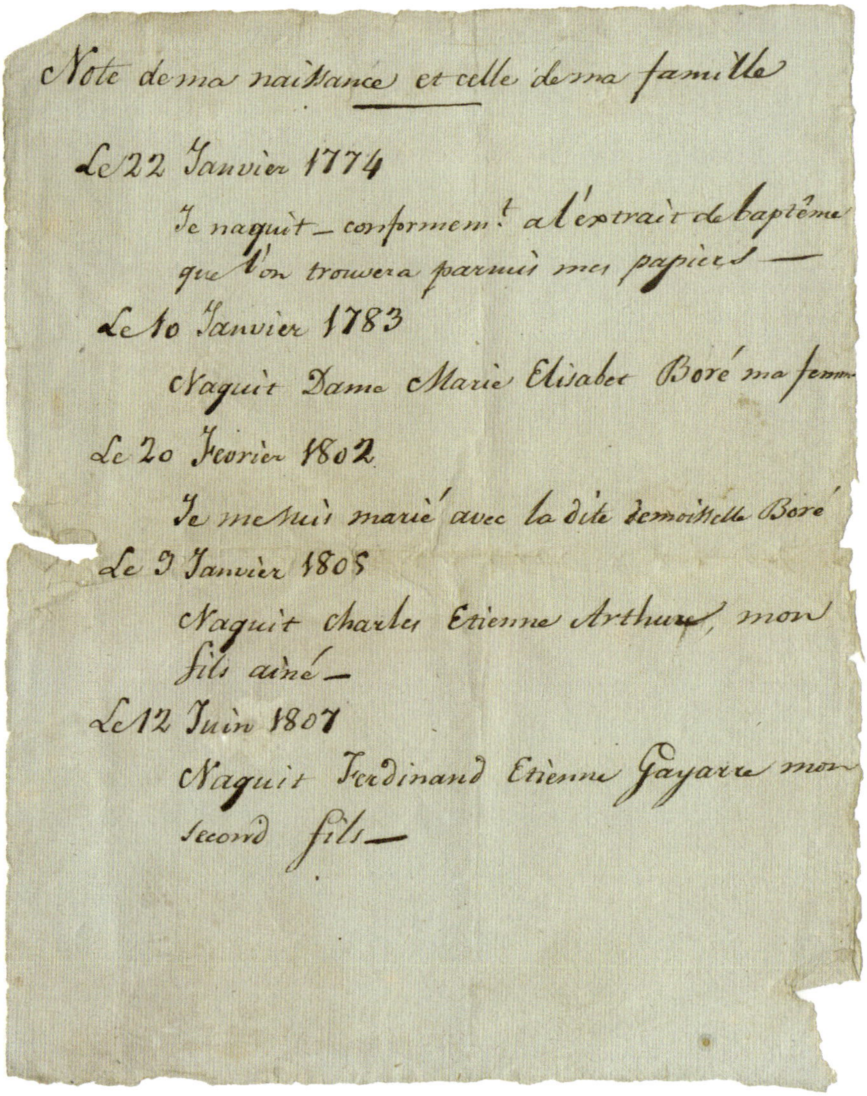

Note de ma naissance et celle de ma famille

Le 22 Janvier 1774

Je naquit — conformem.t a l'extrait de baptême que l'on trouvera parmi mes papiers —

Le 10 Janvier 1783

Naquit Dame Marie Elisabet Boré ma femme

Le 20 Fevrier 1802

Je me suis marié avec la dite demoiselle Boré

Le 9 Janvier 1805

Naquit Charles Etienne Arthur, mon fils ainé —

Le 12 Juin 1807

Naquit Ferdinand Etienne Gayarre mon second fils —

FIGURE 9.10
"Note de ma naissance et celle de ma famille." Item 472, Charles Gayarré Papers, Mss 156, Louisiana and Lower Mississippi Valley Collections, LSU Libraries, Baton Rouge. Charles Gayarré was a great collector of books and papers for the state. He also kept papers about various family members. The simplicity of this small description of immediate family has a certain resonance with genealogists' concerns about how little one retains of family records.

a copy of his son's birth certificate, his natural son whom he had reprimanded for trying somehow to rise above his station as a person of color. The birth certificate did not leave the universe of remembering. Of course, simple forgetfulness may have made it survive there in a stack on his desk. Yet he had always insisted on honesty about slavery itself, not hiding its brutality, for example, in discussions with his protégée, Grace King.[18] Perhaps, melodramatic as his character appears today, he saw the birth certificate as important in the same way: a clue in his life story, not necessarily to an admirable act but to part of his life.

We might also ask if he simply could not give up certain habits. As genealogists said to me, "you have to be a little egotistic to leave behind all your stuff."[19] He might have guessed, as genealogists do, that the "stuff" would be useful to someone. It is so, to us. His recordkeeping enables us (and others in the future) to continue asking questions and even perhaps to understand the environment in which he lived.

Again, there is the obvious idea to which genealogists always returned: what one destroys and what one saves shape what we know of the past. But what we know is also shaped by how the records are handled, how they are accumulated and made accessible, what circumstances of context are known. Creet takes the family tree and the many records on the Internet and demonstrates how what is remembered there has been populated within a veritable forest in which we could well lose our way.[20]

Or is it the stories that provide continuing evolutions of the forest, of context? Finding records, as Elizabeth Yakel and Deborah Torres stated, "frees [genealogists] to search for meaning. . . . As a result they are less concerned about every story being true and can seek identity through more subtle and perhaps metaphorical meaning in the stories."[21] The family historians of New Orleans have revealed in detail how records *and* stories are intricately woven into our identities as Americans.

Do Not Erase

Lucy (b. 1955) again spoke, this time of methods of research, of going over mistakes:

> I don't recommend erasing. I recommend you draw one line through it and continue on because that way you can see where your mistakes were. What direction you started going in . . . you can always go back and see where, what direction you started to go in that you know didn't work.

This simple statement brings me back to my own reasons for beginning this book, for continuing to work on the history of family history well past the interviews with family historians following the flooding from Hurricane Katrina. Their insights offered the chance to be *in* the South, but *out* of it, to be attached to the many cultures who lived and live in this city, to those ancestors who wished their family members farewell from somewhere far away to come to this city of remembering—approaching more closely, then, what we as Americans want to be: a pluralistic community. Genealogy is always that "being in two places, the past and the present," one family historian told me, plus "it's being in the libraries and the courthouses and the state archives . . . and it's a replica of these materials of the past also for the future."[22]

Genealogists feel that they are building something to transform obscurity, something that works against oblivion, and something that contributes to collective memory. As another family historian commented about her ancestor: "It's really frustrating when you just have so little about this person. This person lived this life and left behind children and grandchildren and I have three facts. That's very, very frustrating to me. I try to find out as much as I can." For her, "this person lived a whole life, [and] I have three things to say." Genealogy works both to assuage the truth of this observation (for most people going back five generations have indeed only birth, marriage, and death records; and going back further in time, indeed there are no written records at all for most individuals), and to make a more universal philosophy of humility and communal spirit (since family history can memorialize the whole of humanity, with or without names written down). "After a while," she continued "there are no names, but you know they are there, and who are they but just people? Even the ones you have the names on, well that may be all you have, so you have to look for the bigger picture to even begin to understand them."[23]

Remarking on the reasons he continued family history work, Salvatore Serio (b. 1934) recalled seeing so many family records where children had died before the age of two. Although he was critical of the LDS's baptisms by proxy of Jewish ancestors, "on another level, it's a gift. It's a mark against oblivion. And that's what we are all doing really when we do family history, we are giving that baby that didn't live a sort of equal life with all of us who live our full lifespan." From a city blessed with metaphorical and literal meanings about the progress or failures of democracy, records teach about this sort of effort to honor those who came before us. Records and family history teach also about people always becoming our worst selves or our best selves, but mainly the only selves we have in the brief continuum of our lives, our cumulative steps in making living count.

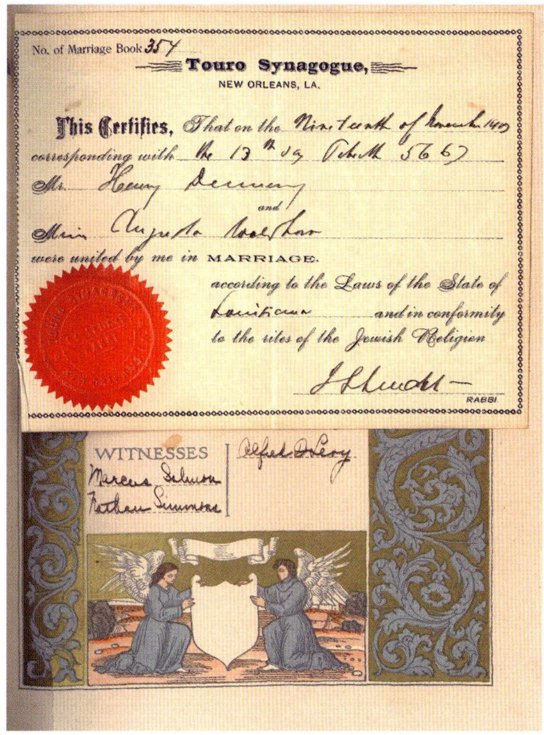

No. of Marriage Book 357
Touro Synagogue,
NEW ORLEANS, LA.
This Certifies, That on the
corresponding with
Mr. Henry Dennery
and
Miss Augusta Waldhorn
were united by me in MARRIAGE.
according to the Laws of the State of
and in conformity
to the rites of the Jewish Religion
RABBI
WITNESSES

FIGURE 9.11
Touro Synagogue Certificate of Marriage of Augusta Waldhorn and Henry Dennery, November 19, 1907, Newcomb Archives and Vorhoff Library Special Collections, Newcomb College Institute, Tulane University. A cliché among genealogists is to say that one is not really present at either one's birth or one's death. Only at one's marriage does one actually become an active participant in the creation of a record. One can see here, however, that neither the bride nor the groom signed the certificate, showing how variable customs can be.

NOTES

Chapter 1

1. Sandra Hargreaves Luebking and Loretto Dennis Szucs, "The Foundations of Family History Research," in *The Source: A Guidebook to American Genealogy*, ed. Sandra Hargreaves Luebking and Loretto Dennis Szucs, 3rd ed. (Provo, UT: Ancestry, 2006), 2.

2. Susan Tucker, "The Most Public of All History: Family History and Heritage Albums in the Transmission of Records/Genealogie en Familiealbums als Dragers van Collectieve Herinnering" (University of Amsterdam, 2009); Tulane University, Susan Tucker, IRB Study, T0010U, *The Vocabularies and Practices of Family History Project, 2006–2009;* interviews and notes on the history and practices of genealogy, Susan Tucker Papers, Newcomb Archives, Tulane University.

3. Luebking and Szucs, "The Foundations of Family History Research," 2.

4. Rob S. Cox, "Finding Aid for Mifflin Family Papers, 1689–1877," William L. Clements Library, University of Michigan, http://quod.lib.umich.edu/c/clementsmss/umich-wcl-M-2722.1mif?view=text, accessed March 15, 2011.

5. National Society of the Colonial Dames of America in the State of Alabama, Historical Activities Committee, *Alabama Portraits prior to 1870* (Mobile, AL: NSCDA, 1969); "Mrs. Calvin Norris (Emily Hare Croom)," Art Inventories Catalog, Smithsonian American Art Museums, http://collections.si.edu/search/results.htm?q=record_ID:siris_ari_216583, accessed January 4, 2011.

6. "Myotonic Muscular Dystrophy," Muscular Dystrophy Association, http://mda.org/disease/myotonic-muscular-dystrophy/causes-inheritance, accessed January 14, 2012.

7. Eviatar Zerubavel, *Time Maps: Collective Memory and the Social Shape of the Past* (Chicago: University of Chicago Press, 2003), 4–5; Eviatar Zerubavel, *Ancestors and Relatives: Genealogy, Identity, and Community* (New York: Oxford University Press, 2012), 77–104.

8. Richard Pearce-Moses, comp., *A Glossary of Archival and Records Terminology* (Chicago: Society of American Archivists, 2005), s.v. "Records"; see also http://www2.archivists.org/glossary/terms/r/record.

Chapter 2

1. David Johnson, ed., *KnowLA: Encyclopedia of Louisiana* (New Orleans: Louisiana Endowment for the Humanities, 2010), s.v. "Edmund Brewster," by Richard Anthony Lewis, http://www.knowla.org/entry/1152/, accessed January 6, 2015; Charles Edwards O'Neill, "'A Quarter Marked by Sundry Peculiarities': New Orleans, Lay Trustees, and Père Antoine," *Catholic Historical Review* 76, no. 2 (April 1990): 235–77.

2. If more than three family historians referred to a method, a belief, or a practice, I have omitted names. When I quote a particular family historian, unless I give

a first and last name, I use pseudonyms (a first name), or a reference to a number assigned to the particular person.

3. O'Neill, "New Orleans, Lay Trustees, and Père Antoine," 247, 255, 256, 257, 258.

4. Ibid., 260–61.

5. Alfred Lemmon, "Trans-Mississippi States: Arkansas, California, Iowa, Louisiana, Minnesota, Missouri, Oregon, and Texas," in *Historical Consciousness in the Early Republic: The Origins of State Historical Societies, Museums, and Collections, 1791–1861*, ed. H. G. Jones (Chapel Hill: North Caroliniana Society; North Carolina Collection, 1995), 188–91; Earl C. Woods and Charles E. Nolan, *Sacramental Record of the Roman Catholic Church of the Archdiocese of New Orleans* (New Orleans: Archdiocese of New Orleans, 1987), 1:xii, xiv; Saint Louis Cathedral, New Orleans, Marriages, 1720–1730, 227; Charles E. Nolan, *A Southern Catholic Heritage*, vol. 1 (New Orleans: Archdiocese of New Orleans, 1976), xxxiii–xxxiv; J. Edgar Bruns, "Annotating for Posterity: The Sacramental Records of Father Antonio de Sedella," in *Cross, Crozier, and Crucible: A Volume Celebrating the Bicentennial of a Catholic Diocese in Louisiana*, ed. Glen Conrad (New Orleans: Archdiocese of New Orleans, 1993), 349–59.

6. Tamar Herzog, "Naming, Identifying and Authorizing Movement in Early Modern Spain and Spanish America," in *Registration and Recognition: Documenting the Person in World History*, Proceedings of the British Academy, ed. Keith Breckenridge and Simon Szreter (Oxford: Oxford University Press, 2012), 200–201.

7. Family History Library Catalog, https://familysearch.org/locations/saltlakecity-library, accessed February 13, 2015.

8. Interviewee no. 21, b. 1959.

9. "History," Research Center and Historical Documents, Notarial Archives, http://www.orleanscivilclerk.com/history.htm, accessed December 28, 2014; Howard Margot, *Guide to the French Colonial Records of the New Orleans Notarial Archives, 1733–1767* (New Orleans: Notarial Archives Research Center, 2007), 14–15; Kate Wallach, *Research in Louisiana Law* (Baton Rouge: Louisiana State University Press, 1958), 167; Hans W. Baade, "Marriage Contracts in French and Spanish Louisiana: A Study in 'Notarial' Jurisprudence," *Tulane Law Review* 53 (December 1978): 1–54.

10. Patricia Nugent, "Pedro Pedesclaux," Orleans Parish Clerk of Civil District Court, http://www.orleanscivilclerk.com/pedrobio.htm, accessed January 6, 2011; Henry Putney Beers, *French and Spanish Records of Louisiana: A Bibliographical Guide to Archive and Manuscript Sources* (Baton Rouge: Louisiana State University Press, 1989), 9; *Digest of the Acts and Deliberations of the Cabildo, 1769–1803*, City Archives, New Orleans Public Library, April 21, 1780, and November 23, 1798, http://nutrias.org/~nopl/inv/digest/digest1.htm, accessed September 3, 2011; *Copia fiel de las actas originales del Cabildo*, Libros 1–2, Archivos de la ciudad de Neuva Orleans, 1938, New Orleans Public Library.

11. John Farmer, "Memoir of John Farmer, M.A., Late Corresponding Secretary of the New Hampshire Historical Society," *New England Historical and Genealogical Register* 1, no. 1 (1847), 9; François Weil, "John Farmer and the Making of American Genealogy," *New England Quarterly* 80, no. 3 (September 2007): 408–34.

12. John Farmer, *A Genealogical Register of the First Settlers of New England* (Lancaster, MA: Carter, Andrews, and Company, 1829), iii.

13. "History of the New England Genealogical Society, from Our Founding in 1845 to Present Day," American Ancestors, http://www.americanancestors.org/About/History/, accessed January 6, 2011; John A. Schutz, *A Noble Pursuit: The Sesquicentennial History of the New England Historic Genealogical Society, 1845–1995* (Boston: New England Historic Genealogical Society, 1995).

14. "Family History," Church of Jesus Christ of Latter-day Saints, http://www.mormon.org/values/family-history, accessed September 22, 2014.

15. James B. Allen and Jessie L. Embry, "Provoking the Brethren to Good Works: Susa Young Gates, the Relief Society, and Genealogy," *BYU Studies* 31 (1991): 115–38.

16. Eric Ketelaar, "The Genealogical Gaze: Family Identities and Family Archives in the Fourteenth to Seventeenth Centuries," *Libraries and the Cultural Record* 44, no. 1 (2009): 9–28.

17. François Weil, *Family Trees: A History of Genealogy in America* (Cambridge, MA: Harvard University Press, 2013), 10–12.

18. Terrick V. H. FitzHugh, *The Dictionary of Genealogy*, rev. ed. (Sherborne, England: Alphabooks, 1988), s.v. "College of Heralds," 35–37; Anthony Richard Wagner, *English Genealogy* (Oxford: Clarendon Press, 1950), 340–41; Michael Sharpe, *Family Matters: A History of Genealogy* (Barnsley, England: Pen and Sword Books, 2011), esp. chapter 3.

19. Ketelaar, "The Genealogical Gaze," 10–11.

20. Weil, *Family Trees*, 12.

21. Simon Szreter, "Registration of Identities in Early Modern English Parishes and amongst the English Overseas," in Breckenridge and Szreter, *Registration and Recognition*, 68–69.

22. Richard Sims, *A Manual for the Genealogist, Topographer, Antiquary, and Legal Professor: Consisting of Descriptions of Public Records, Parochial and Other Registers, Wills, County and Family Histories; Heraldic Collections in Public Libraries, Etc. Etc.* (London: John Russell Smith, 1861), 323; Colleen McDannell, *Material Christianity: Religion and Popular Culture in America* (New Haven, CT: Yale University Press, 1995), 89.

23. Robert M. Taylor Jr. and Ralph J. Crandall, "Historians and Genealogists: An Emerging Community of Interest," in *Generations and Change: Genealogical Perspectives in Social History*, ed. Robert M. Taylor Jr. and Ralph J. Crandall (Macon, GA: Mercer University Press, 1986), 4–5; Weil, "John Farmer and the Making of American Genealogy."

24. See many examples in D. Brenton Simons and Peter Benes, eds., *The Art of Family: Genealogical Artifacts in New England* (Boston: New England Historic Genealogical Society, 2002), chapters 5, 17, 18; Jerome E. Anderson, "Family Record-Keeping: A Rich and Diverse Heritage," *National Genealogical Society Quarterly* 90, no. 4 (December 2002): 247–56; Wendell Garrett, "Families and the Decorative Arts," in Simons and Benes, *The Art of Family*, 1–5; Peter Benes, "Decorated New England Family Registers, 1770–1850," in Simons and Benes, *The Art of Family*, 13–59; Georgia Brady Barnhill, "'Keep Sacred the Memory of Your Ancestors': Family Registers and Memorial Prints," in Simons and Benes, *The Art of Family*, 60–74.

25. Weil, *Family Trees*, 8–10. Weil quotes from a "Letter from Rev. John Walrond of Ottery, Eng., to Rev. William Waldron, Minister of Boston, and Brother of Secretary Waldron, 8 March 1725–26," *New England Historical and Genealogical Register* 1 (January 1847), 66; Weil also cites "Letter of the First Chief-Justice Sewall to His Son, Samuel Sewall, Esq., of Brookline, Giving an Account of His Family," *New England Historical and Genealogical Register* 1 (April 1847): 111–12.

26. Roger Clap, *Memories of Capt. Roger Clap* (Boston: B. Green, 1731).

27. Luke Stebbins, *A Genealogy of the Family of Mr. Samuel Stebbins and Mrs. Hannah Stebbins, His Wife, from the Year 1701 to 1771 . . .* (Hartford, CT: Ebenezer Watson, 1771).

28. Lloyd DeWitt Bockstruck, "Four Centuries of Genealogy: A Historical View," *RQ* 23, no. 2 (Winter 1983), 162; Unidentified compiler, Genealogical chart of the Brid (Bird and Byrd) family, Mss 6:2 B9965:1, Virginia Historical Society, Richmond.

29. Grace King, *Creole Families of New Orleans* (New York: Macmillan, 1921), 265.

30. Weil, *Family Trees*, 26–27; Thomas Jefferson Encyclopedia, s.v. "Coat of Arms," http://www.monticello.org/site/research-and-collections/coat-arms, accessed February 8, 2014.

31. Benes, "Decorated New England Family Registers," 14.

32. Peter Benes, "Selected Checklist of Manuscript, Watercolor and Needlework Family Registers and Family Trees in New England, 1780–1846," in Simons and Benes, *The Art of Family*, 275–82.

33. John Demos, introduction to Simons and Benes, *The Art of Family*, xii.

34. Ola Elizabeth Winslow, *American Broadside Verse* (New Haven, CT: Yale University Press, 1930), xviii.

35. John Bodnar, *Remaking America: Public Memory, Commemoration, and Patriotism in the Twentieth Century* (Princeton, NJ: Princeton University Press, 1992), 28–29.

36. Elizabeth Shown Mills, "Genealogy in the 'Information Age': History's New Frontier?" *National Genealogical Society Quarterly* 91, Centennial Issue (December 2003): 262–63; Wallace Evan Davies, *Patriotism on Parade: The Story of Veterans' and Hereditary Organizations in America, 1783–1900* (Cambridge, MA: Harvard University Press, 1955), 1–27. See also Minor Myers, *Liberty without Anarchy: A History of the Society of the Cincinnati* (Charlottesville: University of Virginia Press, 1983).

37. "Thomas Jefferson to George Washington, April 16, 1784," in Julian P. Boyd et al., eds., *The Papers of Thomas Jefferson* (Princeton, NJ: Princeton University Press, 1953), 7:106. See also Weil, "John Farmer and the Making of American Genealogy," 411.

38. Davies, *Patriotism on Parade*, 19.

39. Beatrice Gottlieb, *The Family in the Western World from the Black Death to the Industrial Age* (New York: Oxford University Press, 1993), 203.

40. Ann J. Abadie et al., *The New Encyclopedia of Southern Culture*, vol. 2: *Geography* (Chapel Hill: University of North Carolina Press, 2006), s.v. "Primogeniture."

41. Judith Prewse Roach, "Genealogy at the Library of Congress," in *Interna-*

tional Genealogy and Local History: Papers Presented by the Genealogy and Local History Section at IFLA General Conferences 2001–2005, ed. Ruth Hedegaard and Elizabeth Anne Melrose (Munich: K. G. Saur, 2008), 6. One can also use the Library of Congress's search engine to find other titles of genealogy that Jefferson owned.

42. "Jefferson's Library," Library of Congress, http://www.loc.gov/exhibits/jefferson/jefflib.html, accessed March 6, 2008; James Sweany, Head, Local History and Genealogy Reading Room, Library of Congress, telephone conversation with the author, January 16, 2009.

43. Alexis de Tocqueville, *Democracy in America*, ed. J. P. Mayer, trans. George Lawrence (New York: Anchor Books, 1969), 570.

44. David J. Russo, *Keepers of Our Past: Local Historical Writing in the United States, 1820s–1930s* (Westport, CT: Greenwood Press, 1988), 12–13.

45. David D. Van Tassel, *Recording America's Past: An Interpretation of the Development of Historical Studies in America, 1607–1884* (Chicago: University of Chicago Press, 1967).

46. Lester J. Cappon, "Genealogy, Handmaid of History," *National Genealogical Society Quarterly* 45, no. 1 (March 1957): 3–4; Jones, *Historical Consciousness in the Early Republic*, vii–viii.

47. Many of the historical societies maintained libraries and followed standard bibliographic practices.

48. James Savage, John Farmer, and Orrando Perry Dexter, *A Genealogical Dictionary of the First Settlers of New England* (Boston: Little Brown, 1860), v–vi.

49. Sally Griffith, *Serving History in a Changing World: The Historical Society of Pennsylvania in the Twentieth Century* (Philadelphia: Historical Society of Pennsylvania, 2001), 21.

50. The term "little democracies" appears to have been a popular phrase for various northeastern communities. See also Anonymous, review of *Historical Sketch of Amherst, in the County of Hillsborough, in New Hampshire, from Its First Settlement to the Year 1837*, by John Farmer, *North American Review* 46, no. 99 (April 1838): 537. For the Louisiana Historical Society, see W. O. Hart, "History of the Louisiana Historical Society," *Louisiana Historical Quarterly* 3, no. 1 (January 1920): 112–29; Faye Phillips, "Writing Louisiana Colonial History in the Mid-Nineteenth Century: Charles Gayarré, Benjamin Franklin French, and the Louisiana Historical Society," *Louisiana History: The Journal of the Louisiana Historical Association* 49, no. 2 (Spring 2008): 163–90; Faye Phillips, "To 'Build upon the Foundation': Charles Gayarré's Vision for the Louisiana State Library," *Libraries and the Cultural Record* 43, no.1 (2008): 56–78.

51. "Joseph Smith: A Prophet of God," Church of Jesus Christ of Latter-day Saints, http://www.mormon.org/beliefs/joseph-smith, accessed October 12, 2014.

52. "Joseph Smith: History," Church of Jesus Christ of Latter-day Saints, https://www.lds.org/scriptures/pgp/js-h/1?lang=eng, accessed December 10, 2014; "Joseph Smith Jr., 1st President of the Church," Church of Jesus Christ of Latter-day Saints, https://www.lds.org/churchhistory/presidents/controllers/potcController.jsp?topic=facts&leader=1.

53."Family History," Church of Jesus Christ of Latter-day Saints, http://www.mormon.org/values/family-history, accessed September 22, 2014.

54. James B. Allen, Jessie L. Embry, and Kahlile B. Mehr, *Hearts Turned to the Fathers: A History of the Genealogical Society of Utah, 1894–1994* (Provo, UT: Brigham Young University Studies, 1995), 33–57; Allen and Embry, "Provoking the Brethren to Good Works."

55. Since genealogists always warn about misspellings and since Gates's given name, Susa, could be easily misinterpreted, it is worth noting that it's a biblical name and the root of similar-sounding names; they all mean "lily." Susa also comes from the name of a place: Shushan, the capital of ancient Hebrew Elam, which became the Persian Susa and is today the city of Shush in Iran.

56. Allen and Embry, "Provoking the Brethren to Good Works,"121, 126.

57. Allen and Embry, "Provoking the Brethren to Good Works," 126, 129–30, 132. The editors of *Utah Genealogical and Historical Magazine* published the lessons written by Gates beginning in October 1911 and later issued them in a forty-five-page book, edited by Nephi Anderson, without mention of Gates. This book, *Lessons in Genealogy* (1915) should be considered, chronologically, the second or third American book on how to practice genealogy. Lemuel Shattuck, *A Complete System of Family Registration* (Boston: William D. Ticknor, 1841); and his *Blank Book Forms for Family Registers* (Boston: Lemuel Shattuck, 1856) are the first manuals. See chapter 4 for more on Shattuck, an amazing genealogist as well as the founder of the movement for public health statistics.

58. Allen, Embry, and Mehr, *Hearts Turned to the Fathers*, 67–70.

59. "Family History Library," FamilySearch, https://familysearch.org/locations/saltlakecity-library, accessed May 27, 2013; "Background," Family History Library, Church of Jesus Christ of Latter-day Saints, http://www.familysearch.org/eng/library/FHL/frameset_library.asp, accessed January 26, 2009.

60. "Newsroom: The Family History Library," Church of Jesus Christ of Latter-day Saints, http://www.mormonnewsroom.org/article/family-history-library, accessed September 22, 2014.

61. Donald Harman Akenson, *Some Family: The Mormons and How Humanity Keeps Track of Itself* (Montreal: McGill–Queen's University Press, 2007), 59.

62. Alex Shoumatoff, *The Mountain of Names: A History of the Human Family* (New York: Simon and Schuster, 1985), 254.

63. "Granite Mountain Records Vault," Newsroom, Church of Jesus Christ of Latter-day Saints, http://www.mormonnewsroom.org/article/granite-mountain-records-vault, accessed September 22, 2014.

64. See the listing of databases at the Ancestry.com wiki, itself composed of information from "The Source: A Guidebook to American Genealogy"; "Red Book: American State, County, and Town Sources"; other Ancestry.com content; and content added by users, http://www.ancestry.com/wiki/index.php?title=Main_Page, accessed August 31, 2014.

65. James B. Allen and Jessie L. Embry, eds., *Encyclopedia of Mormonism: The History, Scripture, Doctrine, and Procedure of the Church of Jesus Christ of Latter-*

day Saints, s.v. "Susa Young Gates," http://eom.byu.edu/index.php/Gates,_Susa_Young, accessed January 6, 2011.

66. The statue, by Karl Quilter, is called *Ever Pressing Forward* and was dedicated in 2001.

67. John Seabrook, "The Reporter at Large: The Tree of Me," *New Yorker* 77, no. 526 (March 2001), 60.

68. Barack Obama, "Inaugural Address," transcript, the New York Times Company, http://www.nytimes .com/2009/01/20/us/politics/20text-obama.html?_r=1, accessed January 25, 2009.

69. Jan Vansina, *Oral Tradition: A Study in Historical Methodology*, trans. H. M. Wright (New Brunswick, NJ: Aldine Transaction, 2006), 156–57.

70. For the numbers of people working on family histories, see Jennifer Fulkerson, "Climbing the Family Tree," *American Demographics* 17, no. 12 (December 1995): 42–50; Margot Hornblower, Melissa August, et al., "Roots Mania," *Time* 153, no. 15 (April 19, 1999): 54–59. Hornblower and others noted that the Internet's top-ranked searches concerned sex, finance, sports, and genealogy. Later studies show similar findings. See Alan Farnham, "Who's Your Daddy? Genealogy Becomes $1.6B Hobby," ABC News, October 24, 2012, http://abcnews.go.com/Business/genealogy-hot-hobby-worth-16b-mormons/story?id=17544242, accessed August 9, 2015. For the quotation, see Richard J. Cox, "Genealogy and Public History: New Genealogical Guides and Their Implications for Public Historians," *Public Historian* 6, no. 2 (Spring 1984): 89–96.

71. Cyndi Howells, Cyndi's List of Genealogy Sites on the Internet, http://www .cyndislist.com, accessed July 31, 2015; "Ancestry.com LLC Reports Fourth Quarter and Full Year 2013 Financial Results," Ancestry.com, http://corporate.ancestry .com/press/press-releases/2014/02/ancestrycom-llc-reports-fourth-quarter-and -full-year-2013-financial-results/, accessed June 1, 2014.

Chapter 3

1. Other important ports of debarkation were New York, Boston, Philadelphia, and Baltimore.

2. Cruzat Family Papers, Box 1, Folder 1, Manuscript Collection 249, Louisiana Research Collection (hereafter LaRC), Tulane University, New Orleans.

3. Ibid.

4. Besides donations to Tulane and the Louisiana State Museum, see Heloise H. Cruzat Papers, 1788–1848, Mss 19, Special and Area Studies Collections, George A. Smathers Libraries, University of Florida, Gainesville.

5. "Joseph William Crozat [*sic*]," *Daily Picayune*, December 21, 1913. See the officers listed in *Louisiana Historical Society Publications* 1–3 (1895–1905).

6. King, *Creole Families of New Orleans*, 334–36.

7. Joseph Émile Ducros family papers, 1784–1992, Collection 893, LaRC, Tulane University, New Orleans; Bill Meneray, former director, Special Collections, Tulane University Library, email to the author, October 23, 2014; Genealogical Paper Series, Group 1, Collection 504 and Genealogical Vertical File, Group 2, Collection

504, Personal Documents Collection, 1671–1959, LaRC, Tulane University, New Orleans.

8. John Franklin Jameson, "The Functions of State and Local Societies with Respect to Research and Publication," in *American Historical Association Annual Report, 1897* (Washington, DC: Government Printing Office, 1898), 51–59. See also E. S. Mills, "Genealogy in the 'Information Age,'" 260–78.

9. Collection policies today will not accept photocopies for the most part, and hence weed out donations of genealogical papers. The phrase used in the 1980s and 1990s was: "We do not accept materials of a purely genealogical nature." Academic libraries often also will not request genealogical materials for researchers via Interlibrary Loan. I wrote about the distancing of genealogists from libraries in Susan Tucker, "Visible Enough to Us: Identity, Archivists, and Genealogical Researchers," *Comma, International Journal on Archives* 2005, no. 3 (2005): 1–11. See also Richard Harvey Brown and Beth Davis-Brown, "The Making of Memory: The Politics of Archives, Libraries, and Museums in the Construction of National Consciousness," *History of the Human Sciences* 11, no. 4 (1998): 17–32.

10. E. S. Mills, "Genealogy in the 'Information Age,'" 260–78; Charles F. Bryan, "What Should We Do about the 'Genies'?," *History News* 41, no. 1 (January 1986): 31–33; Russell E. Bidlack, "The Awakening Genealogy as It Relates to Library Service," *RQ* 23 (Winter 1983): 171–81; Patrick Cadell, "Building on the Past, Investing in the Future through Genealogy and Local History Services," *IFLA Journal* 28, no. 4 (2002): 175–80; Jean Cooper, "The Librarian and the Genealogist Should Be Friends," paper presented at the Virginia Library Association Annual Conference, Williamsburg, Virginia, October 20, 2005, http://www.vla.org/demo/Conference/05Conf/Presentations/IntrotoGenealogy.ppt, accessed October 5, 2008; Christine Kenneally, *The Invisible History of the Human Race: How DNA and History Shape Our Identities and Our Future* (New York: Viking, 2014). Kenneally's first chapter surveys prejudice against genealogists through 2014, and subsequent chapters deal with the complexity of this disfavor.

11. Laura Graham, "Tales from the Vault: A Journey over the Mountain," *Common-Place* 3 (January 2003), http://www.common-place.org/vol-03/no-02/tales/.

12. To understand how genealogists have worked toward professionalism, or, among amateurs, toward evidenced-based work, see Donn Devine, "Defining Professionalism," in *Professional Genealogy: A Manual for Researchers, Writers, Editors, Lecturers, and Librarians*, ed. Elizabeth Shown Mills (Baltimore: Genealogical Publishing, 2001), 7–8; Donn Devine, "Evidence Analysis," in E. S. Mills, *Professional Genealogy*, 327–43; Elizabeth Shown Mills, *Evidence Explained: Citing History Sources from Artifacts to Cyberspace* (Baltimore: Genealogical Publishing, 2007), 15–38.

13. Manuals on genealogical methods regularly warn family historians of the multiple places where records are kept. See, for example, Charles Anderson, "Colonial English Research," in *The Source: A Guidebook of American Genealogy*, ed. Arlene Eakle and Johni Cerny, 1st ed. (Salt Lake City: Ancestry, 1984), 679–98.

14. Johni Cerny, "Vital Records," in Eakle and Cerny, *The Source*, 49; Centers for Disease Control and Prevention, "Appendix 2: History and Organization of the Vi-

tal Statistics System, Historical Development," in *U.S. Vital Statistics System: Major Activities and Developments, 1950–95* (Washington, DC: Government Printing Office, 1954), 43–44; Robert Gutman, "The Accuracy of Vital Statistics in Massachusetts, 1842–1901" (PhD dissertation, Columbia University, 1956), 1–11, 26–70.

15. William Henry Whitmore, *A Handbook of American Genealogy, Being a Catalogue of Family Histories and Publications Containing Genealogical Information* (Albany, NY: J. Munsell, 1862); Bockstruck, "Four Centuries of Genealogy," 164.

16. Emilie Gagnet Leumas, "Mais, I Sin in French, I Gotta Go to Confession in French: A Study of the Language Shift from French to English within the Louisiana Catholic Church" (PhD dissertation, Louisiana State University, 2009). Leumas lists the dates priests began to write in the registries in English, rather than French, which is helpful in understanding the different neighborhoods in which French predominated. See also Lawrence E. Estaville Jr., "The Louisiana French Language in the Nineteenth Century," *Southeastern Geographer* 30, no. 2 (November 1990): 107–20; Guillermo Náñez Falcón, ed., *The Favrot Family Papers: A Documentary Chronicle of Early Louisiana*, 3 vols. (New Orleans: Howard-Tilton Memorial Library, Tulane University, 1988–2001), esp. vol. 1.

17. Nathalie Dessens, *From Saint-Domingue to New Orleans: Migration and Influences* (Gainesville: University Press of Florida, 2007), 50–52.

18. Charles Patton Dimitry, "Sketches," *Times-Democrat*, January 10, 1892–January 22, 1893 (biweekly); Grace King, *Creole Families of New Orleans* (New York: Macmillan, 1921); Stanley Clisby Arthur and George Campbell Huchet de Kernion, *Old Families of Louisiana* (New Orleans: Harmanson, 1931).

19. Phillips, "Writing Louisiana Colonial History," 163–90; Phillips, "To 'Build upon the Foundation,'" 56–78.

20. Michael G. Kammen, "Some Patterns and Meanings of Memory Distortion in American History," in *Memory Distortion: How Minds, Brains, and Societies Reconstruct the Past*, ed. Daniel L. Schacter and Joseph T. Coyle (Cambridge, MA: Harvard University Press, 1995), 334.

21. E. S. Mills, "Genealogy in the 'Information Age,'" 263.

22. John J. Appel, *Immigrant Historical Societies in the United States, 1880–1950* (New York: Arno Press, 1980); Elisabeth Kaplan, "We Are What We Collect, We Collect What We Are: Archives and the Construction of Identity," *American Archivist* 63 (Spring–Summer 2000): 135. None of the immigrant societies active in New Orleans, for example, appear in W. Fitzhugh Brundage, *The Southern Past: A Clash of Race and Memory* (Cambridge, MA: Belknap Press of Harvard University Press, 2005).

23. Robert M. Taylor Jr., "Summoning the Wandering Tribes: Genealogy and Family Reunions in American History," *Journal of Social History* 16, no. 2 (Winter 1982): 22, 23.

24. Bockstruck, "Four Centuries of Genealogy," 162–70; Rick J. Ashton, "Curators, Hobbyists, and Historians: Ninety Years of Genealogy at the Newberry Library," *Library History* 47, no. 2 (1977): 149–62; Bidlack, "The Awakening Genealogy," 171–81.

25. Samuel Muller, Johan Adriaan Feith, and Robert Fruin, *Manual for the Ar-*

rangement and Description of Archives (1898), 2nd ed., trans. Arthur H. Leavitt (1940; repr., Chicago: Society of American Archivists, 2003); Marjorie Rabe Barritt, "Coming to America: Dutch *Archivistiek* and American Archival Practice," *Archival Issues* 18 (1993): 43–54; Richard C. Berner, *Archival Theory and Practice in the United States: A Historical Analysis* (Seattle: University of Washington Press, 1983), 7.

26. Luke J. Gilliland-Swetland, "The Provenance of a Profession: The Permanence of the Public Archives and Historical Manuscripts Traditions in American Archival History," *American Archivist* 54, no. 2 (Spring 1991): 160–75.

27. Much more work could be done examining the combination of these two models of archives and libraries in New Orleans. That New Orleans was the exception in the American South is one aspect that could be studied. For information on the formation of the other southern institutions of memory, see Brundage, *The Southern Past*, 107–37.

28. Weil, *Family Trees*, 101–11, 153–59.

29. Mark Twain, "Autobiography of Mark Twain," *Harper's Monthly Magazine* 144 (1922): 279–80.

30. Francesca Constance Morgan, "A Noble Pursuit? Bourgeois America's Uses of Lineage," in *The American Bourgeoisie: Distinction and Identity in the Nineteenth Century*, ed. Sven Beckert and Julia B. Rosenbaum, 135–52 (New York: Palgrave Macmillan, 2010); Francesca Constance Morgan, "Lineage as Capital: Genealogy in Antebellum New England," *New England Quarterly* 83, no. 2 (June 2010): 250–82; Francesca Constance Morgan, "'Home and Country': Women, Nation, and the Daughters of the American Revolution, 1890–1939" (PhD dissertation, Columbia University, 1998), 139–42, 151–54, 170–75; Davies, *Patriotism on Parade*, 58–63, 227–32.

31. Kory L. Meyerink, ed., *Printed Sources: A Guide to Published Genealogical Records* (Provo, UT: Ancestry, 1998), 474; see, for example, Daughters of the American Revolution, Delaware State Society, *Old Bible Records, Delaware* (Newark, DE: DAR, Delaware Societies, 1944–1967).

32. Mary Ann Sheble, "Genealogical Libraries and Collections," in *The Encyclopedia of Library History*, ed. Wayne A. Wiegand and Donald G. Davis Jr., Garland Reference Library of Social Science, vol. 503 (New York: Garland Publishing, 1994), 232.

33. Penelope Papailias, *Genres of Recollection: Archival Poetics and Modern Greece* (New York: Palgrave Macmillan, 2005) does an especially good job of looking at the marginalization of local historians.

34. Taylor and Crandall, "Historians and Genealogists," 8–9.

35. "*WMQ* Mission Statement," Omohundro Institute of Early American History and Culture, http://oieahc.wm.edu/wmq/mission.html, accessed April 1, 2009.

36. Donald Lines Jacobus, *Genealogy as Pastime and Profession* (New Haven, CT: Tuttle, Morehouse and Taylor, 1930). Jacobus founded what came to be called the New Haven School of Genealogy in the 1920s, and the *New Haven Genealogical Magazine* in 1922, which became the *American Genealogist* ten years later; David L. Greene, "Donald Lines Jacobus, Scholarly Genealogy, and the *American Ge-*

nealogist," *American Genealogist* 72, nos. 3–4 (July–October 1997): 159–80; E. S. Mills, "Genealogy in the 'Information Age,'" 264–65; "The Source: A Guidebook to American Genealogy," Ancestry.com, http://www.ancestry.com/wiki/index.php?title=The_Source:_A_Guidebook_to_American_Genealogy, accessed August 9, 2015.

37. These can be found in Collection 504, LaRC.

38. New Orleans Public Library, Louisiana Division, Monthly Reports. See especially the reports for 1944, 1949, 1953, and 1959.

39. Both societies mention the preservation of records prominently in their mission statements.

40. Archibald F. Bennett, "The Record Copying Program of the Utah Genealogical Society," *American Archivist* 16, no. 3 (July 1953): 227–32.

41. Kahlile Mehr, conversation and email with the author, January 6 and January 18, 2011; Khalile Mehr, "Acquisitions, 1950–1970," unpublished paper on the history of microfilming, 3, copy in possession of the author.

42. Interviewee no. 25, b. 1949.

43. Interviewee no. 17, b. 1937.

44. Alex Haley, *Roots* (Garden City, NY: Doubleday, 1976).

45. Gary B. Mills and Elizabeth Shown Mills, "*Roots* and the New 'Faction': A Legitimate Tool for Clio?," *Virginia Magazine of History and Biography* 89, no. 1 (January 1981): 9.

46. See articles by Russell E. Bidlack, Anne Billeter, Yvette Guillot Boling, Charles F. Bryan, Thomas Jay Kemp, Elizabeth Shown Mills, Gail R. Redman, Judith P. Reid, and others in Susan Tucker, "Archivists and Genealogical Researchers: A Bibliography," Tulane University, http://www.tulane.edu/~wclib/archivists/archivists.html, accessed February 14, 2015. Boling discusses Louisiana in particular.

47. John Patrick Dulong, "Genealogical Groups in a Changing Organizational Environment: From Lineage to Heritage" (PhD dissertation, Wayne State University, 1986); James Hijiya, "Roots: Family and Ethnicity in the 1970s," *American Quarterly* 30, no. 4 (Autumn 1978): 549.

48. Coralie Guarino Davis Collection, Boxes 4–6, Newcomb Archives, Newcomb College Institute, Tulane University, New Orleans; Susan Tucker, "Coralie Guarino Davis (1926–2004): Claiming Status and Constructing Legacies," in *Louisiana Women*, vol. 2, ed. Shannon Frystak and Mary Kaiser Farmer (Athens: University of Georgia Press, 2016).

49. Davis Collection, Box 6, Diary entry, April 10, 2004.

50. Morgan, "Lineage as Capital," 250–51.

51. Zerubavel, *Time Maps*, 4–5; Jeannette A. Bastian, "The Records of Memory, the Archives of Identity: Celebrations, Texts and Archival Sensibilities," *Archival Science* 13 (2013): 121–31.

Chapter 4

1. Annette Gordon-Reed, *Thomas Jefferson and Sally Hemings: An American Controversy* (Charlottesville: University of Virginia Press, 1997); Annette Gordon-Reed, *The Hemingses of Monticello* (New York: W. W. Norton, 2008), 12.

2. Annette Gordon-Reed, interview, "The Hemingses of Monticello," Washington Journal Series on Presidents, Book TV, C-Span 2, January 10, 2009.

3. Shannon Lanier and Jane Feldman, *Jefferson's Children: The Story of One American Family* (New York: Random House, 2000), 11.

4. Gordon-Reed, interview, "The Hemingses of Monticello."

5. "Thomas Jefferson and Sally Hemings: A Brief Account," Monticello.org, http://www.monticello.org/site/plantation-and-slavery/thomas-jefferson-and-sally-hemings-brief-account, accessed March 31, 2013.

6. Johnson, *KnowLA*, s.v. "Code Noir," by Michael T. Pasquier, January 6, 2011, http://www.knowla.org/entry/742/. Newspaper examples include "Family Seeks to Disprove Colored Charges, Prados Family Appear in Court as Witnesses in Own Behalf," *Daily Picayune*, February 27, 1914; "Prados Family Decreed White," *Daily Picayune*, March 19, 1914. For examples of scholarly examinations of cases, beliefs, and conversations, see Jennifer M. Spear, "Colonial Intimacies: Legislating Sex in French Louisiana," *William and Mary Quarterly* 60, no. 1, Sexuality in Early America (January 2003): 75–98; Sybil Kein, ed., *Creole: The History and Legacy of Louisiana's Free People of Color* (Baton Rouge: Louisiana State University Press, 2000); Stephanie Rose Bird, *Light, Bright, and Damned Near White: Biracial and Triracial Culture in America* (Westport, CT: Praeger, 2009); Shirley Elizabeth Thompson, *Exiles at Home* (Cambridge, MA: Harvard University Press, 2009); Kimberly S. Hanger, *Bounded Lives, Bounded Places: Free Black Society in Colonial New Orleans, 1769–1803* (Durham, NC: Duke University Press, 1997).

7. Winston De Ville, email to the author, October 19, 2014.

8. An excellent short introduction to this controversy is found in Lawrence N. Powell, "Introduction: A Novelist Turns Historian," in *The New Orleans of George Washington Cable: The 1887 Census Office Report*, ed. Lawrence N. Powell (Baton Rouge: Louisiana State University Press, 2008), 9–35.

9. Over 80 percent of the people to whom I spoke were fifty-five years and older. Statistics were gathered from the Jefferson Genealogical Society and the Genealogical Research Society of New Orleans in 2011. However, the stereotype of the elderly genealogist (over sixty-five) does not hold out in national counts. The National Genealogical Society reported the numbers of "senior members" at 1,655, or some 23 percent, out of 7,815 individual members in April 2008. Jan Alpert, former president of the NGS, email to the author, April 16, 2008.

10. Louisiana Creole Research Association, http://www.lacreole.org, accessed August 20, 2014.

11. Charles Gayarré, *History of Louisiana* (New York: William J. Widdleton, 1867), 3:408, http://penelope.uchicago.edu/Thayer/E/Gazetteer/Places/America/United_States/Louisiana/_Texts/GAYHLA/4/7*.html, accessed September 3, 2011.

12. Ten genealogists mentioned that the Spanish and the Catholic Church in New Orleans (and also in nearby Mobile, which has a similar heritage) were such omnipresent recordkeepers that there was little need for private family records; as one said, "even the family name displayed in needlework."

13. Anonymous, "The History of Louisiana and Some of Its Leading Families," *Louisiana Historical Quarterly* 1, no. 1 (January 1917): 95–98. The article includes a letter from G. Montegut to G. Pitot dated February 5, 1917, telling of family history.

14. See court cases mentioned in Thompson, *Exiles at Home*, 44–45, 67–93; Virginia R. Domínguez, *White by Definition: Social Classification in Creole Louisiana* (New Brunswick, NJ: Rutgers University Press, 1986), 1–5, 26–55, 75–89. Thompson concentrates on cases in 1831, 1834, 1842, 1851, 1854, and 1859; Domínguez writes about government policies and cases from 1803 through the 1980s. See also newspaper accounts, note 6 above.

15. Phillips, "To 'Build upon the Foundation.'"

16. Charles Gayarré to John Dimitry, November 14, 1881, John Minor Wisdom Collection, LaRC, Tulane University (also quoted in L. Powell, "Introduction: A Novelist Turns Historian," 17). In the Wisdom Collection, see especially Box 14 for an extended correspondence between John Dimitry and Gayarré. The latter had many grievances about not being published. John was Charles Patton Dimitry's brother, and also a son of Alexander Dimitry.

17. L. Powell, "Introduction: A Novelist Turns Historian," 17; Wisdom Collection, Box 14, LaRC.

18. *Dictionary of American Biography*, s.v. "Alexander Dimitry."

19. Charles Patton Dimitry, "Sketches," *Times-Democrat*, January 10, 1892–January 22, 1893 (biweekly).

20. Thompson, *Exiles at Home*, 50–51, 62–66.

21. Ibid., 28–66, for quotations, 38, 46, 48; "Archives of Our History," *New Orleans Bee*, February 4, 1854.

22. Thompson, *Exiles at Home*, 60–66, quotations 64, 65. Interestingly, during that trial, it was the Dragon-Dimitry women on whom the court focused (among them Alexander's sister, particularly her hair and skin color). The grandmother was called "as evidence." The notarial act that concerned both Dimitry cases is "Reconnaissance d'un enfant naturel par . . . Michel Dragon de Mme Marie Anne Dragon, épouse de Adrian Dimitry," Acts of Christoval de Armas, vol. 1, folio 159, April 12, 1819. There are two other notarial acts, also from 1819, in which Dragon recognizes his daughter and leaves her money.

23. Cheryl I. Harris, "In the Shadow of *Plessy*," *University of Pennsylvania Journal of Constitutional Law* 7 (2004): 867.

24. Marcus Christian Collection, "Sheep, Goats, and Passer Pour Blanches," Mss 11, Box 12, UNO Library, New Orleans.

25. US Daughters of the War of 1812, Chalmette Chapter, Scrapbooks 48–58, LaRC, Tulane University; Daughters of the War of 1812, Chalmette Chapter, Minute Books, 1921–1935, 1935–1943; Scrapbook 656 (2), 1925–1927, 1931–1937, Box 1, Folder 15; Coralie Guarino Davis (b. 1926), conversation with the author (while compiling entries in the 1990 and 2002 editions of *The New Orleans Guide to Collections on Women*), May 15, 1990; March 10, 2002.

26. "Louisiana Colonials Recently Organize," *Times-Picayune*, July 18, 1917.

27. King, *Creole Families of New Orleans*. On her education, connections, and other writings, see Robert Bush, *Grace King: A Southern Destiny* (Baton Rouge: Louisiana State University Press, 1983).

28. King, *Creole Families of New Orleans*, vii.

29. Ibid., x.

30. Grace King Collection, Box 1, Folders 2–26, LaRC, Tulane University.

31. King, *Creole Families of New Orleans*, 322, 351. Father Lugano maintained the registers for people of color; Josie Cerf oversaw many records and manuscripts and knew, or thought she knew, about Gayarré's Creole of color son, mother, and granddaughter; and Heloise Hulse Cruzat was the translator of the judicial records that included court and notarial records involving mixed-race people.

32. Ibid.

33. Arthur and Kernion, *Old Families of Louisiana*, preface.

34. Ibid., 401–5; Thompson, *Exiles at Home*, 53.

35. Kernion was a member of the International Association of Genealogists, the New Orleans Genealogical and Historical Society, the Louisiana Colonials, the Louisiana Historical Society, and the Louisiana Society for Preservation of Ancient Tombs.

36. Representative titles by Charles Maduell include: *The Census Tables for the French Colony of Louisiana from 1699 through 1732* (Baltimore: Genealogical Publishing, 1972); *Index of Spanish Citizens Entering New Orleans, January 1820 through December 1839* (New Orleans: n.p., n.d.); *Marriage Contracts, Wills and Testaments of the Spanish Colonial Period in New Orleans, 1770-1804* (New Orleans: n.p., 1969).

37. Representative works by De Ville can be found in an extensive bibliography of more than three hundred of his works: Dowell Lafleur, *Winston De Ville: A Bibliography of Genealogical and Other Writings, 1959–2012* (Baton Rouge: Claitor's Law Books and Publishing, 2013).

38. Winston De Ville, email to the author, May 1, 2011.

39. Interviewee no. 34, b. 1946.

40. Emilie Gagnet Leumas (archivist, Archdiocese of New Orleans), conversation with the author, August 1, 2012.

41. Interviewee no. 34, b. 1946.

42. Naomi M. Drake, Appellant, v. Department of Health, Appellee, appeal from the Civil Service Commission of the City of New Orleans, no. 391, 1965, City Archives, New Orleans Public Library; "Civil Service Commission Probes Case," *Times-Picayune*, May 14, 1965. Earlier complaints against her had been made in cases such as Katherine Spriggs et al. v. Mrs. Naomi Drake et al., December 4, 1963, City Archives, New Orleans Public Library.

43. Being 1/32> or more of African descent marked one as Negro. Jane Doe et al. v. State of Louisiana et al., no. 78-9513, C-W no. 81-4201, Civil District Court, Parish of Orleans, Louisiana; Calvin Trillin, "Black or White," *New Yorker*, April 14, 1986.

44. Elizabeth Shown Mills, email to the author, May 2, 2011.

45. Gwendolyn Midlo Hall, "The Louisiana Slave Database and the Louisiana Free Database, 1719–1820," http://www.nps.gov/cari/historyculture/upload/using database.pdf, accessed May 18, 2014.

46. Bliss Broyard, *One Drop: My Father's Hidden Life; A Story of Race and Family Secrets* (New York: Little, Brown, 2007), 461.

47. The most important of these initial works, chronologically listed, are Laura Foner's "The Free People of Color in Louisiana and St. Domingue: A Compara-

tive Portrait of Two Three-Caste Slave Societies," *Journal of Social History* 3, no. 4 (Summer 1970): 406–30; the reprint edition of Rodolphe Desdunes's *Our People and Our History* (Baton Rouge: Louisiana State University Press, 1973); James Haskins, *The Creoles of Color of New Orleans* (New York: Crowell, 1975); Gary B. Mills, *The Forgotten People: Cane River's Creoles of Color* (Baton Rouge: Louisiana State University Press, 1977); David C. Rankin, "The Forgotten People: Free People of Color in New Orleans, 1850–1870" (PhD dissertation, Johns Hopkins University,1976). Sybil Kein also began her research at this time, publishing a book of poetry on Creoles of color in 1981.

48. Interviewee no. 28, b. 1940.

49. Samuel Wilson Jr., Bernard Lemann, Mary Louise Christovich, et al., *New Orleans Architecture*, 8 vols. (Gretna, LA: Pelican, 1971–1997).

50. Pierre Nora, "General Introduction: Between Memory and History," in *Realms of Memory: Rethinking the French Past*, ed. Lawrence D. Kritzman, trans. Arthur Goldhammer (New York: Columbia University Press, 1996), 6–8; Interviewee no. 16, b. 1957.

51. Rebuilding Together New Orleans, http://www.rtno.org/get-involved/advocacy/, accessed September 3, 2011.

52. Interviewee no. 8, b. 1966.

53. "Á Monsieur C.A.N. Gayarré, homme de couleur libre," George Smith Collection, Louisiana State Museum, New Orleans.

54. For the quotation: Peu de jours après votre baptême, dans ce même mois de mai 1826, ou je reconnus publiquement votre status, (ce qui certes n'était pas un acte de malveillance a votre égard, et encore moins un présage de l'hostilité sans cause que vous me suppose avoir contre vous,) je fis cesser ces relations qui avaient donné lieu à votre naissance, et j'allai étudier le Droit à Philadelphie. Translation by the author and Heather Frost.

55. Prenez dans la société le rang qui vous appartient réellement; soyez honnête, laborieux, et humble surtout. C'est ainsi que vous vous ferez estimer et respecter de tout le monde. Ne rougissez pas de vous avouer ce que vous êtes—un home de couleur. J'en connais de fort respectables dans cette classe que vous méprisez, et que je vous recommande de prendre pour modelés. Translation by author and Heather Frost.

56. L'aveu d'une faute, Monsieur, est toujours pénible, et surtout quand des circonstances impérieuses peuvent exiger que cet aveu devienne public. Translation by the author and Heather Frost.

57. Charles Gayarré Papers, Box 14, Folder 3, Mss 156, Louisiana and Lower Mississippi Valley Collections, Louisiana State University Libraries, Baton Rouge. Charles Arthur Nicolas Gayarré lived at least until 1900. In the 1850s, he is identified as working as a clerk, and in the 1880s, as an upholsterer. US Census Bureau (1850), New Orleans Municipality 3, Ward 1, Orleans, Louisiana, Roll M432_238, Page 29A; US Census (1880) New Orleans, Orleans, Louisiana, Roll 462, Page 660B; US Census (1900) New Orleans Ward 7, Orleans, Louisiana, Roll 573, Page 6A. All sources available from Ancestry.com and the Church of Jesus Christ of Latter-day Saints.

58. Earl Noland Saucier, "Charles Gayarré, the Creole Historian" (PhD dissertation, George Peabody College for Teachers, 1935), 29.

Chapter 5

1. Interviewee no. 22, b. 1936.

2. Ibid.

3. Noel Currer-Briggs and Royster Gambier, *Debrett's Family Historian: A Guide to Tracing Your Ancestry* (Exeter, England: Webb and Bower, 1982), 33; Daniel Woolf, *The Social Circulation of the Past: English Historical Culture, 1500–1730* (Oxford: Oxford University Press, 2003), 99–137; McDannell, *Material Christianity*, 89.

4. The Samuel Andrews Bible is housed at Harvard University's Houghton Library; the Richards Bible is located at the New England Historic and Genealogical Society in Boston.

5. These Bibles are available in the Newberry Library in Chicago; see also Barnhill, "Keep Sacred the Memory," 64.

6. "Revolutionary War Pension and Bounty-Land Warrant Application Files" (NARA microfilm publication M804, 2,670 rolls), records of the Department of Veterans Affairs, Record Group 15, National Archives, Washington, DC; "U.S., Revolutionary War and Bounty-Land Warrant Application Files, 1800–1900," Ancestry.com, 2010, http://search.ancestry.com/search/db.aspx?dbid=1995.

7. DAR Library File Collection, "Special Collections," Daughters of the American Revolution, http://www.dar.org/library/special-collections, accessed February 11, 2015.

8. David Ferriero, "The Family Bible," AOTUS National Archives, August 2, 2013, http://blogs.archives.gov/aotus/?p=5096 (Ferriero is the tenth archivist of the United States); NGS Bible Records, "Become a Member," National Genealogical Society, http://www.ngsgenealogy.org/cs/individual_member_benefits; Bible Records Online, http://www.biblerecords.com; "Family Bible Records," Library of Virginia, http://www.lva.virginia.gov/public/guides/bible.htm; "Bible Records" search, Ancestry.com, http://search.ancestry.com/search/db.aspx?dbid=29765. There are many other such listings electronically available through the Family History Library; see https://familysearch.org/learn/wiki/en/United_States_Bible_Records. (All sites were accessed on January 30, 2015.)

9. Benes, "Decorated New England Family Registers," 21–36; James Hall, *Illustrated Dictionary of Symbols in Eastern and Western Art* (Cambridge: John Murray, 1994), 59–60; Mary Bouquet, "Family Trees and Their Affinities: The Visual Imperative of the Genealogical Diagram," *Journal of the Royal Anthropological Institute* 2, no. 1 (March 1996): 43–66; Maureen A. Taylor, "Tall Oaks from Little Acorns Grow: The Family Tree Lithograph in America," in Simons and Benes, *The Art of Family*," 75–89.

10. Tim Ingold, *Lines: A Brief History* (New York: Routledge, 2007), 104–19. For an exquisite look at the tree as visual symbol, see Manuel Lima, *The Book of Trees: Visualizing Branches of Knowledge* (New York: Princeton Architectural Press, 2014).

11. Mary Bouquet, "Figures of Relations: Reconnecting Kinship Studies and Museum Collections," in *Cultures of Relatedness: New Approaches to the Study of Kinship*, ed. Janet Carsten (New York: Cambridge University Press, 2000), 174–78, 184; Bouquet, "Family Trees and Their Affinities," 43–66; M. Taylor, "Tall Oaks from Little Acorns Grow," 75–76.

12. "New Confucius Genealogy Out Next Year," China Internet Information Center, http://www.china.org.cn/china/features/content_16696029.htm, accessed May 2, 2015.

13. Lima, *The Book of Trees*, 57. The scroll of the tree is held by the British Museum; Elizabeth Armstrong, "Robert Peril and His 1524 Privilege," *Bibliothèque d'Humanisme et Renaissance* 61, no. 1 (1999): 85–93.

14. Michael A. Kennedy, emails to the author, January 22, February 3, February 4, 2015.

15. Sigrid Weigel, "Genealogy: On the Iconography and Rhetorics of an Epistemological Topos," Enciclopédia e Hipertexto, http://www.educ.fc.ul.pt/hyper/resources/sweigel/, accessed March 6, 2014. See also Sigrid Weigel, "Foreign-Language Publications," http://www.zfl-berlin.org/tl_files/zfl/downloads/personen/weigel/publications_foreign_languages_sigrid_weigel.pdf.

16. Henry de Bray, *The Estate Book of Henry de Bray of Harleston, Co. Northants*, ed. Dorothy Willis (London: Royal Historical Society, 1916), http://www.archive.org/details/estatebookofhenroobray, accessed March 21, 2015.

17. Ibid; see also Ketelaar, "The Genealogical Gaze."

18. Corinne Earnest and Russell Earnest, *To the Latest Posterity: Pennsylvania-German Family Registers in the Fraktur Tradition* (University Park: Pennsylvania State University Press, 2004), 17, 30–31, 35, 40, 81, 99, 107–11, 114.

19. Ibid., 6–8; Gloria Seaman Allen, *Family Record: Genealogical Watercolors and Needlework* (Washington, DC: Daughters of the American Revolution Museum, 1989), 7.

20. William Hyde Family Papers, 1652–1816 (Mss 653), NEHGS, Boston; Tim Salls, NEHGS archivist, emails to the author, December 8, 2008, and May 7, 2009.

21. John Flint, 1722–1792, "In Memory of the Family of the Flints," Lemuel Shattuck Papers (Mss A S53), NEHGS, Boston.

22. Keeping Memories Alive, "KMA History: We Invented Scrapbooking," http://www.scrapbooks.com/history.php, accessed October 6, 2008.

23. Ibid.; Susan Tucker, "Reading and Rereading: The Scrapbooks of Girls Growing into Women, 1900–1940," in *Defining Print Culture for Youth: The Cultural Work of Children's Literature*, ed. Anne Lundin and Wayne Wiegand (Westport, CT: Libraries Unlimited, 2003), 10.

24. "Scrapbooking Statistics," My Creative Memory, http://www.mycreativememory.com/main.asp?page=%7B3B764E60-ACFE-4555-B447-4AE0BFBF7D69%7D, accessed January 16, 2009.

25. Ronald J. Zboray and Mary Saracino Zboray, "Is It a Diary, Commonplace Book, Scrapbook, or Whatchamacallit? Six Years of Exploration in New England's Manuscript Archives," *Libraries and the Cultural Record* 44, no. 1 (February 2009): 101.

26. Sarah McNair Vosmeier, "Picturing Love and Friendship: Photograph Albums and Networks of Affection in the 1860s," in *The Scrapbook in American Life*, ed. Susan Tucker, Katherine Ott, and Patricia Buckler (Philadelphia: Temple University Press, 2006), 209–10.

27. Elizabeth E. Siegel, "'Miss Domestic' and 'Miss Enterprise'; or, How to Keep a Photograph Album," in Tucker, Ott, and Buckler, *The Scrapbook in American Life*, 254–55.

28. "Centre-Table Gossip: Photographic Albums," *Godey's Lady's Book* 64 (February 1862): 208; Siegel, "'Miss Domestic' and 'Miss Enterprise,'" 254.

29. Extant copies of Platt's album are found in the George Eastman House International Museum of Photography, Sipley Collection/3M Collection, and the National Museum of American History, Smithsonian Institution. See Siegel, "'Miss Domestic' and 'Miss Enterprise,'" 318n23.

30. Siegel, "'Miss Domestic' and 'Miss Enterprise,'" 258–63.

31. A copy of *The Family Memorial* is in the New England Historic Genealogical Society Library.

32. See, for example, "Family Trees," De la Fé–Vadillo–Flores–Iturrioz and Matos–Ortega–García–Vadel Family Directory, http://www.delafe.com/familydirectory/trees.htm, accessed October 10, 2008.

33. Suzanne Johnson, "Testimonial," Family Tree DNA, http://www.familytreedna.com/testimonials.aspx, accessed June 1, 2014.

34. John B. Windham, "Windham Family DNA Project, Background," Family Tree DNA, http://www.familytreedna.com/public/windhamfamily/default.aspx?section=yresults, accessed August 29, 2014.

35. "Welcome to Family Tree DNA," Family Tree DNA, http://www.familytreedna.com/, accessed January 27, 2015.

36. Paul A. Lombardo, *A Century of Eugenics in America: From the Indiana Experiment to the Human Genome Era* (Bloomington: Indiana University Press, 2011), 1–95, 192; Alexandra Minna Stern, *Eugenic Nation: Faults and Frontiers of Better Breeding in Modern America* (Berkeley: University of California Press, 2005), esp. chapter 1; Kenneally, *The Invisible History of the Human Race*, esp. chapters 3–4. See also Lutz Kaelber, "Eugenics: Compulsory Sterilization in 50 American States," University of Vermont Today, http://www.uvm.edu/~lkaelber/eugenics/, accessed January 27, 2015.

37. David C. Mountain and Jeanne Kay Guelke, "Genetics, Genealogy, and Geography," in *Geography and Genealogy: Locating Personal Pasts*, ed. Dallen J. Timothy and Jeanne Kay Guelke (Burlington, VT: Ashgate Publishing, 2008), 153.

38. *African American Lives Special*, PBS, first aired in January 2007; See also Henry Louis Gates Jr., *Finding Oprah's Roots: Finding Your Own* (New York: Crown, 2007). PBS also created a DVD of *Oprah's Roots*, featuring thirty minutes of excerpts from the broadcast plus more than an hour of additional comments and research guidance from genealogists, historians, and geneticists featured in the program and in the original African American Lives series. The prototype of many genealogical television series was the British *Who Do You Think You Are?*, which began in 2004. An American series with the same title began in 2010.

39. L. Luca Cavalli-Sforza, Paolo Menozzi, and Alberto Piazza, *The History and Geography of Human Genes* (Princeton, NJ: Princeton University Press, 1994).

40. National Geographic Society, Genographic Project, https://genographic.nationalgeographic.com/about/, accessed January 25, 2015.

41. Kenneally, *The Invisible History of the Human Race*, 210–11.

42. "Ancestry.com Launches New Ancestry DNA Service: The Next Generation of DNA Science Poised to Enrich Family History Research," Ancestry.com, http://corporate.ancestry.com/press/press-releases/2012/05/ancestry.com-dna-launches/, accessed January 6, 2015.

43. CeCe Moore, Your Genetic Genealogist, http://www.yourgeneticgenealogist.com, accessed February 12, 2015; "For DNA Newbies," International Society of Genetic Genealogy, http://www.isogg.org, accessed February 12, 2015; Family Tree DNA Learning Center, https://www.familytreedna.com/learn/test-types/, accessed February 12, 2015.

44. "List of DNA Testing Companies," International Society of Genetic Genealogy, http://www.isogg.org/wiki/List_of_DNA_testing_companies, accessed December 11, 2014; "DNA, Genetics, and Family Health: Professional Services and DNA Testing," Cyndi's List of Genealogy Sites on the Internet, http://www.cyndislist.com/dna/professional-services-and-dna-testing/, accessed October 6, 2014.

45. Interviewee no. 5, b. 1927.

46. "Maternal Ancestry," Oxford Ancestors, http://www.oxfordancestors.com/content/view/35/55/, accessed January 15, 2015.

47. Blaine Bettinger, "Genetic Genealogy: A Powerful Tool for the Family Historian," *The World*, Public Radio International, March 22, 2012; Virtual Institute of Genealogical Research, "Genetic Genealogy for Professional Genealogists," course announcement, 2015, http://vigrgenealogy.com/schedule/bettinger-genetic-pro/, accessed July 29, 2015.

48. "I Don't Want Death to Be Such a Downer," *All Things Considered*, National Public Radio, March 21, 2015.

49. Valerie Atkisson, https://www.valerieatkisson.com. Accessed August 15, 2015.

50. Morgan, "Lineage as Capital," 269–74.

51. Lemuel Shattuck, *A Complete System of Family Registration* (Boston: William D. Ticknor, 1841), introduction.

52. Ibid. Shattuck also issued *Blank Book Forms for Family Registers* (1856), containing pages that could be inserted in other books. A copy of the 1856 edition is available in the Library of Congress, but otherwise this book is very rare.

53. Gutman, "The Accuracy of Vital Statistics," 142–47; James Cassedy, "Lemuel Shattuck," in *American National Biography*, ed. John A. Garraty and Mark C. Carnes (New York: Oxford University Press, 1999), vol. 19.

54. I could find no information indicating whether Shattuck considered New Orleans and its system of vital records, which began in 1790.

55. Walter F. Willcox, "Lemuel Shattuck, Statist, Founder of the American Statistical Association," *American Statistician* 1, no. 1 (August 1947): 13.

56. United States Census Bureau, *Heads of Families at the First Census of the*

United States Taken in the Year 1790, volumes by state (Washington, DC: Government Printing Office, 1908).

57. "Accelerated Indexing Systems, US Census Indexes on Microfilm," Family Search, https://familysearch.org/learn/wiki/en/Accelerated_Indexing_Systems_U.S._Census_Indexes_(on_Microfiche), accessed January 30, 2015.

58. See, for two examples among thousands of pre-Internet indexing and transcription projects, Gaius Marcus Brumbaugh, *Maryland Records, Colonial, Revolutionary, County and Church, from Original Sources*, 2 vols. (Baltimore: Williams and Wilkins, 1915, 1928); Maduell, *The Census Tables for the French Colony of Louisiana*.

59. Sheble, "Genealogical Libraries and Collections," 232.

Chapter 6

1. Laura Porteous to El Reverendo Padre Rector de los Archivos de la Iglesia Metropolitana, Santiago, Cuba, March 31, 1930; Laura Porteous to Monsieur le Directeur de Ministre des Colonies French, October 20, 1930, Laura Porteous Collection, Mss 1200, Special Collections, Hill Memorial Library, Louisiana State University (hereafter, Porteous Collection, LSU). I thank Jenny Marie Forsythe for her work on Porteous; see Jenny Marie Forsythe and Susan Tucker, "'The Most Wonderful Collection of Original Documents in the United States': Notes on the Lives and Work of Two New Orleans Translators," *Collections: A Journal for Museum and Archives Professionals* 11, no. 3 (2015).

2. "My dear Sister Monica," New Orleans, April 15, 1927, scanned copy of letter provided by Sister Debbie Lloyd and Sister Agatha Fitzgerald, OSU, Ursulines of Brown County, in email to the author, January 6, 2015.

3. "History," New Orleans Notarial Archives, http://www.notarialarchives.org/history.htm, accessed September 3, 2011.

4. Pearce-Moses, *A Glossary of Archival and Records Terminology*, s.v. "Notarial Archives."

5. Interviewee no. 20, b. 1947.

6. Pearce-Moses, *A Glossary of Archival and Records Terminology*, s.v. "Notarial Archives."

7. Baade, "Marriage Contracts in French and Spanish Louisiana," 1488, 1490.

8. Nugent, "Pedro Pedesclaux"; Beers, *French and Spanish Records of Louisiana*, 9.

9. Nugent, "Pedro Pedesclaux"; Gilbert Din and John Harkins, *The New Orleans Cabildo: Colonial Louisiana's First City Government, 1769–1803* (Baton Rouge: Louisiana State University Press, 1996), 74–78.

10. Johnson, *KnowLA*, s.v. "Pierre Clément de Laussat," by Catherine Mizell-Nelson, August 23, 2013, http://www.knowla.org/entry/919/; Alfred Lemmon, "The Archival Legacy of Spanish Louisiana's Colonial Records," *American Archivist* 55, no. 1 (Winter 1992): 145–46; Beers, *French and Spanish Records of Louisiana*, 131.

11. Beers, *French and Spanish Records of Louisiana*, 9–11; Nugent, "Pedro Pedesclaux."

12. Lemmon, "The Archival Legacy of Spanish Louisiana's Colonial Records," 145–46; Beers, *French and Spanish Records of Louisiana*, 131; Howard Margot, "Outline of the History of Louisiana," unpublished document in the author's possession, 4.

13. Beers, *French and Spanish Records of Louisiana*, 11.

14. Faye Phillips, conversation with the author, 2012; Howard Margot, conversation with the author, October 25, 2009; Winston De Ville, email to the author, October 21, 2014. Most archivists and family historians do not believe that the judicial records ever left New Orleans for Baton Rouge, which had housed the capitol since 1849 and therein the room set aside for the LHS, the books and records of the state. If the judicial records did make their way to Baton Rouge, they might have been returned to New Orleans on orders of General Benjamin Butler in 1862. Or they might have been rescued by a local citizen who took some five thousand volumes of other library materials to a secure location outside of Baton Rouge. Or they might have been thrown from the windows when Union soldiers started a fire in the interior of one part of the capitol, and after that gathered up by some unknown persons—bibliophiles, vandals, or simply responsible citizens or soldiers.

15. Alcée Fortier, "Report of Prof. Fortier," *Publications of the Louisiana Historical Society* 1, no. 1 (1895): 4. Fortier says that Charles Gayarré in his 1846 and 1854 histories of the state used the records, but I can find no evidence of this use by comparing cases to Gayarré's text.

16. Beers, *French and Spanish Records of Louisiana*, 12.

17. John Hanno Deiler, *The Settlement of the German Coast of Louisiana and the Creoles of German Descent* (Philadelphia: German American Historical Society, 1909), 119–20.

18. Grace King, "The Black Boxes," *Louisiana Historical Quarterly* 7, no. 1 (1913): 11.

19. Henry Plauché Dart, "Courts and Law in Colonial Louisiana," *Louisiana Historical Quarterly* 4, no. 3 (1921): 256.

20. Grace King, "Preface," *Louisiana Historical Quarterly* 8, no. 1 (1914): 9; William Price, "Work of Indexing Louisiana 'Black Boxes,'" *Louisiana Historical Quarterly* 8, no. 1 (1914): 8–20.

21. Louisiana State Museum, *Biennial Report of the Board of Curators for 1920–21* (New Orleans: Louisiana State Museum, 1922), 38. Boyd Cruise published an overall index to the records as they appear in the *Louisiana Historical Quarterly*, vol. 33.

22. Louisiana State Museum, *Biennial Report of the Board of Curators for 1941–42* (New Orleans: Louisiana State Museum, 1942), 22–23.

23. Complaints began in the 1970s. In early 1972, leaders of the Friends of the Cabildo sent letters to the membership announcing that articles highlighting the failure of the museum to protect the documents were to appear soon in the local newspapers. See Friends of the Cabildo, Louisiana State Museum Files, Vertical Files, New Orleans Public Library, Louisiana Division. See also *Times-Picayune*, October 9, 10, 11, 13, 14, 15, 16, 1972; Wayne Morris and Larry Telford, LDS microfilmers, interview with the author, January 8, 2011, Salt Lake City.

24. Winston De Ville, "Manuscript Sources in Louisiana for the History of the French in the Mississippi Valley," in *The French in the Mississippi Valley*, ed. John Francis McDermott (Urbana: University of Illinois Press, 1965): 218.

25. Alice D. Forsyth wrote a series of listings and indexes to the records of the Superior Council of Louisiana in *Genesis* from 1988 to 1992; Jack Belsom, "A Guide to Abstracts of the Records of the Superior Council and the Spanish Judicial Records as They Appeared in the *Louisiana Historical Quarterly*," *Genesis* 32, no. 126 (1993): 144–55.

26. Samuel Wilson Jr. and Leonard Victor Huber, *The Presbytère on Jackson Square* (New Orleans: Friends of the Cabildo, 1981), sec. 20.

27. "Genealogical Information on Family of Laura L. Porteous," Box 7, Porteous Collection, LSU.

28. Porteous Collection, LSU; Cassandra Knobloch (great-niece of Laura Porteous), email to the author, May 30, 2014.

29. Interviewee no. 18, b. 1935.

30. "Genealogy," Archdiocese of New Orleans, Office of Archives, http://archives.arch-no.org/genealogy.php, accessed January 30, 2014.

31. Woods and Nolan, *Sacramental Records of the Roman Catholic Church*, 1:xii–xiii.

32. Interviewee no. 28, b. 1940; Interviewee no. 34, b. 1946.

33. Interviewee no. 34, b. 1946; Woods and Nolan, *Sacramental Records of the Roman Catholic Church*.

34. Diocese of Baton Rouge, *Catholic Church Records* (Baton Rouge, 1978). The series originally included twenty-two volumes covering the period 1707 to 1900. A volume for 1900–1905 is also now available.

35. Donald J. Hébert, *Southwest Louisiana Records: Church and Civil Records of Settlers*, 42 vols. (Eunice, LA: Claitor's Law Books and Publishing, 1974–1998).

36. Checking both the Library of Congress and Family History Library websites, as well as genealogical manuals such as the *Red Book* by Alice Eichholz, one finds only some five to seven published listings of sacramental records.

37. Winston De Ville, email to the author, April 10, 2011.

38. Interviewee no. 30, b. 1935.

39. Interviewee no. 20, b. 1947.

40. Kimberly S. Hanger, "Personas de Varias Clases: Free People of Color in Spanish New Orleans, 1769–1803" (PhD dissertation, University of Florida, 1991), 10, 34, 14n.

41. Interviewee no. 41, b. 1953.

42. Jari Honora, radio interview with Zoe Sullivan, "New Orleans Archdiocese Releases Sacramental Records," WWNO-FM News Feature, February 24, 2011.

43. Dick Eastman, *Eastman's Online Genealogy Newsletter*, March 19, 2006, http://blog.eogn.com/eastmans_online_genealogy/2006/03/americas_geneal.html.

44. Interviewee no. 26, b. 1940.

45. Betty Jarboe, *Obituaries: A Guide to Sources* (Boston: G. K. Hall, 1982), 295–98. Jarboe lists eighteen states that have obituary card files. Nineteenth-century

coverage is indicated for the Hawaii State Archives, three libraries in Indiana, New Orleans Public Library, the Maryland Historical Society, the Montana Historical Society, Cleveland Public Library, the Virginia Historical Society, and the State Historical Society of Wisconsin. New Hampshire may have nineteenth-century coverage, but this is not specifically stated. A poll of librarians and archivists in the summer of 2012 led me to other, smaller obituary indexes, notably in Akron, Ohio; Boston; Charlotte, North Carolina; Springfield, Missouri; Evansville, Indiana; and Atlanta. The Connecticut State Library and the New Jersey State Library also have such indexes. Only the last mentions the work of the WPA.

46. Sam Bass Warner Jr., "The Shame of the Cities: Public Records of the Metropolis," *Midwestern Archivist* 2, no. 2 (1977): 27–34.

47. New Orleans Public Library, Louisiana Division, monthly reports for 1946–1956.

48. Ibid.

49. Ibid.

50. Irene Wainwright, archivist, New Orleans Public Library, conversation with the author, October 15, 2005.

51. Wayne Morris and Larry Telford, interviews with the author, Salt Lake City, January 8, 2011.

52. Collin Hamer, email to the author, August 3, 2012.

53. Morris and Telford, interviews.

Chapter 7

1. Richard Campanella, *Geographies of New Orleans: Urban Fabrics before the Storm* (Lafayette, LA: Center for Louisiana Studies, 2006), 255, 261.

2. Leonard V. Huber, Peggy McDowell, and Mary Louise Christovich, *The Cemeteries*, vol. 3 of *New Orleans Architecture*, ed. Samuel Wilson Jr., Bernard Lemann, and Mary Louis Christovich (Gretna, LA: Pelican, 1974), 49.

3. Sigmund Freud, "A Note upon the 'Mystic Writing Pad,'" in *Collected Papers*, ed. James Strachey, trans. Joan Riviere (New York: Basic Books, 1959), 5:175–80; Douwe Draaisma, *Metaphors of Memory: A History of Ideas about the Mind*, trans. Paul Vincent (Cambridge: Cambridge University Press, 2000), 7–21.

4. Paul Ricoeur, *Memory, History, Forgetting*, trans. Kathleen Blamey and David Pellauer (Chicago: University of Chicago Press, 2004), 84, 208, 212, 258; Draaisma, *Metaphors of Memory*, 7, 8, 9, 21, 27, 45, 103, 111, 190, 202; Michael Schudson, *Watergate in American Memory: How We Remember, Forget, and Reconstruct the Past* (New York: Basic Books, 1992), 217; José van Dijck, *Mediated Memories: Personal Cultural Memory as Object of Cultural Analysis* (Stanford, CA: Stanford University Press, 2007), 5.

5. Verne Harris, "Claiming Less, Delivering More: A Critique of Positivist Formulations on Archives in South Africa," *Archivaria* 44 (Fall 1997): 136.

6. Wendy M. Duff and Catherine A. Johnson, "Where Is the List with All the Names? Information-Seeking Behavior of Genealogists," *American Archivist* 66, no. 1 (Spring–Summer 2003): 94; Elizabeth Yakel, "Seeking Information, Seeking

Connections, Seeking Meaning: Genealogists and Family Historians," *Information Research* 10, no. 1 (October 2004), paper 205, http://InformationR.net/ir/10-1/paper205.html; Elizabeth Yakel and Deborah A. Torres, "Genealogists as a 'Community of Records,'" *American Archivist* 70, no. 1 (Spring–Summer 2007): 102.

7. Eric Ketelaar, "Tacit Narratives: The Meanings of Archives," *Archival Science* 1, no. 2 (2001): 133.

8. Michael Schudson, "Dynamics of Distortion in Collective Memory," in *Memory Distortion: How Minds, Brains, and Societies Reconstruct the Past,* ed. Daniel L. Schacter and Joseph T. Coyle (Cambridge, MA: Harvard University Press, 1995), 348; Michael Schudson, "The Present in the Past versus the Past in the Present," *Communication* 11 (1989): 109–12.

9. Schudson, "Dynamics of Distortion," 348.

10. Francis X. Blouin and William G. Rosenberg, *Processing the Past: Contesting Authority in History and the Archives* (New York: Oxford University Press, 2011), 366, 371–72. Blouin and Rosenberg note a similar experience of French historian Jules Michelet. At the end of the nineteenth century, Michelet imbued his findings with passion, "not only in the excitement" of discovery but in what he believed was a resurrection of the dead. He wrote them into life as he wrote their words. The archives revealed to him what "was really meant."

11. Geoffrey Yeo, "Concepts of Record (1): Evidence, Information, and Persistent Representations," *American Archivist* 70, no. 2 (Fall–Winter 2007): 315–43; Geoffrey Yeo, "Concepts of Record (2): Prototypes and Boundary Objects," *American Archivist* 71, no. 1 (Spring–Summer 2008): 118–43.

12. Brien Brothman, "Archives, Life Cycles, and Death Wishes: A Helical Model of Record Formation," *Archivaria* 61 (Spring 2006): 242n13, 264, 269.

13. Michael Young, *The Metronomic Society: Natural Rhythms and Human Timetables* (Cambridge: Cambridge University Press, 1988), 100.

14. Ketelaar, "Tacit Narratives," 137.

15. Thomas Blanton, "The World's Right to Know," *Foreign Policy* 131 (July–August 2002): 50–58.

16. Eric Ketelaar, "Archival Temples, Archival Prisons: Modes of Power and Protection," *Archival Science* 2, nos. 3–4 (September 2002): 237; Verne Harris, "Of Fragments, Fictions and Powers: Resisting Neat Theorising about 'The Record,'" cited in Ketelaar, "Archival Temples, Archival Prisons," as available at www.rmaa.com.au/events/natcon2001/papers, accessed March 10, 2008; Jacques Derrida, *Archive Fever: A Freudian Impression,* trans. Eric Prenowitz (Chicago: University of Chicago Press, 1995), 3, 11; Catherine C. Marshall, "Rethinking Personal Digital Archiving, Part One," *D-Lib Magazine* 14, nos. 3–4 (March–April 2008), http://www.dlib.org/dlib/march08/marshall/03marshall-pt1.html.

17. Augusta Elmwood, "Augusta Elmwood's Website," Rootsweb, http://freepages.genealogy.rootsweb.ancestry.com/~saintdomingue/, accessed February 16, 2015.

18. Tamara K. Hareven, "The Search for Generational Memory: Tribal Rites in Industrial Society," *Daedalus* 107, no. 4 (Fall 1978): 137.

19. Ibid., 137–49.

20. See, for example, "Family Trees," De la Fé–Vadillo–Flores–Iturrioz and Ma-

tos–Ortega–García–Vadel Family Directory, http://www.delafe.com/familydirectory/trees.htm, accessed October 10, 2008.

21. Daniel R. Woolf, "Memory and Historical Culture in Early Modern England," *Journal of the Canadian Historical Association*, n.s., 2 (1991): 285, 307.

22. Van Dijck, *Mediated Memories*, 163; Papailias, *Genres of Recollection*, 16.

23. Barbara Reed, "Beyond Perceived Boundaries: Imagining the Potential of Pluralised Recordkeeping," *Archives and Manuscripts* 33, no. 1 (May 2005): 177–78.

24. Ibid., 177, 189, 192–93.

25. Rick E. Barry, "Barry Family Journal," http://www.mybestdocs.com/barry-r-familyjournal.htm, accessed April 1, 2009.

26. Sue McKemmish, cited in Michael Steemson, "Confident Australian Records Managers Pick Up the Challenge of the Future," Caldeson Consultancy, http://www.caldeson.com/confidnt.html, accessed March 14, 2009.

27. Susan Stewart, *On Longing: Narratives of the Miniature, the Gigantic, the Souvenir, the Collection* (Durham, NC: Duke University Press, 1993), 152.

Chapter 8

1. For notice of the policy prohibiting genealogical researchers, see "Genealogy," Archdiocese of New Orleans, Office of Archives, http://archives.arch-no.org/genealogy.php, accessed January 30, 2014.

2. Ina J. Fandrich, *The Mysterious Voodoo Queen, Marie Laveaux: A Study of Powerful Female Leadership in Nineteenth-Century New Orleans* (New York: Routledge, 2005).

3. Interviewee no. 4, b. 1940.

4. Pamela J. Drake, "Findings from the Fullerton Genealogy Study, A Master's Thesis Project" (California State University, Fullerton, 2001), http://psych.fullerton.edu/genealogy/#RESULT, accessed January 16, 2009; Cooper, "The Librarian and the Genealogist Should Be Friends." Note that Cooper quotes statistics from the American Library Association's "Fact Sheet 6: Public Library Use" (2002), http://www.ala.org/tools/libfactsheets/alalibraryfactsheet06, accessed February 23, 2015. Women make up 77 percent, 62 percent, and 71 percent, respectively, of current members of three genealogical societies studied extensively from 2006 to 2009 in Alabama and Louisiana, and reported on in Tucker, "The Most Public of All History."

5. "Find a Genealogist," Board for Certification of Genealogists, http://www.bcgcertification.org/associates/index.php, accessed March 15, 2009.

6. Ronald D. Lambert, "Looking for Genealogical Motivation," *Families* 34, no. 3 (August 1995): 158–59; Ronald D. Lambert, "Profile of the Membership of the Ontario Genealogical Society," *Families* 34, no. 2 (May 1995): 74–75. See also Roy Rosenzweig and David P. Thelen, *The Presence of the Past: Popular Uses of History in American Life* (New York: Columbia University Press, 1998), 23.

7. Pierre Bourdieu et al., *Photography: A Middle Brow Art*, trans. Shaun Whiteside (1965; repr., Stanford, CA: Stanford University Press, 1990), 19; Claire Grey, "Theories of Relativity," in *Family Snaps: The Meanings of Domestic Photography*,

ed. Patricia Holland and Jo Spence (London: Virago, 1991), 107; Deborah Chambers, "Family as Place: Family Photograph Albums and the Domestication of Public and Private Space," in *Picturing Place: Photography and the Geographical Imagination*, ed. Joan M. Schwartz and James Ryan (New York: Palgrave, Macmillan, 2003), 97.

8. Van Houts, *Memory and Gender in Medieval Europe*, 66.

9. Patrick J. Geary, *Phantoms of Remembrance: Memory and Oblivion at the End of the First Millennium* (Princeton, NJ: Princeton University Press, 1994), 48–80; Daniel R. Woolf, "A Feminine Past? Gender, Genre, and Historical Knowledge in England, 1500–1800," *American Historical Review* 102, no. 3 (June 1997): 645–79.

10. Connerton, *How Societies Remember*, 39; Van Houts, *Memory and Gender in Medieval Europe*, 67; Shils, *Tradition*, 170.

11. Griffith, *Serving History in a Changing World*, 21, 24. This effort, however, also muddied the waters when later leaders of the society considered genealogists to be less appealing users. Women were not given full membership until 1860.

12. Griffith, *Serving History in a Changing World*, 24.

13. William Carroll Hill, *A Century of Genealogical Progress, Being a History of the New England Historic Genealogical Society, 1845–1945* (Boston: New England Historic Genealogical Society, 1945), 41, 42–43. In 1898, thirty-six women were immediately allowed to join this prestigious group.

14. Bonnie G. Smith, *The Gender of History: Men, Women, and Historical Practice* (Cambridge, MA: Harvard University Press, 1998), 165. In Louisiana, Grace King avoided this designation by almost always aligning herself with men, proving at once her own status as exceptional and proving her equality with them.

15. Cappon, "Genealogy, Handmaid of History," 1–9.

16. For the term "genres of recollection," see Papailias, *Genres of Recollection*. For centuries backward, see Brown and Davis-Brown, "The Making of Memory"; Geary, *Phantoms of Remembrance*; Papailias, *Genres of Recollection*; B. Smith, *The Gender of History*; van Houts, *Memory and Gender in Medieval Europe*; Woolf, "A Feminine Past?" See also accounts in Griffith, *Serving History in a Changing World*; Hill, *A Century of Genealogical Progress*; Davies, *Patriotism on Parade*, 58–63, 227–32; Morgan, "Home and Country," 151–217.

17. Bethany Bultman Collection, Box 1, Folders 2–27, Newcomb Archives, Newcomb College Institute, Tulane University, New Orleans.

18. Schudson, "Dynamics of Distortion," 355.

19. Meigs O. Frost, "Strange Romance of 4 Sisters, Acadian Exiles, in Teche: 4 Parted in Youth Are Joined at Life's Eve; Prejean Sisters Found Numerous Family in Bayou Teche," *New Orleans States*, March 16, 1924, 1–2. The headline on page 2 of the continuation of this story from the title page is "Strange Romance of Acadian Exiles: 4 Prejean Sisters, Parted in Youth, Reunited in Life's Sunset."

20. Thomas Frère Kramer, *A Family Montage* (Lafayette, LA: Center for Louisiana Studies, 2002), 81.

21. Bethany Ewald Bultman and Mary Anne de Boisblanc, *A String of Pearls: The Lustrous Lives of Acadian Women*, exhibition catalog (Saint Martinville, LA: Acadian Memorial Foundation, 2007), 1.

22. Ibid., 1–7. Exhibits were held at the Acadian Memorial Foundation in Saint

Martinville (2005, 2007), the Louisiana State Old Courthouse Museum, Natchitoches (2008), and the Newcomb Archives, Tulane University, New Orleans (2009).

23. Harry Hansen, *Longfellow's New England* (New York: Hastings House, 1972), 96–97.

24. A. J. B. (John) Johnston, "Evangeline," in *France and the Americas: Culture, Politics, and History*, ed. Bill Marshall, Will Kaufman, and Cristina Johnston (Santa Barbara, CA: ABC-CLIO, 2005), 2:421–22; Barbara LeBlanc, "Evangeline as Identity Myth," *Canadian Folklore Canadien* 15, no. 2 (1993): 139–51.

25. Barbara LeBlanc, "The Dynamic Relationship between Historic Site and Identity Construction: Grand-Pré and the Acadians" (PhD dissertation, Université Laval, 1994), 97.

26. Ted Fitzgerald, "Evangeline Mourns in Louisiana," *Western Catholic Reporter*, October 29, 2003, http://www.wcr.ab.ca/columns/tedfitzgerald/2003/fitzgerald110303.shtml; LeBlanc, "The Dynamic Relationship," 109–13.

27. LeBlanc, "The Dynamic Relationship," 109.

28. As in the previous example, because of the public nature of this family's story, the actual names have been used. Gustave Rathe, *The Wreck of the Barque* Stefano *off the North West Cape of Australia in 1875* (Victoria Park, Australia: Hesperian Press, 1990; Edinburgh: Cannongate Press, 1992).

29. Rathe, *The Wreck of the Barque* Stefano, illustrations section in the middle of the book (unnumbered).

30. I found some fifteen different types of records, manuscripts, and artifacts that now tell the story of the shipwreck. See Tucker, "The Most Public of All History," 239–41. See also Josko Petkovic, *The* Stefano *Shipwreck of 1875: An Introduction*, http://wwwmcc.murdoch.edu.au/nass/issue3/pdf/Stefano_1.1_Introduction.pdf, accessed December 10, 2014.

31. Sally Kittredge Reeves, *Legacy of a Century: Academy of the Sacred Heart in New Orleans* (New Orleans: Walsworth Press, 1987), 55–56, 100–101.

32. Josko Petkovic, "The 1920 Translation of the Stefano Manuscript: Notes from the Editor," http://nass.murdoch.edu.au/docs/STEFANO_EDITING_TRANSLATION.pdf, accessed March 16, 2009; Josko Petkovic, "Who Is the Author of the 1876 Stefano Manuscript?," http://nass.murdoch.edu.au/docs/STEFANO_AUTHORSHIP.pdf, accessed March 16, 2009.

33. Rathe, *The Wreck of the Barque* Stefano (Edinburgh ed.), 114.

34. Ibid.

35. Laurel Thatcher Ulrich, "Creating Lineages," in Simons and Benes, *The Art of Family*, 5.

36. Stefan Helmreich, "Kinship in Hypertext: Transubstantiating Fatherhood and Information Flow in Artificial Life," in *Relative Values: Reconfiguring Kinship Studies*, ed. Sarah Franklin and Susan McKinnon (Durham, NC: Duke University Press, 2001), 116–17.

37. Laurel Thatcher Ulrich, *The Age of Homespun: Objects and Stories in the Creation of an American Myth* (New York: Alfred A. Knopf, 2001), 137.

38. Akenson, *Some Family*, 75, 80–81.

39. Ibid., 75.

40. Winterthur Museum, "Who's Your Daddy? Families in Early American Needlework," exhibition, October 4, 2008–August 17, 2009, http://www.winterthur.org/?p=804, accessed August 13, 2012.

41. Morgan, "Lineage as Capital," 263–69.

42. Interviewee no. 9, b. 1955.

43. Interviewee no. 20, b. 1947.

44. Ibid.

45. Pierre Bourdieu, "The Cult of Unity and Cultivated Differences," in Bourdieu et al., *Photography: A Middle-Brow Art*, 19, 22, 22–23.

46. Tom Nesmith, "Still Fuzzy, But More Accurate: Some Thoughts on the 'Ghosts' of Archival Theory," *Archivaria* 47 (Spring 1999): 144, 147.

47. Derrida, *Archive Fever*, 10; Michel Foucault, *The Archaeology of Knowledge*, trans. A. Sheridan Smith (New York: Pantheon, 1972), 129.

Chapter 9

1. Susan Cavin, "Missing Women: On the Voodoo Trail to Jazz," *Journal of Jazz Studies* 3, no. 1 (Fall 1975): 4–27; Fandrich, *The Mysterious Voodoo Queen*, esp. chapters 2, 3.

2. Pearce-Moses, *A Glossary of Archival and Records Terminology*, s.v. "Records Continuum."

3. Ibid.

4. E. S. Mills, "Genealogy in the 'Information Age,'" 262.

5. Robert M. Warner, *Diary of a Dream: A History of the National Archives Independence Movement, 1980–1985* (Metuchen, NJ: Scarecrow Press, 1995), 15, 79, 109, 131.

6. Amy M. Smith, *Tracing Family Lines: The Impact of Genealogy Research on Family Communication* (Lanham, MD: Lexington Books, 2012).

7. "Du Bois Albums of Photographs of African Americans in Georgia Exhibited at the Paris Exposition Universelle in 1900," Daniel Murray Collection, Rare Book and Special Collections Division, Library of Congress; Shawn Michelle Smith, *American Archives: Gender, Race, and Class in Visual Culture* (Princeton, NJ: Princeton University Press, 1999), 158, 177–86 (for quotations, 158, 182–83).

8. Gwendolyn Midlo Hall, "The Louisiana Slave Database and the Louisiana Free Database, 1819–1820, http://www.nps.gov/cari/historyculture/upload/usingdatabase.pdf, accessed May 18, 2014.

9. Angel Adams Parham, "Race, Memory, and Family History," *Social Identities* 14, no. 1 (January 2008): 13–32, 27; for quotation, Rosenzweig and Thelen, *Presence of the Past*, 28.

10. Parham, "Race, Memory, and Family History," 28.

11. Bultman and de Boisblanc, "A String of Pearls," 13; "Toussaint L'Ouverture," exhibition label, the Historical Impressionism of Mary Anne de Boisblanc, Louisiana State Archives, February 22–March 22, 2013.

12. Parham, "Race, Memory, and Family History," 19–24.

13. Personal Documents Collection, Folder 13, LaRC, Tulane University, New Orleans, LA.

14. Pearce-Moses, *A Glossary of Archival and Records Terminology*, s.v. "Artificial Collection," http://www2.archivists.org/glossary/terms/a/artificial-collection.

15. Interviewee no. 11, b. 1943; Akenson, *Some Family*, 204; Kimberly Powell, "Top Five Places to Put Your Family History Online," About.com: Genealogy, http://genealogy.about.com/od/publishing/tp/web_sites.htm, accessed December 11, 2008.

16. Julia Creet, "Arborescent Archives; or, The Aesthetic Roots of the Family Tree," http://www.humanities.mcmaster.ca/~english/JDT/archiveandeverydaylife/PDF/Creet.pdf, accessed December 9, 2014.

17. Atina Grossmann, "Out of the Closet and into the Archives? German Jewish Papers," in *Archives, Documentation, and Institutions of Social Memory: Essays from the Sawyer Seminar*, ed. Francis X. Blouin and William G. Rosenberg (Ann Arbor: University of Michigan Press, 2007), 89–100.

18. Robert Bush, "Charles Gayarré and Grace King: Letters of a Louisiana Friendship," *Southern Literary Journal* 7, no. 1 (Fall 1974): 100–131, esp. 105, 112, 122; "Extrait du [*sic*] Onzième Registre des Actes de Baptisme des Blancs de l'Eglise Cathédrale et Paroissiale de St. Louis," Charles Gayarré Papers, Mss 0156, Box 14, Folder 3, Louisiana and Lower Mississippi Valley Collections, Louisiana State University Libraries, Baton Rouge. The Nota on the side of the Extrait proclaims, as noted in an earlier chapter, that this entry in the register for the whites was a mistake.

19. Interviewee no 21, b. 1959.

20. Creet, "Arborescent Archives."

21. Yakel and Torres, "Genealogists as a 'Community of Records,'" 108.

22. Interviewee no. 16, b. 1957.

23. Interviewee no. 15, b. 1970. For a similar sentiment, see Michael Moss, "Choreographed Encounter: The Archive and Public History," *Archives* 32, no. 116 (2007): 42; Buzzy Jackson, video interview with Dick Eastman, Roots Television, October 29, 2008, http://www.rootstelevision.com/ players/player_conferences .php?bctid=2474688001, accessed December 12, 2008.

SOURCES

Much of the work for this book is based on interviews conducted with family historians and archivists during the years 2006–2015. Those interviews not restricted by interviewees, along with notes on the work, are available within my collection listed below under Newcomb Archives. Choosing sources was a difficult process because local genealogy itself has so many publications. There are many books and articles that I regret omitting, such as some of the Bible records copied by patriotic societies, the many tombstone inscriptions transcribed and compiled that I so enjoy glancing through, and the short but so meaningful family histories contributed as unique volumes to libraries. I trust that others will continue the quest for examples far beyond the works cited here.

Manuscripts

Amistad Research Center, New Orleans
- Harrietta Harris Papers
- Henry Hugh and Adeline L. Davis Proctor Family Papers

Earl K. Long Library, University of New Orleans, New Orleans
- Marcus Christian Collection
- René Grandjean Collection
- Nell Pomeroy O'Brien Collection

Louisiana Research Center, Tulane University, New Orleans
- Augustin, Wogan, and Labranche Families Papers
- Cruzat Family Papers
- Degas and Musson Families Papers
- Joseph Émile Ducros Family Papers
- Genealogical Paper Series and Genealogical Vertical File
- Grace King Collection
- Personal Documents Collection, 1671–1959
- US Daughters of the War of 1812, Chalmette Chapter, Papers
- John Minor Wisdom Collection

Library of Congress, Washington, DC
- Daniel Murray Collection

Louisiana and Lower Mississippi Valley Collections, Louisiana State University Libraries, Baton Rouge
- Charles Gayarré Papers
- Laura Porteous Collection

Louisiana State Museum, Historical Center, New Orleans
George Smith Collection
Judicial Records of the French Superior Council
Judicial Records of the Spanish Superior Council

New England Historic Genealogical Society, Boston
William Hyde Family Papers
Lemuel Shattuck Papers

Newcomb Archives, Tulane University, New Orleans
Bethany Bultman Papers
Coralie Guarino Davis Collection
Mary Anne de Boisblanc Papers
Augusta Waldhorn Dennery Scrapbook
Susan Tucker Papers

Virginia Historical Society, Richmond
Bryan Family Papers
Bruce Family Papers
Genealogical chart of the Brid (Bird and Byrd) family
George Hannah Family Papers
Peyton Family Papers

Books, Articles, Dissertations, and Papers

Abadie, Ann J., et al. *The New Encyclopedia of Southern Culture*. Vol. 2, *Geography*. Chapel Hill: University of North Carolina Press, 2006.

Akenson, Donald Harman. *Some Family: The Mormons and How Humanity Keeps Track of Itself*. Montreal: McGill–Queen's University Press, 2007.

Allen, Gloria Seaman. *Family Record: Genealogical Watercolors and Needlework*. Washington, DC: Daughters of the American Revolution Museum, 1989.

Allen, James B., and Jessie L. Embry, eds. *Encyclopedia of Mormonism: The History, Scripture, Doctrine, and Procedure of the Church of Jesus Christ of Latter-day Saints*. Available at http://eom.byu.edu/index.php/Encyclopedia_of_Mormonism.

———. "Provoking the Brethren to Good Works: Susa Young Gates, the Relief Society, and Genealogy." *BYU Studies* 31 (1991): 115–38.

Allen, James B., Jessie L. Embry, and Kahlile B. Mehr. *Hearts Turned to the Fathers: A History of the Genealogical Society of Utah, 1894–1994*. Provo, UT: Brigham Young University Studies, 1995.

Anderson, Charles. "Colonial English Research." In Eakle and Cerny, *The Source*, 679–98.

Anderson, Jerome E. "Family Record-Keeping: A Rich and Diverse Heritage." *National Genealogical Society Quarterly* 90, no. 4 (December 2002): 247–56.

Anonymous. "The History of Louisiana and Some of Its Leading Families." *Louisiana Historical Quarterly* 1, no. 1 (January 1917).

———. Review of *Historical Sketch of Amherst, in the County of Hillsborough, in New Hampshire, from Its First Settlement to the Year 1837*, by John Farmer. *North American Review* 46, no. 99 (April 1838): 536–38.

Appel, John J. *Immigrant Historical Societies in the United States, 1880–1950*. New York: Arno Press, 1980.

Armstrong, Elizabeth. "Robert Peril and His 1524 Privilege." *Bibliothèque d'Humanisme et Renaissance* 61, no. 1 (1999): 85–93.

Arthur, Stanley Clisby, and George Campbell Huchet de Kernion. *Old Families of Louisiana*. New Orleans: Harmanson, 1931.

Ashton, Rick J. "Curators, Hobbyists, and Historians: Ninety Years of Genealogy at the Newberry Library." *Library History* 47, no. 2 (1977): 149–62.

Baade, Hans W. "Marriage Contracts in French and Spanish Louisiana: A Study in 'Notarial' Jurisprudence." *Tulane Law Review* 53 (December 1978): 1–54.

Barnhill, Georgia Brady. "'Keep Sacred the Memory of Your Ancestors': Family Registers and Memorial Prints." In Simons and Benes, *The Art of Family*, 60–74.

Barritt, Marjorie Rabe. "Coming to America: Dutch *Archivistiek* and American Archival Practice." *Archival Issues* 18 (1993): 43–54.

Bastian, Jeannette A. "The Records of Memory, the Archives of Identity: Celebrations, Texts and Archival Sensibilities." *Archival Science* 13 (2013): 121–31.

Beers, Henry Putney. *French and Spanish Records of Louisiana: A Bibliographical Guide to Archive and Manuscript Sources*. Baton Rouge: Louisiana State University Press, 1989.

Belsom, Jack. "A Guide to Abstracts of the Records of the Superior Council and the Spanish Judicial Records as They Appeared in the *Louisiana Historical Quarterly*." *Genesis* 32, no. 126 (1993): 144–55.

Benes, Peter. "Decorated New England Family Registers, 1770–1850." In Simons and Benes, *The Art of Family*, 13–59.

———. "Selected Checklist of Manuscript, Watercolor and Needlework Family Registers and Family Trees in New England, 1780–1846." In Simons and Benes, *The Art of Family*, 275–82.

Bennett, Archibald F. "The Record Copying Program of the Utah Genealogical Society." *American Archivist* 16, no. 3 (July 1953): 227–32.

Berner, Richard C. *Archival Theory and Practice in the United States: A Historical Analysis*. Seattle: University of Washington Press, 1983.

Bidlack, Russell E. "The Awakening Genealogy as It Relates to Library Service." *RQ* 23 (Winter 1983): 171–81.

Bird, Stephanie Rose. *Light, Bright, and Damned Near White: Biracial and Triracial Culture in America*. Westport, CT: Praeger, 2009.

Blanton, Thomas. "The World's Right to Know." *Foreign Policy* 131 (July–August 2002): 50–58.

Blouin, Francis X., and William G. Rosenberg. *Processing the Past: Contesting Authority in History and the Archives*. New York: Oxford University Press, 2011.

Bockstruck, Lloyd DeWitt. "Four Centuries of Genealogy: A Historical View." *RQ* 23, no. 2 (Winter 1983): 162–70.

Bodnar, John. *Remaking America: Public Memory, Commemoration, and Patriotism in the Twentieth Century*. Princeton, NJ: Princeton University Press, 1992.

Boling, Yvette Guilott. *The How and Where of Research in New Orleans and the Surrounding Area*. Jefferson, LA: Y. G. Boling, 1987.

Bolton, Charles K. "Genealogy and History." *Annual Report of the American Historical Association for the Year 1912*. Washington, DC: Smithsonian Institution, 1914.

Bouquet, Mary. "Family Trees and Their Affinities: The Visual Imperative of the Genealogical Diagram." *Journal of the Royal Anthropological Institute* 2, no. 1 (March 1996): 43–66.

———. "Figures of Relations: Reconnecting Kinship Studies and Museum Collections." In *Cultures of Relatedness: New Approaches to the Study of Kinship*, edited by Janet Carsten, 167–90. New York: Cambridge University Press, 2000.

Bourdieu, Pierre. "The Cult of Unity and Cultivated Difference." In Bourdieu et al., *Photography: The Middle-Brow Art*, 232–41.

Bourdieu, Pierre, et al. *Photography: The Middle-Brow Art*. Translated by Shaun Whiteside. 1965. Reprint, Stanford, CA: Stanford University Press, 1990.

Boyd, Julian P., et al., eds. *The Papers of Thomas Jefferson*. Vol. 7. Princeton, NJ: Princeton University Press, 1953.

Brasseaux, Carl. *The "Foreign French": Nineteenth-Century French Immigration into Louisiana*. 3 vols. Lafayette, LA: Center for Louisiana Studies, 1990–1993.

Breckenridge, Keith, and Simon Szreter, eds. *Registration and Recognition: Documenting the Person in World History*. Proceedings of the British Academy. Oxford: Oxford University Press, 2012.

Brothman, Brien. "Archives, Life Cycles, and Death Wishes: A Helical Model of Record Formation." *Archivaria* 61 (Spring 2006): 235–69.

Brown, Richard Harvey, and Beth Davis-Brown. "The Making of Memory: The Politics of Archives, Libraries and Museums in the Construction of National Consciousness." *History of the Human Sciences* 11, no. 4 (1998): 17–32.

Broyard, Bliss. *One Drop: My Father's Hidden Life; A Story of Race and Family Secrets*. New York: Little, Brown, 2007.

Brumbaugh, Gaius Marcus. *Maryland Records, Colonial, Revolutionary, County and Church, from Original Sources*. 2 vols. Baltimore: Williams and Wilkins, 1915, 1928.

Brundage, W. Fitzhugh. *The Southern Past: A Clash of Race and Memory*. Cambridge, MA: Belknap Press of Harvard University Press, 2005.

Bruns, J. Edgar. "Annotating for Posterity: The Sacramental Records of Father Antonio de Sedella." In *Cross, Crozier, and Crucible: A Volume Celebrating the Bicentennial of a Catholic Diocese in Louisiana*, edited by Glen Conrad, 349–59. New Orleans: Archdiocese of New Orleans, 1993.

Bryan, Charles F. "What Should We Do about the 'Genies'?" *History News* 41, no. 1 (January 1986): 31–33.

Bultman, Bethany Ewald, and Mary Anne de Boisblanc. *A String of Pearls: The*

Lustrous Lives of Acadian Women. Exhibition Catalog. Saint Martinville, LA: Acadian Memorial Foundation, 2007.

Bush, Robert. "Charles Gayarré and Grace King: Letters of a Louisiana Friendship." *Southern Literary Journal* 7, no. 1 (Fall 1974): 100–131.

———. *Grace King: A Southern Destiny*. Baton Rouge: Louisiana State University Press, 1983.

Cadell, Patrick. "Building on the Past, Investing in the Future through Genealogy and Local History Services." *IFLA Journal* 28, no. 4 (2002): 175–80.

Campanella, Richard. *Geographies of New Orleans: Urban Fabrics Before the Storm*. Lafayette, LA: Center for Louisiana Studies, 2006.

Cappon, Lester J. "Genealogy, Handmaid of History." *National Genealogical Society Quarterly* 45, no. 1 (March 1957): 1–9.

Cassedy, James. "Lemuel Shattuck." In *American National Biography*, edited by John A. Garraty and Mark C. Carnes, vol. 19. New York: Oxford University Press, 1999.

Cavalli-Sforza, L. Luca, Paolo Menozzi, and Alberto Piazza. *The History and Geography of Human Genes*. Princeton, NJ: Princeton University Press, 1994.

Cavin, Susan. "Missing Women: On the Voodoo Trail to Jazz." *Journal of Jazz Studies* 3, no. 1 (Fall 1975): 4–27.

Centers for Disease Control and Prevention. "Appendix 2: History and Organization of the Vital Statistics System, Historical Development." In *U.S. Vital Statistics System: Major Activities and Developments, 1950–95*, 43–44. Washington, DC: Government Printing Office, 1954.

Cerny, Johni. "Vital Records." In Eakle and Cerny, *The Source*.

Chambers, Deborah. "Family as Place: Family Photograph Albums and the Domestication of Public and Private Space." In *Picturing Place: Photography and the Geographical Imagination*, edited by Joan M. Schwartz and James Ryan. New York: Palgrave, Macmillan, 2003.

Clap, Roger. *Memories of Capt. Roger Clap*. Boston: B. Green, 1731.

Connerton, Paul. *How Societies Remember*. Cambridge: Cambridge University Press, 1989.

Cooper, Jean. "The Librarian and the Genealogist Should Be Friends." Paper presented at the Virginia Library Association Annual Conference, Williamsburg, Virginia, October 20, 2005. Available at http://www.vla.org/demo/Conference/05Conf/Presentations/IntrotoGenealogy.ppt.

Cox, Richard J. "Genealogy and Public History: New Genealogical Guides and Their Implications for Public Historians." *Public Historian* 6, no. 2 (Spring 1984): 89–96.

Creet, Julia. "Arborescent Archives; or, The Aesthetic Roots of the Family Tree." Available at http://www.humanities.mcmaster.ca/~english/JDT/archiveandeverydaylife/PDF/Creet.pdf.

Currer-Briggs, Noel, and Royster Gambier. *Debrett's Family Historian: A Guide to Tracing Your Ancestry*. Exeter, England: Webb and Bower, 1982.

Daily Picayune, "Family Seeks to Disprove Colored Charges, Prados Family Appear in Court as Witnesses in Own Behalf," February 27, 1914.

Dart, Henry Plauché. "Courts and Law in Colonial Louisiana." *Louisiana Historical Quarterly* 4, no. 3 (1921): 255–89.

Davies, Wallace Evan. *Patriotism on Parade: The Story of Veterans' and Hereditary Organizations in America, 1783–1900*. Cambridge, MA: Harvard University Press, 1955.

De Bray, Henry. *The Estate Book of Henry de Bray of Harleston, Co. Northants*. Edited by Dorothy Willis. London: Royal Historical Society, 1916. Available at http://www.archive.org/details/estatebookofhenroobray.

Deiler, John Hanno. *The Settlement of the German Coast of Louisiana and the Creoles of German Descent*. Philadelphia: German American Historical Society, 1909.

Demos, John. Introduction to Simon and Benes, *The Art of Family*, xii.

Derrida, Jacques. *Archive Fever: A Freudian Impression*. Translated by Eric Prenowitz. Chicago: University of Chicago Press, 1995.

Desdunes, Rodolphe. *Our People and Our History*. Reprint of the 1911 edition. Baton Rouge: Louisiana State University Press, 1973.

Dessens, Nathalie. *From Saint-Domingue to New Orleans: Migration and Influences*. Gainesville: University Press of Florida, 2007.

De Ville, Winton. "Manuscript Sources in Louisiana for the History of the French in the Mississippi Valley." In *The French in the Mississippi Valley*, edited by John Francis McDermott, 217–32. Urbana: University of Illinois Press, 1965.

Devine, Donn. "Defining Professionalism." In E. S. Mills, *Professional Genealogy*, 3–14.

———. "Evidence Analysis." In E. S. Mills, *Professional Genealogy*, 327–43.

Dimitry, Charles Patton. "Sketches." *Times-Democrat*, January 10, 1892–January 22, 1893 (biweekly).

Din, Gilbert, and John Harkins. *The New Orleans Cabildo: Colonial Louisiana's First City Government, 1769–1803*. Baton Rouge: Louisiana State University Press, 1996.

Diocese of Baton Rouge. *Catholic Church Records*. 23 vols. Baton Rouge, 1978.

Domínguez, Virginia R. *White by Definition: Social Classification in Creole Louisiana*. New Brunswick, NJ: Rutgers University Press, 1986.

Draaisma, Douwe. *Metaphors of Memory: A History of Ideas about the Mind*. Translated by Paul Vincent. Cambridge: Cambridge University Press, 2000.

Drake, Pamela J. "Findings from the Fullerton Genealogy Study: A Master's Thesis Project." California State University, Fullerton, 2001. Available at http://psych.fullerton.edu/genealogy/#RESULT.

Duff, Wendy M., and Catherine A. Johnson. "Where Is the List with All the Names? Information-Seeking Behavior of Genealogists." *American Archivist* 66, no. 1 (Spring–Summer, 2003): 79–95.

Dulong, John Patrick. "Genealogical Groups in a Changing Organizational Environment: From Lineage to Heritage." PhD dissertation, Wayne State University, 1986.

Eakle, Arlene, and Johni Cerny, eds. *The Source: A Guidebook of American Genealogy*. 1st ed. Salt Lake City: Ancestry, 1984.

Earnest, Corinne, and Russell Earnest. *To the Latest Posterity: Pennsylvania-German Family Registers in the Fraktur Tradition*. University Park: Pennsylvania State University Press, 2004.

Eastman, Dick. *Eastman's Online Genealogy Newsletter*. March 19, 2006. Available at http://blog.eogn.com/eastmans_online_genealogy/2006/03/americas_ge neal.html.

Elmwood, Augusta. "Augusta Elmwood's Website." Rootsweb. Available at http:// freepages.genealogy.rootsweb.ancestry.com/~saintdomingue/.

Estaville, Lawrence E., Jr. "The Louisiana French Language in the Nineteenth Century." *Southeastern Geographer* 30, no. 2 (November 1990): 107–20.

Fandrich, Ina J. *The Mysterious Voodoo Queen, Marie Laveaux: A Study of Powerful Female Leadership in Nineteenth-Century New Orleans*. New York: Routledge, 2005.

Farmer, John. *A Genealogical Register of the First Settlers of New England*. Lancaster, MA: Carter, Andrews, and Company, 1829.

———. "Memoir of John Farmer, M.A., Late Corresponding Secretary of the New Hampshire Historical Society." *New England Historical and Genealogical Register* 1, no. 1 (1847): 9.

Farnham, Alan. "Who's Your Daddy? Genealogy Becomes $1.6B Hobby." ABC News, October 24, 2012. Available at http://abcnews.go.com/Business/geneal ogy-hot-hobby-worth-16b-mormons/story?id=17544242.

Fitzgerald, Ted. "Evangeline Mourns in Louisiana." *Western Catholic Reporter*, October 29, 2003. Available at http://www.wcr.ab.ca/columns/tedfitzgerald/2003/ fitzgerald110303.shtml.

FitzHugh, Terrick V. H. *The Dictionary of Genealogy*. Rev. ed. Sherborne, England: Alphabooks, 1988.

Foner, Laura. "The Free People of Color in Louisiana and St. Domingue: A Comparative Portrait of Two Three-Caste Slave Societies." *Journal of Social History* 3, no. 4 (Summer 1970): 406–30.

Forsyth, Alice Daly, comp. *Louisiana Marriages*. Vol. 1, *A Collection of Marriage Records from the St. Louis Cathedral in New Orleans . . . 1784–1806*. New Orleans: Polyanthos, 1977.

Forsythe, Jenny Marie, and Susan Tucker. "'The Most Wonderful Collection of Original Documents in the United States': Notes on the Lives and Work of Two New Orleans Translators." *Collections: A Journal for Museum and Archives Professionals* 11, no. 1 (2015).

Fortier, Alcée. "Report of Prof. Fortier." *Publications of the Louisiana Historical Society* 1, no. 1 (1895).

Foucault, Michel. *The Archaeology of Knowledge*. Translated by A. Sheridan Smith. New York: Pantheon, 1972.

Freud, Sigmund. "A Note upon the 'Mystic Writing Pad.'" In *Collected Papers*, 5:175–80. Edited by James Strachey. Translated by Joan Riviere. New York: Basic Books, 1959.

Frost, Meigs O. "Strange Romance of 4 Sisters, Acadian Exiles, in Teche: 4 Parted in Youth Are Joined at Life's Eve; Prejean Sisters Found Numerous Family in Bayou Teche." *New Orleans States*, March 16, 1924, 1–2.

Fulkerson, Jennifer. "Climbing the Family Tree." *American Demographics* 17, no. 12 (December 1995): 42–50.

Garrett, Wendell. "Families and the Decorative Arts." In Simons and Benes, *The Art of Family*, 1–5.

Gates, Henry Louis, Jr. *Finding Oprah's Roots: Finding Your Own*. New York: Crown, 2007.

Gayarré, Charles. *History of Louisiana*. 4 vols. New York: William J. Widdleton, 1867.

Geary, Patrick J. *Phantoms of Remembrance: Memory and Oblivion at the End of the First Millennium*. Princeton, NJ: Princeton University Press, 1994.

Genesis. Genealogical Research Society of New Orleans, 1962–present.

Gilliland-Swetland, Luke J. "The Provenance of a Profession: The Permanence of the Public Archives and Historical Manuscripts Traditions in American Archival History." *American Archivist* 54, no. 2 (Spring 1991): 160–75.

Gordon-Reed, Annette. *The Hemingses of Monticello*. New York: W. W. Norton, 2008.

———. *Thomas Jefferson and Sally Hemings: An American Controversy*. Charlottesville: University of Virginia Press, 1997.

Gottlieb, Beatrice. *The Family in the Western World from the Black Death to the Industrial Age*. New York: Oxford University Press, 1993.

Graham, Laura. "Tales from the Vault: A Journey over the Mountain." *Common-Place* 3 (January 2003). Available at http://www.common-place.org/vol-03/no-02/tales/.

Greene, David L. "Donald Lines Jacobus, Scholarly Genealogy, and the *American Genealogist*." *American Genealogist* 72, nos. 3–4 (July–October 1997): 159–80.

Grey, Claire. "Theories of Relativity." In *Family Snaps: The Meanings of Domestic Photography*, edited by Patricia Holland and Jo Spence. London: Virago, 1991.

Griffith, Sally. *Serving History in a Changing World: The Historical Society of Pennsylvania in the Twentieth Century*. Philadelphia: Historical Society of Pennsylvania, 2001.

Grossmann, Atina. "Out of the Closet and into the Archives? German Jewish Papers." In *Archives, Documentation, and Institutions of Social Memory: Essays from the Sawyer Seminar*, edited by Francis X. Blouin and William G. Rosenberg, 89–100. Ann Arbor: University of Michigan Press, 2007.

Gutman, Robert. "The Accuracy of Vital Statistics in Massachusetts, 1842–1901." PhD dissertation, Columbia University, 1956.

Haley, Alex. *Roots*. Garden City, NY: Doubleday, 1976.

Hall, Gwendolyn Midlo. "The Louisiana Slave Database and the Louisiana Free Database, 1719–1820." Available at http://www.nps.gov/cari/historyculture/upload/usingdatabase.pdf.

Hall, James. *Illustrated Dictionary of Symbols in Eastern and Western Art*. Cambridge: John Murray, 1994.

Hamer, Collin B. *Genealogical Materials in the New Orleans Public Library*. New Orleans: Friends of the New Orleans Public Library, 1984.

Hamer, Collin B., Wayne M. Everard, and Irene Wainwright. *Genealogical Materi-*

als in the New Orleans Public Library's Louisiana Division and City Archives. New Orleans: Friends of the New Orleans Public Library, 1998.

Hanger, Kimberly S. *Bounded Lives, Bounded Places: Free Black Society in Colonial New Orleans, 1769–1803.* Durham, NC: Duke University Press, 1997.

———. "Personas de Varias Clases: Free People of Color in Spanish New Orleans, 1769–1803." PhD dissertation, University of Florida, 1991.

Hansen, Harry. *Longfellow's New England.* New York: Hastings House, 1972.

Hareven, Tamara K. "The Search for Generational Memory: Tribal Rites in Industrial Society." *Daedalus* 107, no. 4 (Fall 1978): 137–49.

Harris, Cheryl I. "In the Shadow of *Plessy*," *University of Pennsylvania Journal of Constitutional Law* 7 (2004): 867–901.

Harris, Verne. "Claiming Less, Delivering More: A Critique of Positivist Formulations on Archives in South Africa." *Archivaria* 44 (Fall 1997): 132–44.

———. "Of Fragments, Fictions and Powers: Resisting Neat Theorising about 'The Record.'" Cited in Ketelaar, "Archival Temples, Archival Prisons." Available at www.rmaa.com.au/events/natcon2001/papers.

Hart, W. O. "History of the Louisiana Historical Society," *Louisiana Historical Quarterly* 3, no. 1 (January 1920): 112–29.

Haskins, James. *The Creoles of Color of New Orleans.* New York: Crowell, 1975.

Hébert, Donald J. *Southwest Louisiana Records: Church and Civil Records of Settlers.* 42 vols. Eunice, LA: Claitor's Law Books and Publishing, 1974–1998.

Helmreich, Stefan. "Kinship in Hypertext: Transubstantiating Fatherhood and Information Flow in Artificial Life." In *Relative Values: Reconfiguring Kinship Studies,* edited by Sarah Franklin and Susan McKinnon. Durham, NC: Duke University Press, 2001.

Herzog, Tamar. "Naming, Identifying and Authorizing Movement in Early Modern Spain and Spanish America." In Breckenridge and Szreter, *Registration and Recognition,* 200–201.

Hijiya, James. "Roots: Family and Ethnicity in the 1970s." *American Quarterly* 30, no. 4 (Autumn 1978): 548–56.

Hill, William Carroll. *A Century of Genealogical Progress, Being a History of the New England Historic Genealogical Society, 1845–1945.* Boston: New England Historic Genealogical Society, 1945.

Hornblower, Margot, Melissa August, et al. "Roots Mania." *Time* 153, no. 15 (April 19, 1999): 54–59.

Huber, Leonard V., Peggy McDowell, and Mary Louise Christovich. *The Cemeteries.* Vol. 3 of *New Orleans Architecture,* edited by Samuel Wilson Jr., Bernard Lemann, and Mary Louis Christovich. Gretna, LA: Pelican, 1974.

Ingold, Tim. *Lines: A Brief History.* New York: Routledge, 2007.

Jacobus, Donald Lines. *Genealogy as Pastime and Profession.* New Haven, CT: Tuttle, Morehouse and Taylor, 1930.

Jameson, John Franklin. "The Functions of State and Local Societies with Respect to Research and Publication." In *American Historical Association Annual Report, 1897,* 51–59. Washington, DC: Government Printing Office, 1898.

Jane Doe et al. v. State of Louisiana et al., no. 78-9513, C-W no. 81-4201, Civil District Court, Parish of Orleans, Louisiana.

Jarboe, Betty. *Obituaries: A Guide to Sources.* Boston: G. K. Hall, 1982.

Johnson, David, ed. *KnowLA: Encyclopedia of Louisiana.* New Orleans: Louisiana Endowment for the Humanities, 2010. Available at http://www.knowla.org/.

Johnson, Suzanne. "Testimonial." Family Tree DNA. Available at http://www.familytreedna.com/testimonials.aspx.

Johnston, A. J. B. (John). "Evangeline." In *France and the Americas: Culture, Politics, and History*, edited by Bill Marshall, Will Kaufman, and Cristina Johnston, 2:421–22. Santa Barbara, CA: ABC-CLIO, 2005.

Jones, H. G. [Houston Gwynne]. *Historical Consciousness in the Early Republic: The Origins of State Historical Societies, Museums, and Collections, 1791–1861.* Chapel Hill: North Caroliniana Society; North Carolina Collection, 1995.

Kaelber, Lutz. "Eugenics: Compulsory Sterilization in 50 American States." University of Vermont Today. Available at http://www.uvm.edu/~lkaelber/eugenics/.

Kammen, Michael G. "Some Patterns and Meanings of Memory Distortion in American History." In *Memory Distortion: How Minds, Brains, and Societies Reconstruct the Past*, edited by Daniel L. Schacter and Joseph T. Coyle, 329–45. Cambridge, MA: Harvard University Press, 1995.

Kaplan, Elisabeth. "We Are What We Collect, We Collect What We Are: Archives and the Construction of Identity." *American Archivist* 63 (Spring–Summer 2000): 126–51.

Kein, Sybil, ed. *Creole: The History and Legacy of Louisiana's Free People of Color.* Baton Rouge: Louisiana State University Press, 2000.

Kenneally, Christine. *The Invisible History of the Human Race: How DNA and History Shape Our Identities and Our Future.* New York: Viking, 2014.

Ketelaar, Eric. "Archival Temples, Archival Prisons: Modes of Power and Protection." *Archival Science* 2, nos. 3–4 (September 2002): 221–38.

———. "The Genealogical Gaze: Family Identities and Family Archives in the Fourteenth to Seventeenth Centuries." *Libraries and the Cultural Record* 44, no. 1 (2009): 9–28.

———. "Tacit Narratives: The Meanings of Archives." *Archival Science* 1, no. 2 (2001): 131–41.

King, Grace. "The Black Boxes." *Louisiana Historical Quarterly* 7, no. 1 (1913): 11–13.

———. *Creole Families of New Orleans.* New York: Macmillan, 1921.

———. "Preface." *Louisiana Historical Quarterly* 8, no. 1 (1914): 9–11.

Kramer, Thomas Frère. *A Family Montage.* Lafayette, LA: Center for Louisiana Studies, 2002.

Lafleur, Dowell. *Winston De Ville: A Bibliography of Genealogical and Other Writings, 1959–2012.* Baton Rouge: Claitor's Law Books and Publishing, 2013.

Lambert, Ronald D. "Looking for Genealogical Motivation." *Families* 34, no. 3 (August 1995): 149–60.

———. "Profile of the Membership of the Ontario Genealogical Society." *Families* 34, no. 2 (May 1995): 73–80.

Lanier, Shannon, and Jane Feldman. *Jefferson's Children: The Story of One American Family*. New York: Random House, 2000.

LeBlanc, Barbara. "The Dynamic Relationship between Historic Site and Identity Construction: Grand-Pré and the Acadians." PhD dissertation, Université Laval, 1994.

———. "Evangeline as Identity Myth." *Canadian Folklore Canadien* 15, no. 2 (1993): 139–51.

Lemmon, Alfred. "The Archival Legacy of Spanish Louisiana's Colonial Records." *American Archivist* 55, no. 1 (Winter 1992): 142–55.

———. "Trans-Mississippi States: Arkansas, California, Iowa, Louisiana, Minnesota, Missouri, Oregon, and Texas." In Jones, *Historical Consciousness in the Early Republic*, 188–216.

Leumas, Emilie Gagnet. "Mais, I Sin in French, I Gotta Go to Confession in French: A Study of the Language Shift from French to English within the Louisiana Catholic Church." PhD dissertation, Louisiana State University, 2009.

Lima, Manuel. *The Book of Trees: Visualizing Branches of Knowledge*. New York: Princeton Architectural Press, 2014.

Lombardo, Paul A. *A Century of Eugenics in America: From the Indiana Experiment to the Human Genome Era*. Bloomington: Indiana University Press, 2011.

Louisiana Creole Association. *La Créole: A Journal of Creole History and Genealogy*. New Orleans: Louisiana Creole Research Association, 2008–.

Louisiana Historical Quarterly. "The History of Louisiana and Some of Its Leading Families." *Louisiana Historical Quarterly* 1, no. 1 (January 1917): 95–98.

Louisiana State Museum. *Biennial Report of the Board of Curators for 1920–21*. New Orleans: Louisiana State Museum, 1922.

———. *Biennial Report of the Board of Curators for 1941–42*. New Orleans: Louisiana State Museum, 1942.

Lowenthal, David. "History and Memory." *Public Historian* 19, no. 2 (Spring 1997): 38–39.

Luebking, Sandra Hargreaves, and Loretto Dennis Szucs. "The Foundations of Family History Research." In *The Source: A Guidebook to American Genealogy*, edited by Sandra Hargreaves Luebking and Loretto Dennis Szucs, 2–16. 3rd ed. Provo, UT: Ancestry, 2006.

Maduell, Charles R., Jr., ed. *The Census Tables for the French Colony of Louisiana from 1699 through 1732*. Compiled and translated by the editor. Baltimore: Genealogical Publishing, 1972.

———. *Index of Spanish Citizens Entering New Orleans, January 1820 through December 1839*. New Orleans: n.p., n.d.

———. *Marriage Contracts, Wills and Testaments of the Spanish Colonial Period in New Orleans, 1770–1804*. Compiled and indexed by the editor. New Orleans: n.p., 1969.

Margot, Howard. *Guide to the French Colonial Records of the New Orleans Notarial Archives, 1733–1767*. New Orleans: Notarial Archives Research Center, 2007.

———. "Outline of the History of Louisiana." Unpublished document in the author's possession.

Marshall, Catherine C. "Rethinking Personal Digital Archiving, Part One." *D-Lib Magazine* 14, nos. 3–4 (March–April 2008). Available at http://www.dlib.org/dlib/march08/marshall/03marshall-pt1.html.

McDannell, Colleen. *Material Christianity: Religion and Popular Culture in America*. New Haven, CT: Yale University Press, 1995.

Meyerink, Kory L., ed. *Printed Sources: A Guide to Published Genealogical Records*. Provo, UT: Ancestry, 1998.

Mills, Elizabeth Shown. *Evidence Explained: Citing History Sources from Artifacts to Cyberspace*. Baltimore: Genealogical Publishing, 2007.

———. "Genealogy in the 'Information Age': History's New Frontier?" *National Genealogical Society Quarterly* 91, Centennial Issue (December 2003): 260–78.

———, ed. *Professional Genealogy: A Manual for Researchers, Writers, Editors, Lecturers, and Librarians*. Baltimore: Genealogical Publishing, 2001.

Mills, Gary B. *The Forgotten People: Cane River's Creoles of Color*. Baton Rouge: Louisiana State University Press, 1977.

Mills, Gary B., and Elizabeth Shown Mills. "*Roots* and the New 'Faction': A Legitimate Tool for Clio?" *Virginia Magazine of History and Biography* 89, no. 1 (January 1981): 5–26.

Morgan, Francesca Constance. "'Home and Country': Women, Nation, and the Daughters of the American Revolution, 1890–1939." PhD dissertation, Columbia University, 1998.

———. "Lineage as Capital: Genealogy in Antebellum New England." *New England Quarterly* 83, no. 2 (June 2010): 250–82.

———. "A Noble Pursuit? Bourgeois America's Uses of Lineage." In *The American Bourgeoisie: Distinction and Identity in the Nineteenth Century*, edited by Sven Beckert and Julia B. Rosenbaum, 135–52. New York: Palgrave Macmillan, 2010.

Moss, Michael. "Choreographed Encounter: The Archive and Public History." *Archives* 32, no. 116 (2007): 41–57.

Mountain, David C., and Jeanne Kay Guelke. "Genetics, Genealogy, and Geography." In *Geography and Genealogy: Locating Personal Pasts*, edited by Dallen J. Timothy and Jeanne Kay Guelke, 153–74. Burlington, VT: Ashgate Publishing, 2008.

Muller, Samuel, Johan Adriaan Feith, and Robert Fruin. *Manual for the Arrangement and Description of Archives*. 1898. Reprint of the second edition (1940), translated by Arthur H. Leavitt. Chicago: Society of American Archivists, 2003.

Myers, Minor. *Liberty without Anarchy: A History of the Society of the Cincinnati*. Charlottesville: University of Virginia Press, 1983.

Náñez Falcón, Guillermo, ed. *The Favrot Family Papers: A Documentary Chronicle of Early Louisiana*. 3 vols. New Orleans: Howard-Tilton Memorial Library, Tulane University, 1988–2001.

Naomi M. Drake, Appellant, v. Department of Health, Appellee. Appeal from the Civil Service Commission of the City of New Orleans, no. 391, 1965. New Orleans Public Library.

Nesmith, Tom. "Still Fuzzy, But More Accurate: Some Thoughts on the 'Ghosts' of Archival Theory." *Archivaria* 47 (Spring 1999): 136–49.

New Orleans Public Library. Louisiana Division. *Monthly Reports* for 1946–1956.

Nolan, Charles E. *A Southern Catholic Heritage*. Vol. 1. New Orleans: Archdiocese of New Orleans, 1976.

Nora, Pierre. "General Introduction: Between Memory and History." In *Realms of Memory: Rethinking the French Past*, 1–23. Edited by Lawrence D. Kritzman. Translated by Arthur Goldhammer. New York: Columbia University Press, 1996.

Nugent, Patricia. "Pedro Pedesclaux." Orleans Parish Clerk of Civil District Court. Available at http://www.orleanscivilclerk.com/pedrobio.htm.

O'Neill, Charles Edwards. "'A Quarter Marked by Sundry Peculiarities': New Orleans, Lay Trustees, and Père Antoine." *Catholic Historical Review* 76, no. 2 (April 1990): 235–77.

Papailias, Penelope. *Genres of Recollection: Archival Poetics and Modern Greece*. New York: Palgrave Macmillan, 2005.

Parham, Angel Adams. "Race, Memory, and Family History." *Social Identities* 14, no. 1 (January 2008): 13–32.

Pearce-Moses, Richard, comp. *A Glossary of Archival and Records Terminology*. Chicago: Society of American Archivists, 2005.

Petkovic, Josko. "The 1920 Translation of the Stefano Manuscript: Notes from the Editor." Available at http://nass.murdoch.edu.au/docs/STEFANO_EDITING_TRANSLATION.pdf.

———. *The* Stefano *Shipwreck of 1875: An Introduction*. Available at http://www.mcc.murdoch.edu.au/nass/issue3/pdf/Stefano_1.1_Introduction.pdf.

———. "Who Is the Author of the 1876 Stefano Manuscript?" Available at http://nass.murdoch.edu.au/docs/STEFANO_AUTHORSHIP.pdf.

Phillips, Faye. "To 'Build upon the Foundation': Charles Gayarré's Vision for the Louisiana State Library." *Libraries and the Cultural Record* 43, no.1 (2008): 56–78.

———. "Writing Louisiana Colonial History in the Mid-Nineteenth Century: Charles Gayarré, Benjamin Franklin French, and the Louisiana Historical Society." *Louisiana History: The Journal of the Louisiana Historical Association* 49, no. 2 (Spring 2008): 163–90.

Powell, Kimberly. "Top Five Places to Put Your Family History Online." About.com: Genealogy. Available at http://genealogy.about.com/od/publishing/tp/web_sites.htm.

Powell, Lawrence N. "Introduction: A Novelist Turns Historian." In *The New Orleans of George Washington Cable: The 1887 Census Office Report*, edited by Lawrence N. Powell, 9–35. Baton Rouge: Louisiana State University Press, 2008.

Price, William. "Work of Indexing Louisiana Black Boxes." *Louisiana Historical Quarterly* 8, no. 1 (1914): 8–20.

Rankin, David C. "The Forgotten People: Free People of Color in New Orleans, 1850–1870." PhD dissertation, Johns Hopkins University, 1976.

Rathe, Gustave. *The Wreck of the Barque* Stefano *off the North West Cape of Australia in 1875*. Victoria Park, Australia: Hesperian Press, 1990; Edinburgh: Cannongate Press, 1992.

Reed, Barbara. "Beyond Perceived Boundaries: Imagining the Potential of Pluralised Recordkeeping." *Archives and Manuscripts* 33, no. 1 (May 2005): 177–98.

Reeves, Sally Kittredge. *Legacy of a Century: Academy of the Sacred Heart in New Orleans*. New Orleans: Walsworth Press, 1987.

Ricard, Ulysses S. *African Americans in Louisiana: Selected Works along with Some Genealogical References*. New Orleans: Chicory Society of Afro-Louisiana History and Culture, 1989.

Ricoeur, Paul. *Memory, History, Forgetting*. Translated by Kathleen Blamey and David Pellauer. Chicago: University of Chicago Press, 2004.

Riffel, Judy. *New Orleans Register of Free People of Color, 1840–1864*. Baton Rouge: Le Comité des Archives de la Louisiane, 2008.

Roach, Judith Prewse. "Genealogy at the Library of Congress." In *International Genealogy and Local History: Papers Presented by the Genealogy and Local History Section at IFLA General Conferences 2001–2005*, edited by Ruth Hedegaard and Elizabeth Anne Melrose, 13–18. Munich: K. G. Saur, 2008.

Rosenzweig, Roy, and David P. Thelen. *The Presence of the Past: Popular Uses of History in American Life*. New York: Columbia University Press, 1998.

Ruff, Verda Jenkins. *The Cabildo Records of New Orleans, 1769–1785: An Index to Abstracts in the* Louisiana Historical Quarterly. 2nd ed. Ville Platte, LA: Provincial Press, 1997.

Russo, David J. *Keepers of Our Past: Local Historical Writing in the United States, 1820s–1930s*. Westport, CT: Greenwood Press, 1988.

Saucier, Earl Noland. "Charles Gayarré, the Creole Historian." PhD dissertation, George Peabody College for Teachers, 1935.

Savage, James, John Farmer, and Orrando Perry Dexter. *A Genealogical Dictionary of the First Settlers of New England*. Boston: Little, Brown, 1860.

Schudson, Michael. "Dynamics of Distortion in Collective Memory." In *Memory Distortion: How Minds, Brains, and Societies Reconstruct the Past*, edited by Daniel L. Schacter and Joseph T. Coyle, 346–64. Cambridge, MA: Harvard University Press, 1995.

———. "The Present in the Past versus the Past in the Present." *Communication* 11 (1989): 105–12.

———. *Watergate in American Memory: How We Remember, Forget, and Reconstruct the Past*. New York: Basic Books, 1992.

Schutz, John A. *A Noble Pursuit: The Sesquicentennial History of the New England Historic Genealogical Society, 1845–1995*. Boston: New England Historic Genealogical Society, 1995.

Seabrook, John. "The Reporter at Large: The Tree of Me." *New Yorker* 77, no. 526 (March 2001): 58–71.

Sharpe, Michael. *Family Matters: A History of Genealogy*. Barnsley, England: Pen and Sword Books, 2011.

Shattuck, Lemuel. *Blank Book Forms for Family Registers*. Boston: Lemuel Shattuck, 1856.

———. *A Complete System for Family Registration*. Boston: William D. Ticknor, 1841.

Sheble, Mary Ann. "Genealogical Libraries and Collections." In *The Encyclopedia of Library History*, edited by Wayne A. Wiegand and Donald G. Davis Jr., 232–33. Garland Reference Library of Social Science, vol. 503. New York: Garland Publishing, 1994.

Shils, Edward Albert. *Tradition*. Chicago: University of Chicago Press, 1981.

Shoumatoff, Alex. *The Mountain of Names: A History of the Human Family*. New York: Simon and Schuster, 1985.

Siegel, Elizabeth E. "'Miss Domestic' and 'Miss Enterprise'; or, How to Keep a Photograph Album." In Tucker, Ott, and Buckler, *The Scrapbook in American Life*, 251–67.

Simons, D. Brenton, and Peter Benes, eds. *The Art of Family: Genealogical Artifacts in New England*. Boston: New England Historic Genealogical Society, 2002.

Sims, Richard. *A Manual for the Genealogist, Topographer, Antiquary, and Legal Professor: Consisting of Descriptions of Public Records, Parochial and Other Registers, Wills, County and Family Histories; Heraldic Collections in Public Libraries, Etc. Etc.* London: John Russell Smith, 1861.

Smith, Amy M. *Tracing Family Lines: The Impact of Genealogy Research on Family Communication*. Lanham, MD: Lexington Books, 2012.

Smith, Bonnie G. *The Gender of History: Men, Women, and Historical Practice*. Cambridge, MA: Harvard University Press, 1998.

Smith, Shawn Michelle. *American Archives: Gender, Race, and Class in Visual Culture*. Princeton, NJ: Princeton University Press, 1999.

Spear, Jennifer M. "Colonial Intimacies: Legislating Sex in French Louisiana." *William and Mary Quarterly* 60, no. 1, Sexuality in Early America (January 2003): 75–98.

Stebbins, Luke. *A Genealogy of the Family of Mr. Samuel Stebbins and Mrs. Hannah Stebbins, His Wife, from the Year 1701 to 1771 . . .* Hartford, CT: Ebenezer Watson, 1771.

Stern, Alexandra Minna. *Eugenic Nation: Faults and Frontiers of Better Breeding in Modern America*. Berkeley: University of California Press, 2005.

Stewart, Susan. *On Longing: Narratives of the Miniature, the Gigantic, the Souvenir, the Collection*. Durham, NC: Duke University Press, 1993.

Szreter, Simon. "Registration of Identities in Early Modern English Parishes and amongst the English Overseas." In Breckenridge and Szreter, *Registration and Recognition*, 68–69.

Taylor, Maureen A. "Tall Oaks from Little Acorns Grow: The Family Tree Lithograph in America." In Simons and Benes, *The Art of Family*, 75–89.

Taylor, Robert M., Jr. "Summoning the Wandering Tribes: Genealogy and Family Reunions in American History." *Journal of Social History* 16, no. 2 (Winter 1982): 21–37.

Taylor, Robert M., Jr., and Ralph J. Crandall, eds. *Generations and Change: Genealogical Perspectives in Social History*. Macon, GA: Mercer University Press, 1986.

———. “Historians and Genealogists: An Emerging Community of Interest.” In Taylor and Crandall, *Generations and Change*, 3–28.

Thompson, Shirley Elizabeth. *Exiles at Home*. Cambridge, MA: Harvard University Press, 2009.

Times-Picayune. “Louisiana Colonials Recently Organize,” July 18, 1917.

Tocqueville, Alexis de. *Democracy in America*. Edited by J. P. Mayer. Translated by George Lawrence. New York: Anchor Books, 1969.

Trillin, Calvin. “Black or White.” *New Yorker*, April 14, 1986, 62–78.

Tucker, Susan. “Archivists and Genealogical Researchers: A Bibliography.” Tulane University. Available at http://www.tulane.edu/~wclib/archivists/archivists.html.

———. “Coralie Guarino Davis (1926–2004): Claiming Status and Constructing Legacies.” In *Louisiana Women*, vol. 2, edited by Shannon Frystak and Mary Kaiser Farmer. Athens: University of Georgia Press, 2015.

———. “The Most Public of All History: Family History and Heritage Albums in the Transmission of Records/Genealogie en Familiealbums als Dragers van Collectieve Herinnering.” PhD dissertation, University of Amsterdam, 2009.

———. *The New Orleans Guide to Collections on Women*. New Orleans: Newcomb College Center for Research on Women, 1989.

———. “Reading and Rereading: The Scrapbooks of Girls Growing into Women, 1900–1940.” In *Defining Print Culture for Youth: The Cultural Work of Children's Literature*, edited by Anne Lundin and Wayne Wiegand. Westport, CT: Libraries Unlimited, 2003.

———. “Visible Enough to Us: Identity, Archivists, and Genealogical Researchers.” *Comma, International Journal on Archives* 2005, no. 3 (2005): 1–11.

Tucker, Susan, Katherine Ott, and Patricia Buckler, eds. *The Scrapbook in American Life*. Philadelphia: Temple University Press, 2006.

Twain, Mark. “Autobiography of Mark Twain.” *Harper's Monthly Magazine* 144 (1922): 273–80, 455–60.

Ulrich, Laurel Thatcher. *The Age of Homespun: Objects and Stories in the Creation of an American Myth*. New York: Alfred A. Knopf, 2001.

———. “Creating Lineages.” In Simons and Benes, *The Art of Family*, 5–11.

United States Census Bureau. *Heads of Families at the First Census of the United States Taken in the Year 1790*. Volumes by state. Washington, DC: Government Printing Office, 1908.

Van Dijck, José. *Mediated Memories: Personal Cultural Memory as Object of Cultural Analysis*. Stanford, CA: Stanford University Press, 2007.

Van Houts, Elisabeth. *Memory and Gender in Medieval Europe, 900–1200*. Toronto: University of Toronto Press, 1999.

Vansina, Jan. *Oral Tradition: A Study in Historical Methodology*. Translated by H. M. Wright. New Brunswick, NJ: Aldine Transaction, 2006.

Van Tassel, David D. *Recording America's Past: An Interpretation of the Development of Historical Studies in America, 1607–1884*. Chicago: University of Chicago Press, 1967.

Vosmeier, Sarah McNair. "Picturing Love and Friendship: Photograph Albums and Networks of Affection in the 1860s." In Tucker, Ott, and Buckler, *The Scrapbook in American Life*, 207–19.

Wagner, Anthony Richard. *English Genealogy*. Oxford: Clarendon Press, 1950.

Wallach, Kate. *Research in Louisiana Law*. Baton Rouge: Louisiana State University Press, 1958.

Walrond, John. "Letter from Rev. John Walrond of Ottery, Eng., to Rev. William Waldron, Minister of Boston, and Brother of Secretary Waldron, 8 March 1725–26." *New England Historical and Genealogical Register* 1, no. 1 (January 1847), 66.

Warner, Robert M. *Diary of a Dream: A History of the National Archives Independence Movement, 1980–1985*. Metuchen, NJ: Scarecrow Press, 1995.

Warner, Sam Bass, Jr. "The Shame of the Cities: Public Records of the Metropolis." *Midwestern Archivist* 2, no. 2 (1977): 27–34.

Weigel, Sigrid. "Foreign-Language Publications." Available at http://www.zfl-berlin.org/tl_files/zfl/downloads/personen/weigel/publications_foreign_languages_sigrid_weigel.pdf.

———. "Genealogy: On the Iconography and Rhetorics of an Epistemological Topos." Enciclopédia e Hipertexto. Available at http://www.educ.fc.ul.pt/hyper/resources/sweigel/.

Weil, François. *Family Trees: A History of Genealogy in America*. Cambridge, MA: Harvard University Press, 2013.

———. "John Farmer and the Making of American Genealogy." *New England Quarterly* 80, no. 3 (September 2007): 408–34.

Whitmore, William Henry. *A Handbook of American Genealogy, Being a Catalogue of Family Histories and Publications Containing Genealogical Information*. Albany, NY: J. Munsell, 1862.

Wilcox, Shirley Langdon. "The National Genealogical Society: A Look at Its First One Hundred Years." October 31, 2003. Available at http://www.ngsgenealogy.org/galleries/aboutngs/history_of_ngs_4.0.pdf.

Willcox, Walter F. "Lemuel Shattuck, Statist, Founder of the American Statistical Association." *American Statistician* 1, no. 1 (August 1947): 11–13.

Wilson, Samuel, Jr., and Leonard Victor Huber. *The Presbytère on Jackson Square*. New Orleans: Friends of the Cabildo, 1981.

Wilson, Samuel, Jr., Bernard Lemann, Mary Louise Christovich, et al. *New Orleans Architecture*. 8 vols. Gretna, LA: Pelican, 1971–1997.

Windham, John B. "Windham Family DNA Project, Background." Family Tree DNA. Available at http://www.familytreedna.com/public/windhamfamily/default.aspx?section=yresults.

Winslow, Ola Elizabeth. *American Broadside Verse*. New Haven, CT: Yale University Press, 1930.

Winterthur Museum. "Who's Your Daddy? Families in Early American Needlework." Exhibition, October 4, 2008–August 17, 2009. Available at http://www.winterthur.org/?p=804.

Woods, Earl C., and Charles E. Nolan. *Sacramental Records of the Roman Catholic Church of the Archdiocese of New Orleans*. 19 vols. New Orleans: Archdiocese of New Orleans, 1987–2003.

Woolf, Daniel R. "A Feminine Past? Gender, Genre, and Historical Knowledge in England, 1500–1800." *American Historical Review* 102, no. 3 (June 1997): 645–79.

———. "Memory and Historical Culture in Early Modern England." *Journal of the Canadian Historical Association*, n.s., 2 (1991): 283–308.

———. *The Social Circulation of the Past: English Historical Culture, 1500–1750*. Oxford: Oxford University Press, 2003.

Yakel, Elizabeth. "Seeking Information, Seeking Connections, Seeking Meaning: Genealogists and Family Historians." *Information Research* 10, no. 1 (October 2004), paper 205. Available at http://InformationR.net/ir/10-1/paper205.html.

Yakel, Elizabeth, and Deborah A. Torres. "Genealogists as a 'Community of Records.'" *American Archivist* 70, no. 1 (Spring–Summer 2007).

Yeo, Geoffrey. "Concepts of Record (1): Evidence, Information, and Persistent Representations." *American Archivist* 70, no. 2 (Fall–Winter 2007): 315–43.

———. "Concepts of Record (2): Prototypes and Boundary Objects." *American Archivist* 71, no. 1 (Spring–Summer 2008): 118–43.

Young, Michael. *The Metronomic Society: Natural Rhythms and Human Timetables*. Cambridge: Cambridge University Press, 1988.

Zboray, Ronald J., and Mary Saracino Zboray. "Is It a Diary, Commonplace Book, Scrapbook, or Whatchamacallit? Six Years of Exploration in New England's Manuscript Archives." *Libraries and the Cultural Record* 44, no. 1 (February 2009): 101–23.

Zerubavel, Eviatar. *Ancestors and Relatives: Genealogy, Identity, and Community*. New York: Oxford University Press, 2012.

———. *Time Maps: Collective Memory and the Social Shape of the Past*. Chicago: University of Chicago Press, 2003.

Radio and Television Productions

African American Lives, PBS, first aired January 2007.

Bettinger, Blaine. "Genetic Genealogy: A Powerful Tool for the Family Historian." *The World*. Public Radio International, March 22, 2012.

Gordon-Reed, Annette. Interview. "The Hemingses of Monticello." Washington Journal Series on Presidents. Book TV, C-Span 2, January 10, 2009.

Honora, Jari. Radio interview with Zoe Sullivan. "New Orleans Archdiocese Releases Sacramental Records." WWNO–FM News Feature, February 24, 2011.

Jackson, Buzzy. Video interview with Dick Eastman. Roots Television, October 29, 2008. Available at http://www.rootstelevision.com/players/ player_conferences.php?bctid=2474688001.

INDEX

Page numbers in **bold** refer to illustrations.